Industrialization in Nineteenth-century Europe

Industrialization in Nineteenth-century Europe

TOM KEMP

Longmans

LONGMANS, GREEN AND CO LTD
London and Harlow
*Associated companies, branches and representatives
throughout the world*

© *Longmans, Green and Co Ltd 1969*
First published 1969

SBN 582 48024 8   Cased

   582 48025 6   Paper

*Printed in Great Britain
by Ebenezer Baylis and Son, Limited
The Trinity Press, Worcester, and London*

Contents

37104

Contents

Preface

This book is intended as a guide for the specialist undergraduate or postgraduate student of European economic history. It therefore takes for granted on the reader's part much of the factual knowledge imparted by existing textbooks and directs his attention principally to problems of interpretation. It embarks upon this by putting forward a synthesis and explanation of its own. In this way the student or general reader is offered a coherent view of the field covered and is invited to further study.

The main theme of the following chapters is the industrialization of the European countries in the nineteenth century. The starting point is the Industrial Revolution in Britain, but this is dealt with only to bring out its salient features and to offer a standard of comparison when dealing with industrialization in other national settings. To France, Germany, Russia and Italy the same synthetic treatment is applied. This is not because the author is inclined to believe that the big questions in the economic history of these countries have been solved: on the contrary most of them are still very open. It is considered, however, that it is useful to offer the student some firm hypotheses to begin with rather than to confuse him with a mass of perhaps conflicting data and a diversity of views. Because many economic historians are unwilling to commit themselves on many of the larger matters of interpretation—for reasons which may in themselves be sound—the student is frequently baffled and finds himself at sea amidst a swelling mass of monographs and articles. Here, then, is an attempt to bring him a lifeline on which he can steady himself to deal with the flood of conflicting opinion and detailed research which will later confront him.

The emphasis on European economic history is intended to

counteract what appears to be a distinctly insular trend in much of the teaching which takes place in British universities at the present day. Probably in no other country in the world has the discipline of economic history assumed such an important place in the universities, yet interest in the economic history of other countries is not very strong. As can be seen from the bibliography, there is remarkably little writing in English on the economic history of countries which have been so important for Britain as, for example, Germany. Practically no research has been done on the economic history of nineteenth-century Europe by British economic historians until comparatively recent years. Yet as study of the British industrial revolution proceeds it becomes increasingly apparent that it cannot be understood in isolation from developments outside the British Isles, or without fuller study of comparable processes elsewhere. Such a study should begin with those countries which were nearest to Britain geographically as well as in their cultural heritage. Perhaps no aspect of modern European history has been more neglected than the economic side, yet recent political, as well as economic, developments show how dangerous this ignorance can be.

It may seem that this book gives the reader readymade opinions. That is not the intention. By presenting a firm interpretation he is being called upon at the same time to think about it and, if he is curious enough, as he should be, to test it. In any case, he will need to refer to other works for description and narrative and in the bibliography his attention is called to the principal books and articles in which the problems may be considered further. As an additional aid to orientation in study and research a list of problems for further investigation, or perhaps for classroom discussion, has been placed at the end of each chapter. The problems themselves have not necessarily been dealt with adequately in the text, but help in pursuing them will be found in the items in the bibliography.

Chronologically the treatment is limited to the pre-1914 period. The justification for this is that the main emphasis is on the conditions in which the foundations were laid for industrialization, not with the further working out of the process of economic growth in advanced industrial societies. Furthermore, the First World War marked the end of a distinctive era in European economic history and brought onto the scene a complex of new problems which change considerably the character of the next period. There are more books available to the student dealing with this later period than for the nineteenth century, yet an understanding of the problems of current economic development requires a firm foundation in nineteenth-century economic history. It was in this period that the economies of Europe assumed their specific characteristics and direction; their subsequent problems were set and in large measure worked out under the shadow of their earlier history. In the case of Britain, for example, it is impossible to approach the current problems of the economy without searching for their historical roots which, as shown in chapter 7, lay well back in the nineteenth century. Perhaps, too, a fuller understanding of history will not only show what is new on the contemporary economic scene, but will also reveal the constants in the economic and social life of the various countries which have to be taken into consideration at the present time. In some ways it is true that the exigencies of industrialism and urban living tended to make the advanced countries of the world more alike, but underneath appearances they retain specific features derived from their history which these chapters may do something to demonstrate and explain.

Note to the Reader

As this does not claim to be a work of original research or erudition footnotes have been avoided. Its principal sources in English are indicated in the Bibliography. The source of quotations used in the text and the works of authors mentioned by name will be found on page 220.

Industrialization in Nineteenth-century Europe

1 British and European Industrialization

Britain was the pioneer industrial country, the classic theatre for the transformation of a traditional agrarian economy into an urban society based on machine technology. This first Industrial Revolution, while it has been intensively studied by several generations of academic economic historians, has still far from yielded all its secrets. In recent years the increasing interest displayed both by historians and by economists in the problems of economic growth has given it a new importance. The result is that the complexity of the industrialization process is now more clearly recognized, if not understood, and the explanation of its origins and nature has been shown to be more difficult than was once assumed.

At present it can at least be said that the study of the Industrial Revolution has become infused with a greater amount of theoretical analysis and some of its aspects have been given more quantitative precision in the past decade or so. Writings on the subject, while now appearing at an accelerated rhythm, show that the question of causes or origins remains controversial and perhaps unanswerable. The accumulation of knowledge and the advances made in theoretical understanding have not, as yet, produced anything like a consensus of opinion among the experts. On the other hand, great positive advances have undoubtedly been made both in accumulating evidence and in revealing the full extent of the problems which remain to be investigated. Research has thus tended to be oriented in new directions, operating with more advanced theoretical tools and aiming at greater quantitative verification for general statements and conclusions.

While this is a healthy sign so far as the development of economic history as an academic discipline is concerned it does not make things easier for the student. He is confronted with a mounting volume of specialist writings in articles and monographs. He quickly learns to distrust much of what he reads in the older textbooks without finding available anything positive to put in its place. In place of the firm general conclusion come the conflicting versions of contending authorities. Today's fashionable theory may become suspect as a result of tomorrow's article.

There is no intention here to deal in detail with the British Industrial Revolution since this book is primarily concerned with the pattern of industrialization in European countries. However, its general historical importance and the immense influence which it exercised on the economic development of the Continent requires something to be said about it. It was the first in a long line of similar processes and is therefore often taken as the classic case or model. Some theories of industrialization, such as Rostow's, are virtually based on a generalization of the British case, with the result that a pattern has been imposed on the industrial development of other countries which the facts do not support. However, despite dangers of this sort, the industrialization of Europe cannot be understood without a consideration of the British case. The other side of this, not always clearly recognized, is that an understanding of the British industrialization process cannot be obtained in isolation. Not only do its interrelations with the development of the world economy have to be examined, but a comparative study with other countries in a similar stage of economic development may enable its specific character to be understood. One of the purposes of this study is to bring out the specific features of each national industrialization process.

For these reasons something has to be said about the peculiar and special features of the British Industrial Revolution, which distinguished it from the similar process in the other countries which will be examined. Let it first be emphasized that the transformation of the British economy by the application of the techniques and forms of organization of industrial capitalism could only have taken place as part of a worldwide movement. The needs of an industrializing economy for supplies of raw materials and for markets brought into being a new international division of labour between it and the mainly agrarian regions and then with the other industrializing countries as well. The creation of this world market injected forces of change and disturbance into societies of different forms and levels of development throughout the nations. The great drama of modern world history thereby began. In particular, the disparities in technical and economic levels between the countries of economic development and the areas of the world with traditional agrarian and often primitive economies led to the economic and political subjugation of the latter by the former. The areas which first saw the rise of modern industry, inhabited by Europeans, thus became dominant for a whole historical epoch.

This global historical context should be kept in mind. It was productive of colonial expansion and imperialist rivalries between the advanced countries. It impinged on the industrialization process continually and in many ways. It led, in time, to the growth of nationalist movements and a desire on the part of the old or newly created élites in the underdeveloped countries to emulate the advanced countries by discovering the secret of economic growth. In time it produced also an awareness of the growing disparity between income levels in the fortunate industrial countries and the backward agrarian ones. From this stemmed the interest in problems of growth among politicians and economists and advances in theory and an accumulation of empirical material which, in turn, fructified the study of the economic development of the advanced countries.

It is not the intention here to pursue further the worldwide repercussions of the Industrial Revolution as a crucial determinant of the modern world. Rather is the emphasis in this chapter on the characteristic features of industrialization in its original home, Britain, with a view to explaining how and why they differed in the countries of Europe which followed closest on her heels. Britain was the pioneer; it was here that the physical, social and cultural factors proved most favourable for the autonomous operation of the basic economic forces which generated industrialization. The advantages which enabled British entrepreneurs, commercial and financial as well as industrial, to be first in the field persisted for a long time. Undoubtedly the first 'latecomers' were in many ways at a comparative disadvantage. In time – the tendency becomes perceptible towards the end of the nineteenth century, though perhaps more to later generations than to contemporaries – the pioneer country began to suffer disabilities from its early start. Whether economic 'maturity' then became a handicap to economic change and adjustment will be analysed in the concluding chapter. It is certain, however, that the latecomers were by this time able to take over much of the technique and apparatus of an advanced society as a going concern and reshape their institutions around it, where conditions were otherwise favourable, and reduce within a short time the income gap between themselves and the pioneer. This is what happened, with varying degrees of success and by different paths, in the European countries examined here. A study of these experiences can, it is believed, cast light on the essential nature of industrialization and the special form which it took, of necessity, in the first industrial country. It can also reveal the special physiognomy of the later industrializing countries, account for the degree to which they succeeded in making good their initial lag and perhaps help in the understanding of the problems of the present day developing countries.

All these industrializing processes had certain common features and required the prior existence of a favourable sociocultural environment as well as the necessary physical resources. What makes Britain the 'classic' model is that it is possible to trace these conditions with some precision, in part, of course, because so much research has been done on the question. Indeed, successive textbook systematizations have made the marshalling of the necessary 'prerequisites' and their favourable combination and interaction appear more straightforward than they are in practice. The controversy about origins and causes already referred to turns on the relative weight to be ascribed to these different factors, and views about which factors were decisive in a causal sense. In Britain industrialization was not part of a preconceived plan or programme. It resulted strictly from the operations of many competing business firms spontaneously pursuing their own self-interest in a climate and an institutional setting extremely favourable to the full and free operation of market forces. This organic or autonomous nature of British industrialization was its most original and outstanding characteristic. Nowhere else could these conditions be exactly reproduced. Britain could become a model to be consciously followed, but once an element of conscious emulation and example or the transplanting of technique, capital and enterprise are introduced the process assumes a different character. This provides the basic difference between British industrialization and the models later to be examined.

The continental countries did not and could not simply duplicate British experience. As latecomers they did not have to go through all the stages by means of which the conditions for industrialization were autonomously prepared in Britain. Their ability to leap over stages, in this sense, was their principal advantage and the key to the rapidity with which the initial gap with Britain could be closed in the course of the late nineteenth and early twentieth centuries.

At the same time, all industrialization processes, whether or not based mainly on the spontaneous result of individual decisions taken according to market indicators, had certain common features. The most difficult point of all, perhaps, is to define what were the necessary social and cultural conditions for industrialization to succeed. Certainly the reshaping and discarding of much of the traditional order was indispensable. A new institutional framework and legal system had to be created to suit the needs of a complex industrial society with private ownership geared to the needs of the market. The nearer the pre-existing institutions, laws, social habits and so on were to those required by an industrial society the more likely it was to come into being as a spontaneous process. In general it can be said that European society, with its antecedents in the classical world, was more favourable in these respects than the civilized societies found in other parts of the world. Within Europe, the preparatory conditions for industrialism had been worked out as a result of expanding trade and the growth of a market-oriented economy over a span of many centuries. Especially favoured in this respect were the countries of the north-west which became the pivot of the commercial links with other continents established from the late fifteenth century onwards. Subsequently social and political change in this area was rapid. The spread of new knowledge, and the challenging of old religious beliefs and social rigidities produced a receptivity to change and innovation, including that in the sphere of production, which had no previous parallel in human history.

The European background therefore seems important. But so, in a detailed examination, would the special conditions prevailing in the British Isles which enabled these favourable factors to operate most freely. The special situation arising in Britain provided a particularly fertile field for the operation of the specifically economic forces which produced indstrialization as a spontaneous process. However, Britain was culturally part of Europe and some of these conditions were derived from sources which the Continent shared. Various other circumstances – political, religious and social – conspired to hold back development on the Continent and to stimulate it in Britain, and thus to account for the priority and originality of the British Industrial Revolution.

The common features in industrialization are to be found principally in the economic forces which produce it. Here we come back to the 'prerequisites' which, while so useful for purposes of exposition, do, it should be pointed out, tend to simplify a complex process. In particular, because they act together – indeed cannot act apart – in a closely integrated and complex matrix it is impossible to isolate one as the main or compelling cause. We have to do this to explain the process. It is virtually impossible to attach weights to each factor and the order in which they are referred to should not therefore be taken as an order of causal importance.

Industrialization involved a more productive use of the factors of production obtained partly by altering the proportions in which they were applied, partly by improving their efficiency and partly by introducing new techniques. The active agents of this process were men interested in buying and selling at a profit, and they operated under the spur of self-interest, although other motives may have been present. The expansion of markets was therefore a condition for the application of new techniques and methods of organization to production. The expansion of production required that part of current output should be used not for consumption but to add to the stock of productive equipment. In fact the prior accumulation of capital in the sense of direct and indirect aids to production requiring investment outlays had been going on for a long time before industrialization began, and was a necessary condition for it.

The profitable utilization of productive equipment required the expenditure of human muscular and mental powers. The owners of capital depended, therefore, upon the existence of an adquate supply of labour provided by people who were obliged to work for wages because they had no other adequate means of support. Such a class appeared, at least in Britain, many centuries before the rise of modern industry. The principal problems of industrialization arose in recruiting it from the older sorts of employment and fitting it to the exigencies of the new technology. The existence of a free labour force, of people able and willing to move into the occupations and areas where employers required it in response to market forces, was a further vital condition for industrialization.

The Industrial Revolution made possible a great increase in the productivity of human labour, in output per head. Production could expand, and larger aggregate, perhaps proportionate, amounts of current production could be used to add to the stock of productive equipment. To some extent this could be done through a better use of existing means and improvements in organization. The great breakthrough required, however, the provision of new technical means to raise output per head greatly in excess of what the existing methods made possible. New machines and new sources of power were thus indispensable. Changes in technology arose out of the specific conditions of the British economy at a particular stage in its development. Their application to industry, their ability to serve the needs of profit-seeking entrepreneurs competing with their rivals for a place in an expanding market, was decisive.

The profit-making entrepreneur, bound to accumulate to stay in the competitive race and thus receptive to technical improvements which could lower costs and increase profits, was central to the process. He was the human agent of change in industry, the actual mobilizer of the factors of production who sought out market opportunities and sank or swam according to the accuracy or good fortune with which he judged the situation. Of course he was not alone in providing the conditions for industrialization. He was, after all, only extending into production itself the practices of a long line of merchant capitalists whose activities in opening up markets, developing a demand for foreign imports and accumulating capital had prepared the ground over many centuries. Indeed, the successes they had achieved had the character of a commercial revolution and the ability of British merchants and shipowners to win a dominant position in the developing world market in the period before and concurrent with the Industrial Revolution of the eighteenth century was undoubtedly a major factor in accounting for the head start which British industry achieved.

If we take these as the main generating factors in economic growth it is clear that British priority in industrialization has to be seen as part of a broad historical process. It was part of a movement which was bound up with the nature of European civilization and the connection of Europe with the wider world. But, for a variety of reasons, it was in Britain that it led, autonomously, to a revolution in production. In other countries the conditions for industrialization were not altogether absent but the old institutional framework was still largely intact. The opportunities for the profit-seeking entrepreneur were narrowed by the slow growth of the internal market and by the continued social dominance of the landowning nobility. The receptivity to change, including technical change, was on the whole much less than in England. However, if one overriding reason can be given for the slower transformation of the Continent, despite the fact that in the West there were many signs of growth and change in the eighteenth century, it must be the continued prevalence of the traditional agrarian structures. For this reason the relationship between agrarian revolution or reform and industrialization will be examined separately in the following chapter.

To sum up, British industrialization had definite and unique characteristics, the result of deeply rooted historical forces and the timing and conditions under which it began and was continued. Once it had begun a stock of technical and organizational innovations was brought into existence. These could be transferred to other environments either by British entrepreneurs or through borrowing by foreigners. Capital and labour, as well as enterprise, could flow across national frontiers. Obviously, then, the British experience was exactly reproduced nowhere else. On the other hand, an example was now available and in direct ways British capitalists transplanted the Industrial Revolution to Europe.

On the Continent, as each country felt the impact of industrialization, what might be called its national economic physiognomy began to take form. In considering this aspect a considerable weight has to be given to national structures and traditions. Especially in the period after the French Revolution, nationalism was one of the great forces in European history. New nation-states were formed and the old dynastic states took on a new complexion. The expansion of a trading and industrial middle class took place within the context of these states. Indeed, consciousness of national identity was strongest among the middle class. Nationalism, as well as liberalism, was thus fed by economic growth. The state, whether national or dynastic, had economic relevance through its tariff frontiers, its monetary units and the whole body of civil and commercial law which regulated economic dealings and distinguished nationals from aliens. In the course of the nineteenth century, as economic life became more complex and nationalism became an increasingly important political force, it defined itself still more imperiously in the economic sphere.

The rise of modern industry therefore took place within the confines of the national state. At the very time when improvements in communications and transport seemed to make the world smaller and the involvement of these states with the international division of labour became more intense, identification with the state or nation and rivalry between states became sharper. The interests of the rising commercial and industrial bourgeoisie thus found expression through the state. It looked to the state to provide a favourable climate for its business activities at home and to promote its interests against those of its foreign rivals. Distinct national economic policies therefore emerged. Industrialization thus tended to reinforce national differences and rivalries even though, technically and socially, it made living conditions more uniform, regardless of linguistic, cultural and other national differences.

Since industrialization was by its nature a geographically uneven process there are some anomalies involved in considering the national state as the growth unit. In all cases the rapid development of industry and urban living in some areas of a country opened up disparities with those which remained mainly agrarian. In certain cases, of which the North-South differential in Italy is a classic, the gap could be very wide and persistent. In most countries the national average in income levels, rates of growth and other significant indices conceals quite wide regional differences which makes national generalizations suspect. For example, there were regions of France which showed quite early in the nineteenth century the symptoms of industrial advance and enterprise which made them leading sectors of the European economy, a position which they retained. However, national averages were dragged down by the backwardness and stagnation which ruled in other parts of the country. Indeed, in some ways it would be more logical to look at European industrialization on a continent-wide basis regardless of national frontiers. What would stand out then would be the importance of physical factors, mainly location and resource endowment, in determining the extent and rate of industrialization. The advanced areas of nineteenth-century Europe had as their core the coalfields of northern France, Belgium and western Germany; from there the influence of industrialization fanned out along convenient lines of communication, including the sea, to other parts of these countries, with some outposts still further to the south and east, including administrative centres, sea and river ports and mineral deposits as the main nodal points. Thus the division between the advancing industrial and mainly agrarian regions cut across state frontiers and, once established, retained considerable influence down to the present day.

This brief review of European industrialization can be complemented with another generalization. Attention tends to be given to the differential between Britain and the Continent in the eighteenth and nineteenth centuries; from a world view, however, it was the differential between Europe and other parts of the world which was significant. Excluding the European transplants in America, scholars have been able to find only relatively weak precursive signs, and then virtually only in parts of India and Japan, of an autonomous process of growth which might have resulted in industrialization in the other continents. Without entering more deeply into a tricky subject it seems possible to say that there was something in the European historical background, and in the adjustment which the population made to physical conditions in some parts of the Continent, which favoured the development of capitalism and thus industrialization. The nature of European feudalism, looser, more individualist and open to commercial influences, together with the fact that Europe was the heir to the property and civil laws, commercial tradition and trade routes of the Greco-Roman world must surely have given an advantage over other areas. Commercial activity and enterprise, and even more productive activity, seem to flourish best within a range of climatic variation into which fell most of Europe but few of the other areas of civilization. The importance of natural resources,

especially coal and ores, to which the new industrial techniques were
applied and on which nineteenth-century industrialization depended,
hardly needs emphasis. But even when such general considerations
have been set out all that has been done is to suggest some of the
conditions which were necessary for development to take place at all
and very little light is cast upon the initiating causes.

What such an approach does suggest is that the course of what
turned out to be the 'preparation' for industrialization occupies a
very lengthy historical span and is bound up with the whole character of European civilization as it emerged from the Middle Ages.
That the breakthrough came first in Europe is in a sense more important than the particular part of Europe in which it came. As it
was, through her geographical and insular position and the possession of the right sort of accessible resources the first act took place on
the British stage. Here, indeed, the adaptation had been taking place
for a very long time in a great variety of ways to the needs of what,
for brevity's sake, can be described as capitalism. The use of money,
the existence of markets, the growth of trade and the establishment
of trade links with a wider world were all important parts of the
prelude to industrialization. But these had, after all, existed in the
Ancient World and had a virtually unbroken history from that time
forward. Moreover, trade, markets and money economy were to be
found in other parts of the world. Surely, then, it is the productive
relations distinctive of the new economic order which were decisive:
that is to say, that some men worked for wages, serving others who
owned the raw material or perhaps the implements and tools of the
industry. The rise of the industrial entrepreneur, whose wealth con-
sists of mobile property enabling him to control the means of
production and dispose of the finished goods, marks a decisive turn
in economic life. However, in a number of places, such as northern
Italy and Flanders, men of this stamp had built up important industries in the Middle Ages without there following a general process of
economic transformation. The establishment of capitalist control over
industry was only a beginning, and might not lead anywhere, unless
accompanied by change in the economy as a whole, that is to say in
the agrarian sector in which the mass of the population was engaged.

What distinguished British, and particularly English, development from continental Europe was the fact that feudal agrarian

relations began to break up earlier and did so more rapidly and completely. Land became a form of individual property to be bought and sold or hired to the highest bidder, not everywhere or completely but to a much greater extent than anywhere else by the sixteenth century. On the other hand, as landowners broke through the old traditional restraints and the land itself was turned into a commercial asset by being used for production for the market, a class of landless wage-earners was created. That some wage-earners existed before, even in agriculture, does not matter a great deal. Large additions were now made to the numbers of the landless needing to work for wages either by the driving of peasants off the land or by the pressure of market forces which favoured the large, efficient producers rather than the smaller and weaker ones. The distinction between freedom and unfreedom passed into one between property-owners and those without property; by the seventeenth century at the latest the change had become complete and had permeated the whole of society.

The emphasis was now on individual acquisition, on the rights of property, on possessiveness. Market relations, not tradition or status, became the main determinant of social position. Wealth became identified with money, or with property which could be transformed into money by sale on the market. To lack money or property meant to depend on the labour market for the means of subsistence. True, even in the eighteenth century many were still shielded from the full effect of market forces by the right to a scrap of land or left-over customary rights from the medieval past. Parliamentary enclosure completed the sway of the market and regulated by law the transformation of the remaining old rights into forms of property consistent with complete individual possession and thus with the full operation of market forces. This often overlooked characteristic of enclosures was perhaps of greater fundamental importance than anything else which they did. It explains the strict observance of due legal forms and the respect for property rights even of the humblest and, at the same time, the far-reaching and irrevocable nature of the social transformation which they produced in rural society.

Changes of this order, which altered fundamentally the relationship between men and the land and men with each other, which changed the nature of property and brought about a new class division, necessarily required a wide range of social and political adjustments. Indeed, the seventeenth century was an age of political revolution the outcome of which was to curtail the pretensions of the Crown, subordinate government to the will of men of property and provide full juridical protection for the new property forms consistent with the development of capitalism. It is difficult to see how industrialization could have taken place as an organic and spontaneous process without the preparation of the environment in this way. In fact a series of piecemeal changes favourable to capitalist property and enabling accumulation and investment to take place in freedom and security provided conditions in England which were completely without parallel in the other European states. That is why, although techniques and forms of organization could be developed and wealth accumulate through trade or financing government activities, individual enterprise and initiative remained stifled by the prevailing medievalism of the social environment, the still extensive and arbitrary powers of the dynastic state, the privileges of the hereditary nobility and the anti-individualist and non-capitalist nature of agrarian relations.

The changes which had been going on in England since the late Middle Ages and which brought into being in the seventeenth century an institutional and political order containing unique elements, did not necessarily result in a significant increase in the wealth-producing capacity of the nation. The basic determinants of *per capita* output were the techniques employed in agriculture, and the numbers and skill of those employed in a still predominantly handicraft industry. In addition, through international trade the merchants of one nation might add to the national capital and income and stimulate domestic activity. It was through the latter channel that a measure of economic growth was achieved in the Low Countries with a remoulding of the social and political environment similar to that which took place in Britain. However, the continental position of this area in a period of endemic wars, lack of physical resources and a large internal market, and scarcity of labour, prevented it from projecting the first industrial revolution, though in the nineteenth century the Walloon area followed closely on Britain's heels.

In a number of other continental areas, too, a measure of commercial and some industrial prosperity was achieved within the confines of the old order but without breaking through the medieval heritage. Until the latter part of the eighteenth century, then, there was nothing unique about the rate or even the character, of the economic development which took place in Britain. It is true, however, that nowhere else was an entire national area being drawn into a market economy to anything like the same extent, nor in any other country was such a large proportion of the population dependent for its very existence on selling commodities or labour. A comparison which confined itself to technique, forms of organization or rates of growth would miss the main and decisive characteristic of the scene in Britain: that it had undergone a structural transformation which, in retrospect, seems to be the necessary groundwork for industrialization.

This does not mean that the origin of the Industrial Revolution has thus been attributed to a single cause. The structural transformation just referred to was an extremely broad and complex process, not composed of separable factors but rather unable to go forward unless change took place on various planes and in many interrelated fields. Market forces had been able to operate as a dissolvent of the old traditional and customary ties over virtually the whole field, though to varying extents in different places. A situation was being brought about, without conscious design, in which growth could be promoted. Within this institutional setting, increasingly hinged upon market relations, it was men in market situations who became the active agents of change and growth. Although wealth may not have grown much, if at all, faster than in other countries, more of it flowed through their hands in an incessant process of buying and selling of commodities and more of it stayed with them to make possible a growth in the scale of their business. The numbers of such men, the scope which they had to carry on their business affairs with little let or hindrance, the opportunities which were opening before them through the development of the home market and the expansion of international trade built up to a situation which was historically new and unique. The capitalist entrepreneurs, dedicated to profit-making and to accumulation, came into their own and personified the forces making for still more far-reaching change.

Of course, the capitalist entrepreneurs had, by the eighteenth century, generations of forebears, and they had their counterparts in all the more developed centres of Europe. In Britain, however, they were able to emancipate themselves to a very large degree from customary restraints, they had an extremely favourable legal environment, and they came to constitute a substantial social force around which clustered those who made up the middle class. This growing middle class derived its income from the practice of trade and the professions, in distinction from the landowners who received rent and the workers who had to sell their labour power to exist. Men of property and substance constituted the core of the middle class and they were, in the eighteenth century, principally engaged in large-scale trade and finance. Such men did not necessarily incline towards industrial production which did not in itself provide a profitable outlet for capital until there had been a considerable extension of the market where, necessarily, the merchant and trader played the decisive role. When merchant capital flowed over into industry it did so mainly through the putting-out system in which the direct producer still worked in his own home or workshop, and for the most part it provided circulating, not fixed, capital. It was only where the technical nature of the process made outlays on fixed capital imperative, as in the mining and metallurgical industries, that industrial capital became predominant. In the textile industries and in the many industries which worked up metal, wood and other materials into consumer goods, the putting-out system or small-scale handicrafts were the rule.

A principal theme of the history of the Industrial Revolution is, therefore, the manner in which industrial capital took command of production, especially in the textile industries, and made possible a great expansion of output in fields in which it was already dominant. Into this story enters a series of economic determinants which find their expression through the behaviour of entrepreneurs and especially the recruitment of new men to the expanding industries. The growing opportunities for individual enterprise in buying and selling were now accompanied by equal if not greater opportunities in the field of production. The growth of the market encouraged greater investment in production and revealed the technical and organizational shortcomings of the existing industrial organization. Where the pressure of demand was felt entrepreneurs had long been experimenting with transitional forms somewhere between the individual craftsman with his tools and the articulated division of labour possible in the mechanized factory. The putting-out system was itself the most successful and widely used of these forms, permitting the realization of certain of the economies of division of labour without heavy investment in fixed capital. Like its successors, it required the existence of people able and willing to work for wages. Supplies of labour had, in fact, been assured by the disintegration of the old self-sufficient peasant economy and the growth of population, specifically of men without land or with insufficient to support themselves and their families. On the other hand it had distinct disadvantages arising from the scattered nature of the work and the lack of supervision or continuity of quality and supply. As pressure of demand built up against it these disadvantages were expressed as sharply rising costs or missed opportunities for profit.

At the level of the productive enterprise employers thus sought to overcome the disadvantage of the traditional forms. Organizing large-scale production while still employing many scattered producers served for a long time and continued to exist in many fields into the nineteenth century or later. But by the eighteenth century it was no longer able to realize further economies in the expanding industries. Another answer was to bring together workers who still performed similar or identical tasks in large workshops. Against the costs of providing buildings and supervision could be set the greater degree of uniformity and the higher quality of the product. This could be important in luxury or semi-luxury trades or where production was for government specifications, as in the case of military or naval supplies. Most probably, however, some splitting up of the work among the various handicrafts would take place either to begin with or as a result of a redistribution of tasks in order to achieve economies of the sort to which Adam Smith drew attention in his analysis of the division of labour. Once a complex handicraft operation had been broken down into its component parts and made repetitive it was but a step to transfer the operation from the worker with his tool to a mechanism driven by some form of power, which performed the operation under the supervision of the worker.

The application of power-driven machinery to industry was only revolutionary when applied to the production of commodities for which a growing market was already in existence or could be found as costs and prices fell. Mechanical invention was not in itself enough, however brilliant in conception. Prototypes of the factory equipped with machines driven by power (generally water) had appeared in a number of fields before the Industrial Revolution. The market for what they produced and their general effect on the economy were, however, restricted, as long as they were confined either to expensive luxury articles or to goods which formed only a small part of total output. The application of machinery to textiles was of a different order. In a mainly agrarian society which is growing in income and becoming entwined in a market economy textile production will be the principal activity moving outside the household. The growth of a market for yarn and cloth, as well as for certain finished goods such as hosiery, provided the basis for the most extensive of the putting-out industries in the period before the Industrial Revolution. It was precisely the series of mechanical innovations in these industries which constituted the core of this process. But it is important to note that it could only have revolutionary consequences because of what was happening to demand and supply outside as well as inside the textile field. In other words, the application of the mechanical inventions and their ability to transform the economy and to contribute to economic growth depended on the existence of opportunities which grew out of a still wider system of change.

There is nothing, to prove, for example, that mechanical skill and inventive capacity were less developed on the Continent than in England during the seventeenth and eighteenth centuries. As technical change took place in the latter country a pool of knowledge was created on which foreigners could draw. English inventors and entrepreneurs went, or were invited, to France and other countries. Finance was provided and labour was recruited. These efforts to transplant the Industrial Revolution to Europe, though they may have sown seeds which were later to bear fruit, did not, for some time to come, initiate anything like an industrialization process. It is true that, by the 1790s, Europe was engulfed in war again and this diverted resources to less productive outlets, though at the same time it kept out English competition. The point is that in Europe the soil was not so well prepared for a rapid transition to an industrial society. A whole complex of circumstances stood in the way:

the agrarian system had yet to be transformed; a disproportionate part of the disposable surplus flowed through the hands of a nobility which thought in terms of consumption rather than investment; the internal market was still narrow and localized. No doubt there were other retarding influences connected with these; together they built up in every sphere a kind of inertia to change. Growth was possible, but it took place mainly within the old structures, there was no sign of a new, industrial form of society coming into existence. The economy remained of the old eighteenth-century type well into the succeeding century for reasons which will be explored more fully in the country studies which follow.

The leading role of textiles must not be exaggerated and it must not be separated from its context. The changes in textiles were themselves piecemeal and long drawn out so that until the second or third decade of the nineteenth century the factory system was virtually synonymous with spinning. They were connected, however, with the growth of a commercial society which had been going on for a long time and which enabled cotton, in particular, to be imported on a massive scale and markets overseas to be found for a high proportion of the output. The success of Lancashire was evidently founded on the prior performance of the economy and required supporting changes in many other fields. Technically there was the stimulus to improve the machines and to develop and apply a prime mover to them, which encouraged the improvement of machine tools and the rise of a machine-making industry. Textile processing also consumed various chemical products and growth was thus related to the ability of the chemical industry to supply them in larger quantities and at lower cost. Similarly, in the field of finance, insurance, transport and business organization generally, associated changes took place which enabled external economies to be realized. To reproduce such conditions anywhere else thus required a rearrangement of economic life, as well as a complex of favourable conditions, which could not rapidly be effected on the Continent.

The growth of the different industrial sectors in eighteenth-century Britain moved on broadly complementary lines. It reflected in the first instance, no doubt, a whole process of demographic and agrarian change which widened markets, not only for textiles, but for everyday household articles, farm implements, tools, leather goods, paper and processed foods and drink. The Industrial Revolution was launched in an economy which was already being transformed and which bore many symptoms of growth, making it different already from the continental economies. But in the period preceding the Industrial Revolution many of the differences were of degree, rather than of kind. In terms of technique and industrial organization the difference had not yet become decisive; the gap was a quantitative one, though it was significant that it was to Britain's advantage. The process of change, too, took place without state assistance and certainly without the prior building up of a capital goods industry. This was another example of the complementary character of the process of industrial change. The textile industry, even, put no great demands on the capital goods industry since the machines which it required were at first simple enough to be constructed locally, as required, by existing skilled workers. The same was true also of the early steam engines. It was only as a market came into existence for textile machinery and steam engines that specialized producers began to turn to standardized quantity production.

It is unlikely that the early stages of industrialization required such a big heave in investment as has sometimes been supposed. The infra-structure required was being laid down and financed already in response to the needs of commerce and an agriculture dependent on markets for its prosperity. The factory entrepreneurs were able to insert themselves into this buoyant commercial environment, the environment which, indeed, had produced them. Their own needs for capital were, to begin with, similar to those of the existing merchant-manufacturers; a relatively small proportion of their capital needed to be laid out in fixed plant and machinery. Certainly it was the need for some fixed capital of a technically higher performance which distinguished them from their predecessors. However, in the financing of purchases of raw materials, payment of wages, holding of stocks and goods in progress, they could make use of the existing web of credit based upon the use of the bill of exchange and of institutions specialized in handling them. While it is true that there were few formal banks in England until the later eighteenth century and that English bankers in any case eschewed long-term industrial investment, the possession of an advanced credit network was of inestimable advantage in forwarding the process of industrialization. The more advanced and intricate system of banking and credit, geared to business needs, to be found in Britain compared with the Continent was an index of the more commercial, market-oriented, nature of the economy. The financial structure, it must be assumed, largely reflected the needs of businessmen. The very origin of banks and financial institutions as outgrowths of business in commodity trade or production bears witness to this. The evolution on the Continent was, outside a few special centres, greatly retarded by comparison. Consequently, industrial entrepreneurs laboured under serious handicaps in obtaining the facilities which they required; in the end the influence of bankers over industry became much greater because of this later development.

In Britain entrepreneurs were on the whole independent of banks and outside financial control. Whether they would have formed joint stock companies and sold shares to the public on a large scale had the law permitted is impossible to say. As it was they adapted themselves successfully to a situation in which such a recourse was excluded. Each entrepreneur had therefore to find his own capital from existing personal or family accumulations, by borrowing on personal security or mortgage, or by entering into partnership with someone having financial means. As in textiles, at least, the initial outlay on fixed capital was comparatively small it was possible for a firm to begin in a modest way. Its expansion would consist principally of ploughing back profits into the business. These methods, imposed by necessity, acquired in the minds of the industrial entrepreneurs a virtue of their own. As their wealth increased and the enterprise became a secure family possession realizing more than sufficient profits to make possible expansion from internal sources they looked with suspicion on the joint stock company. Thus for many decades the great industrial families retained control of their businesses, neither needing, nor looking for, outside finance which might have diluted their control.

The formative period of British industry was thus characterized by the predominance of the family or partnership firm in which ownership and control were embodied in the same people. This left a legacy of competitive individualism which was combined with yet other traits. The success of British industry in this period enabled these firms to grow and to win a secure position in the home and overseas market. The methods by which this had been achieved, on the technical as well as the financial side, thus tended to acquire great prestige. In the technical sphere, for instance, where in the early stages of industrial development the emphasis was bound to be on the practical man, and where for a long time British superiority was unchallenged, habits of mind and practice were formed which at a later stage could be an obstacle to change. Moreover, as long as the actual physical equipment of the firm, in conditions where it had, effectively, a privileged market, enabled profits to be maintained, there was a reluctance to replace it with expensive, but technically more advanced and productive machinery. Since the long-established firms were not prodded by shareholders clamouring for dividends or by bankers with a stake in the firm a tendency towards routine and sluggishness in response to change grew up.

For the first generation of continental entrepreneurs in the period after the restoration of peace in 1815, the situation was very different. In the first place, although a pool of technical know-how was now available and, subject to the restrictions imposed by the British government, machines and skilled workers could be obtained from the more advanced country, these potential advantages must be set against a number of serious disadvantages. In the second place, during the period of the wars and the blockade the industrial gap between Britain and the continental countries had become much wider. Not only had the Industrial Revolution gone forward without abatement while the Continent was absorbed in wars which stunted and distorted economic development but, thanks to this advantage, British industry was now in a position to flood the European market, as well as to retain the international market for manufactured goods which had been carved out in the previous decades. In assessing the prospects for European industrialization, then, it is necessary to take into consideration not only the extent to which internal conditions had matured for an acceleration of growth and a structural change in the economy but the extent to which the head start acquired by Britain acted as a disincentive to industrial investment and innovation.

In the country studies which follow some attempt will be made to show how the conditions for industrialization ripened in the main

2

European countries and the special circumstances which applied to each. Here something will be said about the adjustment to British technical and economic superiority. Of the possible reactions the most obvious was for entrepreneurs to seek to keep control of their own national market by demanding that the government maintain or increase tariffs on imported manufactures. On the whole, continental industry tended to be protectionist on these grounds. It was possible to make good use of the infant industry argument by claiming that unless the new industries received effective tariff protection at the start they would never be able to get off the ground in the face of their low-cost British competitors. While many European agrarians welcomed the free trade campaign in Britain because it would widen the market for their produce and hoped, through lower tariffs at home, to buy manufactured goods at a lower price, industrialists from self-interest tended towards the protectionist camp. As traditional policy was protectionist in any case, and even the agrarians were reluctant to break from it, it is not surprising that free trade ideas found little expression in the policies of the European countries until after the mid-century.

It is difficult to say what effect protection had on the rate of growth of continental industry. Tariff rates were seldom high enough to exclude British competition altogether because the disparity in costs between British and home industry was so great. In some cases, where tariff rates were very high, as for iron in France, it is probably true that industrialists were content to reap high profits behind the tariff wall and neglected improvements in organization and technology which could have brought down costs. High cost producers were kept in existence. Such a policy assumed that little could be done to challenge the British hold on other markets. It was a response conducive to stagnation which, in the long run, could be nationally ruinous. Thus, when railway building began relaxations of tariffs and import restrictions had to be made because home producers were unable to cope with the demand for rails and rolling stock.

Another, more constructive, response was made by those entrepreneurs who, while accepting that there were fields — such as the production of cheap textiles — in which there was little hope of competing with the British firms already entrenched in the market, turned to others in which they had, or could develop, an advantage. The general rise in incomes in Europe and in North America, the appearance of a middle-class consumer market for goods of a higher quality and greater variety, gave opportunities which continental producers were able to exploit. Of course, in the case of many commodities of this sort production was still carried on in small units using handicraft methods; a technical transformation was thus not necessarily required. On the other hand, steady growth could be assured by the further extension of these industries. However, a somewhat similar course could be pursued by capitalist entrepreneurs in the more advanced industrial areas of Europe. This meant an emphasis on high quality and finish, variety, ability closely to follow changing fashions rather than large-scale production of long runs at low unit cost. In short they left that sort of market to Lancashire and concentrated on producing for the higher income market which the Industrial Revolution in England had been largely instrumental in bringing about.

Thus an international division of labour was shaped in which British exports dominated the more distant markets, especially in the primary producing countries, while continental industrialists, so far as they had an export market, found it in the more advanced areas of Europe and North America. As a result the exports of the European industries were, by and large, of high quality specialities which followed on from, or incorporated, the handicraft type production directed at a higher income market. At the same time, the nature of the home market in these lagging areas of early industrialization tended to emphasise the same pattern. Carrying over from the eighteenth century, purchasing power was highly skewed in favour of the nobility and bourgeoisie. A large proportion of the population, still engaged in a mainly self-sufficient agriculture, bought little, and what they did buy constituted a local exchange with artisans or consisted of commodities produced under the putting-out system. Thus a transition to factory production was delayed and the old forms of industry in the countryside had a prolonged life. In much the same way, the heavy weight of the high income groups in the market for manufactured goods made possible the survival of small-scale quality production. Not only was the progress of factory industry thus delayed, but it for long had the characteristic of an alien, artificial growth, confined to a few special areas and existing in an industrial environment still dominated by the traditional forms. Thus the 'dual economy', though not absent in England too, was much more pronounced in Europe and had a longer life.

The workers and entrepreneurs in the old, small-scale and artisan trades, as they became conscious of the threat of factory production, did what they could to arrest its spread. In part, of course, hostility to the factory-made product was, especially in France, an aspect of Anglophobia. In Germany the privileges of the guilds did not legally disappear until the 1860s and the kind of industries which they embraced continued to form a powerful pressure group which, together with the agrarians, tried to resist the advance of industrial society. In Russia a whole school of thinkers idealized the traditional handicrafts and vainly advocated their preservation. Although in Britain there were those who shed nostalgic tears over the fate of the old crafts and the machine-breakers gave the language a new word, Luddism in any literal sense soon died out. If the progress of machine industry was, in many fields, slow and piecemeal the causes were mainly economic; through free trade, factory regulation and the attitude of the law to restraint of trade the older forms of industry were deprived of supports and disappeared when market conditions were ripe.

Continental industrialization displayed some characteristics which flowed naturally from the fact that the entrepreneurs and others who promoted it were both confronted by a powerful and entrenched rival and could make use of British capital, technique and managerial and entrepreneurial ability. In the early decades of the nineteenth century, however, there were few areas or sectors in which such borrowing could yield fruits. It was not enough to have a model, there had also to be propitious conditions for its transference to a different environment. In some cases, such as the textile industry of Alsace and some other parts of French industry, there was a judicious combination of adaptation to the conditions created by British leadership by taking advantage of the opportunities it offered for specialization and adopting advanced techniques and forms of organization worked out in Britain. This type of response was much more fruitful than the earlier transplanting because it bore a closer organic relationship to the economic changes now going on, and could speed them on their way.

The adoption of the railway was an obvious way in which the Industrial Revolution in Britain made a direct impact on the Continent. Because of the long distances which had to be traversed to link up raw materials with producing centres, these centres with their markets, the ports with their hinterlands and so on, the new means of transport was bound to have a more revolutionary effect than it had in its country of origin. But the railway also made great demands for capital which was either not available in sufficient quantity or which prospective investors were unwilling to tie up in such a form without some guarantee, which only the state could give, that a certain return would be forthcoming. In most cases, therefore, railway development in Europe took place under state auspices and required the cooperation of international bankers and financiers. Apart from the political and strategic motives involved, it had the definite character of an economic promotion which was expected to inject new life into the economy. Of course, it did not suffice to build a railway in order to initiate industrialization but, for the latecomers, the building of the railways represented one of the necessary preliminary steps. It brought on to the scene advanced financial and business techniques and made the wealthy familiar with new forms of investment. It was a great stimulant for heavy industry and led to the rapid adoption of techniques of iron-making, coal-mining and engineering which had been available for a long time but which had been comparatively little used.

Without making the contrast too sharp, it can be said that in the experience of the latecomers the capital goods industries played a more important role in the industrialization process than they had done at a comparable stage in British experience. Of course, there were mechanical textile industries in France, parts of Germany and other countries before the railways were built. In some cases these could be described already as the strongholds of the older form of industrial capitalism which the capitalism based on heavy industry was to challenge. The point is clear, however, that the heavy industries, thanks principally to the railways, had greater weight in the transformation of the continental economies. These industries, like the railways, required large outlays of capital. Because of the scale of production and the heavy overhead costs involved competition was unstable; a few large firms tended to dominate the field. There took place a series of technical improvements which emphasized the trend towards bigness and towards integration of the processes under unified control and ownership. While in Britain, even in iron and steel, and still more strikingly in coal mining, industry tended to be organized in many competitive, self-financed family firms, on the Continent many of the enterprises were on a large scale from an early stage, looked to outside sources of finance and sought to limit the effectiveness of competition. Beside the old-style family capitalism, which still predominated in Britain, there grew up in the continental countries, when industrialization seriously began in the third quarter of the nineteenth century, a sector which, by its scale, organization and links with the banks prefigured the typical form of capitalist enterprise in the twentieth century. From a present day perspective, who was then the pioneer?

Once again it is important not to exaggerate these differences, however significant they were. In some ways industrialization followed a common path in all the European countries. The family firm and self-financing were found everywhere, especially in the textile and other consumer goods industries. Even in heavy industry the dynastic firm of the Krupps or de Wendel type was of outstanding importance; such firms did not draw closer to the banks until the steel-making processes of the late nineteenth century required enormous outlays of capital, especially in the Ruhr and Lorraine. In general France, the first latecomer, showed features closer to the British model than did Germany, whose industrialization was later, less spread out in time and more definitely associated with coal and iron.

Throughout the nineteenth century and down to the middle of the twentieth the continental countries remained much less thoroughly industrialized than did Britain. This is shown in the first place by the considerable, if dwindling, weight which agriculture — still largely in the hands of peasants — retained in the structure of the economy. Inevitably the fact that excessive resources were, from a purely economic point of view, pinioned in agriculture, kept the average *per capita* income lower than it might otherwise have been. Some sections of agriculture, and entire regions, were, in every European country, condemned to a relative backwardness which acted as a drag upon the transformation of the national economy as a whole. No doubt there were sociological as well as economic reasons for the disparities between the Paris Basin and Brittany, Wallonia and the Flemish-speaking districts of Belgium, the Ruhr and southern Germany. France, as well as Italy, had its southern problem, though in a less acute form, and the whole Mediterranean area was backward compared with the north-west. To move east was likewise to go back in time, or in levels of economic development; in eastern Europe and Russia the industrial centres were oases in a sea of peasant sloth and bureaucratic inertia. The stranglehold of earlier structures, particularly the effects of belated feudalism and serfdom, were not thrown off until comparatively recently. Invisible economic frontiers separated the advancing from the slowly changing areas to make the national unit an unsatisfactory basis for the measurement of growth in some respects.

As agriculture conserved a considerable weight in the economies of the European states so it tended also to preserve the old structures in industrial production. In the agrarian regions, where genuine industrial towns were few and far between, market towns and administrative centres, often small and sleepy, represented urban living. In these small towns handicraft industry could survive on the market constituted by the peasantry in the surrounding countryside and the petty bourgeoisie in the town itself. These somewhat archaic conditions had a considerable survival power and were an aspect of the economic dualism referred to above. In Britain, where peasant agriculture had to all intents and purposes disappeared by the early nineteenth century, and where, in a compact geographical environment, transport improvements diminished rural isolation and drew all regions into a single 'urbanized' national market, there were few parallels. In this sense the industrial transformation was more thorough than anywhere on the Continent. Even the rural areas were drawn into the mainstream of economic change as part of an economy geared to the market, peopled mainly by wage labourers who had to buy in the market most of what they consumed and therefore bought wherever possible, cheap, factory-made products. Under these conditions rural industries and the rural artisans died out and the market towns became merely distributing centres for the manufactured goods of the industrial areas. As a corollary to this, the urban pattern of living characteristic of a modern industrial society, with its effects on the disposal of income, became established in England earlier and more firmly than on the Continent where the catching up process was still going on well into the twentieth century.

As the European countries industrialized they may be thought of, not only as rivals to Britain, but also as links in the developing international division of labour without which industrialization in Britain would have been slowed down. On the extreme hypothesis of an industrial Britain in an agrarian Europe a severe limit would have been set to the purchasing power of the European economies. This would not only have prevented them from expanding their purchases of British goods but, by restricting their purchase of goods from other parts of the world, would also have curtailed the market for British goods on a world scale. If this is true the free trade picture of an international division of labour in which Britain remained 'the workshop of the world' was as undesirable as it was unrealizable. It is true that the existence of free trade in Britain played a crucial role in the development of the European and world economy in the nineteenth century by offering a market for agrarian surpluses and specialized industrial products and thus encouraging investment of capital in them. On the other hand, had other countries not protected their industries many of them could never have got off the ground and without them the incomes of their people, and thus international purchasing power, would have been held back. The continued industrialization of Britain in the period from the 1840s was certainly assisted by the rise of industry in Europe, even of an industry behind tariff walls.

For a time, beginning with the Anglo-French Treaty of Commerce of 1860, it seemed that all European countries were bent on a liberalization of trade relations. In France, and perhaps in other countries, the lowering of tariff walls had an undoubtedly salutary effect on industrial efficiency. However, most French industrialists remained firmly protectionist and tried unceasingly to reverse what has been called Napoleon III's 'industrial *coup d'état*'. The real blow to the evolution of a European free trade system came as a result of the trade crisis of the 1870s. In all countries investment had expanded rapidly in the closing years of the quarter of a century of

prosperity (1848–73) which coincided with the first phases of industrialization in Western Europe. European industry was still vulnerable to English competition particularly when, under the pressure of
shrinking markets, prices were being sharply lowered by the manufacturers across the Channel. Those industrialists not already converted to at least moderate protection now mostly cried out for
higher tariffs. This time they were joined by the agrarian interests,
often formerly favourable to free trade, who faced the great slide in
agricultural prices as railways and cheap oceanic shipping brought
the grain of America and Russia to their doorsteps. The protectionist
reaction was thus severe and widespread. Trade between the European countries was not halted but it was certainly deformed by the
tariffs. National industries were built up behind tariff walls which
had to have an export market. Some relief was found in the fact that
the British market remained open; and British manufacturers had
the advantage, without protection, of privileged markets and a
particular facility for selling in the less developed countries. However, there was intensified trade competition, especially a search for
privileged market areas which could only be obtained and defended
with political support.

Industry thus became more dependent upon government, but governments saw their responsibilities in different ways. Britain remained
a free trade country because far more, and more vocal, interests
profited from it than stood to gain from protection. There was
nothing paradoxical about that. In the younger industrial countries
the industrialists demanded protection as a right consistent with
national interest, and they obtained it. Britain had acquired a large
formal and informal empire which assured her entrepreneurs of
privileged investment fields, supplies of raw materials and markets
for their industrial goods. With these advantages other forms of
government support were not required. The protectionist reaction
in Britain was mild; colonial development acted as a substitute.
In France, and more particularly Germany, the protectionist reaction was vigorous and was coupled with other government
measures designed to give national industry an advantage. In any
case, in these countries, the older tradition of Government support for industry had never died out but it was revived now
in societies which were being transformed by advanced industrial

techniques and the practices of large-scale business enterprises.

The competitive and noninterventionist climate in which the early steps in industrialization had been taken in Britain were, in fact, quite exceptional. In different degrees in the European late-comers the state was expected to play a more positive role in creating favourable conditions for business. Where industries were established from scratch, as it were, on a large scale and needed support from the banks competitive forces were weakened. New and complex patterns of economic development emerged in the different countries as will be shown in later chapters. In some ways the latecomers appeared to possess advantages. Their entrepreneurs could begin with the most modern plant, located and laid out to take the maximum advantage of the availability of raw materials and the most recent technical knowledge. They had access to wider sources of finance and could look to support from banking institutions. Where new and abundant supplies of raw materials could be tapped, where a growing population ensured an abundant supply of labour power and an expanding internal market, high rates of growth were attainable. Moreover, it was possible, and indeed imperative, to push a way into the world market, both to ensure supplies of raw materials and foodstuffs and to dispose of the output of industries whose capacities developed in excess of domestic demand. No more than in the case of England could it be said of industrial capitalism in Europe that it was a self-contained national development. Its national form concealed the deep and growing involvement with the world market without which industrialization was impossible. Success thus required an ability to make such an adaptation; but, as has been seen, it was in part thwarted by national exclusiveness and the competitive drive for commercial outlets and colonies. In fact, even while Britain lost her industrial and technological leadership the strongly entrenched position of her merchants, financiers and shipowners in the world market remained much less pervious to the challenge of the newer industrial countries.

The advantages of the latecomers have therefore to be seen in perspective. Down to 1914 they continued to be accompanied by many drawbacks and, by comparison with Britain, they remained, in terms of average *per capita* income at least, in an inferior position. It is principally in terms of interindustry comparisons that they appeared to have derived an advantage by the belatedness of their development.

It may be concluded that the British Industrial Revolution did not have a precise parallel in the continental countries. Nowhere else did the industrialization process assume the same autonomous or organic character, nowhere else, as a national phenomenon, was it so complete and so successful in changing the whole social structure. In the European context, indeed, the term tends to take on a different meaning. It covers the process whereby the social and legal conditions for the full development of capitalism were created against the resistance of the beneficiaries of the old, industrial order, a process which in England had begun a century or more before industrialization. Even where, as in Germany, there was a very rapid growth of industry so that what had taken a century or so in England was compressed into a couple of decades, the full impact of the transition was confined to certain regions and, for all its speed, it was less complete. The substantial weight of the agrarian sector, the preindustrial survivals in society and the retention of backward regions bear witness to this.

During the nineteenth century European industrialization tended to be mainly a regional phenomenon and the transformation of whole national economies remained less complete than in Britain. Even Belgium, the smallest of the industrial countries, had its backward agrarian region. Germany, the outstanding industrial success among the great powers, still retained a large peasant sector and some of the characteristics of a dual economy. Although in France too the foundations of a modern economy had been securely laid between the 1880s and 1914 the transformation was still less complete. In Russia promising spurts of rapid industrial growth tended either to grind to a halt or to intensify internal strains and weaknesses because of the constricting influence of the old inherited structures. Italy was disadvantaged by lack of natural resources and the failure of capitalism to carry through a transformation of the agrarian sector and diminish its weight in the economy or to resolve the southern question. Elsewhere industrialization was simply a regional phenomenon and the creation of modern national economies, although going on, was still far from complete. In one sense, then, what can be stressed about the Continent is the incompleteness and the geographical patchiness of the industrial transformation compared with Britain. By comparison with the rest of the world, however, Europe was the area of advanced capitalism *par excellence*. Excluding the European transplants, above all the United States, only in Japan and to a certain extent in India were there precursive signs of an industrial transition to come. In relation to the underdeveloped regions of the world, even the economies of southern or eastern Europe displayed many of the basic features of modern economic life, at any rate in a few urban and industrial areas.

As an already highly developed and built-up industrial area, inheriting from her earlier industrial past a heavy weight of institutionalized habits and productive equipment embodying much which was outmoded and obsolete, the great problem of Britain was to be the slow rate of adaptation to the changing trends of the twentieth century. To some extent, of course, a similar inflexibility afflicted all those areas in which industrialization had its roots in the eighteenth or early nineteenth centuries. It was not so much a specifically British phenomenon as its particularly sharp expression on a national scale in that country led some to believe. More will be said at the end of this book about the penalties of having been first in the field, but it is as well to point out that these penalties had to be paid in some form, sooner or later, by all those areas which had followed on Britain's heels in the development of the industries of coal, iron and textiles upon which earlier industrialization had been based. Then, especially between the wars, Europe as a whole appeared to be ageing and in decline compared with the United States, Japan and Russia which had, in terms of its social-economic system, separated itself from Europe. New forms of industrial technology, business methods and consumption patterns, as well as economic policies, which developed, or realized their full potential, outside Europe contributed after 1945 to make possible a renewed process of rapid growth and carried through industrialization where it had hitherto been incomplete. The possibilities of such a transformation were, on the whole, narrower in Britain than in the continental countries so that a new disparity began to appear between the former, growing sluggishly, and the latter leaping ahead at a 'miraculous' rate. Deeply-rooted historical forces may be said to explain, to an important extent at least, the Britain–Europe growth differentials of the recent period.

Problems for discussion

1. By comparison with the European countries what appear to be the main distinguishing features of industrialization in Britain?
2. Did the industrialization of European countries assume the character of an industrial revolution?
3. Why did (*a*) the state and (*b*) the banks play a more prominent role in the economic development of the continental countries than in Britain?
4. What advantages did the 'latecomers' possess?
5. Compare the effect of railway construction and operation in Britain and in one or more of the European countries.
6. How did continental entrepreneurs react to British industrial predominance in the nineteenth century?
7. Why did Eastern and Southern Europe lag behind the Western European countries?
8. Compare the problems encountered by entrepreneurs in recruiting a labour force for industry in Britain with those in one other country.

2 Agrarian Revolution and Industrialization

A preindustrial economy is one in which, by definition, most of the population obtains its living by tilling the soil and raising animals; that part which is specialized in other pursuits depends for its support on a surplus which derives from the same source. For centuries before industrialization began there is a history of settled agricultural communities in most parts of Europe. Although in many places new land was still being brought into cultivation this was small in extent compared with the area on which a settled agraianr life had been going on for a thousand years or more. Many traits of European agriculture, resulting from an adaptation of man to prevailing conditions of the soil and the climate in the earliest times, had a pretty well continuous existence through this time. For instance, this was an area of dry farming which did not require extensive irrigation works and which was based on a combination of cereal cultivation with animal husbandry. It thus lent itself to the establishment of self-contained rural communities which produced enough to support a ruling class of landowning warriors. In the period after the decline of the Roman Empire there developed the peculiarly European variety of feudalism consisting of the imposition of manorial organization on the groundplan of the village community of an earlier period of tribal settlement. In turn, European feudalism displayed many local variations and began to change as a result of many different factors with unequal local weights.

At least it can be said that European feudalism, in general terms, carried within itself the seeds of change. Whereas in other parts of the world, notably the Orient, more power resided in the hands of the state and civilization can really be correlated with the emergence of a centralized political authority, in Europe the central powers were weak in relation to the manorial lords. The other civilizations tended either not to change or to break up and decay under internal or external pressures. Under European feudalism, however, there was more scope for change and adaptation. The decentralization of power widened the scope for an autonomous development not only of the lords but also of towns and townsmen. Urban activities which required buying and selling, thus the existence of markets and the use of money, while in some ways alien to feudalism as a 'chemically pure' system, were necessary to its rulers if they were to live better and increase their wealth. Taking advantage of this the towns were able to win franchises which extended their ability to govern themselves and expand the operations in which their influential inhabitants were interested. From the towns, therefore, issued dissolvents which penetrated the basically rural foundations of feudalism.

Under agrarian feudalism, as the term is understood here, a ruling class of landowners extracts, by coercive means, a surplus from an underlying population of cultivators. Land was unproductive without people to work it. With the manor, therefore, necessarily went the inhabitants of the village communities. On the manor these inhabitants enjoyed the protection of their overlords whose monopoly of coercive power gave some guarantee of tranquillity and order in an era of internecine baronial wars and lawlessness. Conserving certain rights in the soil which antedated the manor itself, the rural population were not chattel slaves (at least for the most part) but neither were more than a small minority free men. They were bound to the manor and obliged to perform the services and meet the obligations which the lords laid upon them. In short, permitted to use part of the land to support themselves and their families, most of what they produced over and above this, whether or not exacted in the form of compulsory labour services on the demesne lands, went to support the lords and their retainers. The form in which the surplus over and above the bare subsistence of the cultivators was extracted in the manorial economy provides the distinguishing feature of European feudalism.

The ecology of the peasant community in Europe makes an interesting study. Later generations were apt to be impatient of the open fields with their jumbled up strips and apparent wastes and inefficiencies and with the other practices of the village community.

However, for the men who built them up and perpetuated them over many centuries these practices evidently had a rationale of their own which represented an empirical adaptation of means to physical environment. These agrarian communities, like most, were, of course, short of tools, implements and draught animals. They lacked all scientific and technical knowledge except that which had been built up over generations in a slow process of trial-and-error. They operated with a low level of reserves and were vulnerable to every caprice of nature. Under these conditions little could be produced above mere subsistence and most of that went to support the mainly unproductive activities of the ruling seigneurial class.

The layout of the fields and the methods which were employed to cultivate them represented a close adaptation to the force of circumstances. The basic activity of breaking up the land to prepare it for cultivation was necessarily a collective effort requiring the pooling of ploughs and draught animals. There was nothing more natural than that the size and layout of the fields and the individual plots in them should bear a close relationship to the means used to make them ready for cultivation. Likewise, the other collective servitudes linked the villagers in a common effort to extract what they could from a niggardly nature; the sacrifice of individual freedom in one respect was more than compensated for by what was gained in others.

In the economy of the European village an indispensable part was played by the animals, for not only did they provide food and drag the heavy ploughs needed to turn over the clayey soil, they also provided the manure which was required to maintain its fertility. Even this was not sufficient to make possible continuous cropping of the open fields. One-half or one-third of the land lay fallow each year to enable the land to recover some of its fertility. Lack of winter feeds limited the number of animals which could be kept. The variety of crops was also limited since many of the vegetables which became common in the nineteenth century were still unknown.

Besides the arable fields the villagers made use of common and waste lands to which they had rights by custom more or less tolerated by the lords. From these lands fuel, building materials and food were obtained which formed an essential complement to the produce of the open fields. Their use was regulated generally according to the holdings of the villagers in the arable fields but in tolerant periods outsiders, or the village poor, might establish a kind of right of their own to make use of the common or waste and even to set up dwellings on them.

This sketch of the structure of European rural life has an astonishingly wide application. In its essentials it could be still applied to many areas even in the twentieth century, despite detailed changes and accretions. Having existed from time immemorial, in a society without a written culture or any opportunity of developing science and technique, the form of husbandry associated with the village community had a tremendous hold over men's minds and habits. It embodied the powerful momentum of custom and traditions which even the will of the lords was often unable to stop or alter.

European agriculture was composed of two separable components. On the one side it provided a ready means, in various guises, whereby the lords were able to scoop up a surplus of agricultural produce which passed under their control and served to support them materially. On the other it provided the framework of existence for largely self-contained peasant communities with a low level of technique and little capital at their disposal. It contained, therefore, inherent sources of tension between the claims and pretensions of the lords and the strivings of the peasantry to retain a greater share of their product. Peasant discontent was endemic, breaking out from time to time in revolts or in sporadic disorders in times of hardship or when the exactions of the lords became unbearable.

Internal change resulting from the varying pressures of lords and peasants provided only one, and perhaps the lesser, of the forces which made for change in rural society. Its modification and perhaps eventual disintegration took place, in the main, as the result of external forces: the growth of towns and trade, the spread of money economy, the desire of the lords to raise their incomes, the opportunities for individual self-advancement which such changes provided. As the distribution of these forces making for change was very uneven, and their rate of operation different in different places, the pattern from the later Middle Ages becomes increasingly variegated. These forces operated, it must be remembered, in different ways on the two components of rural life. What mattered was both how they brought about the extinction of feudal tenures — also when and under what conditions — and whether at the same time the peasant community was uprooted. Broadly speaking the changes could take place from above, under the control of the state or the nobility, or from below as a result of the successful revolt of the peasantry. In neither case, of course, was the change merely social and political, always it was connected with complex economic forces which substituted new social relations for those characteristic of feudalism as the term is here used. The end result, or we might say the form of capitalist agriculture which emerged, besides appearing at different times from the sixteenth century onwards, varied greatly from place to place. It henceforth became possible to speak of the distinguishing characteristics of the agrarian system within different countries; the later studies show what influence different patterns of agrarian development had on the process of industrialization in each case.

Although European agricultural life gives an impression of stability or stagnation for long periods, even into modern times, and the very predominance of custom and tradition acted against change even in the more advanced areas it certainly went through a slow but appreciable degree of improvement. It was only when the basic structure was affected that we can speak of reform or even of revolution. Peasant cultivators were not receptive to technical improvements except where they arose out of their own experience. Nor was there any desire on the part of the great majority to change the customary servitudes which went with the cultivation of the open fields. Land, after all, was part of an established way of life; for the peasants it did not have the nature of private property in the Roman or modern sense. It was only by a struggle, by beating down peasant opposition, that the lords were able, in places, to establish a new conception of landed property. What the peasants sought to change, at least intermittently, was the situation which condemned them to serfdom and to the payment of an inordinate proportion of their product to the feudal overlord. Where conditions favoured them, therefore, they sought, and in some cases achieved, the abolition of serfdom, though under conditions which still left them paying dues in money and other forms to the lord. Where conditions favoured the lord, and there was the incentive to do so, estates might be cleared of peasants, as happened in places in England during the sixteenth century. By enclosing the open fields and asserting their right to consider the land as their individual private property the English landlords were responding to market opportunities and consciously assuming that land was a source of commercial profit and a marketable asset. For such an attitude to emerge a whole process of change had had to take place outside agriculture which created a market for wool and other products.

Where enclosure took place and peasants were driven off the land they became landless people. The way in which they had been deprived of their land and the social problems which the sudden appearance of rootless people without means of support created drew the attention of government and of reformers. The enclosures have since stood as a monumental example of social injustice perpetrated by the rich upon the poor. For Marx they represented one of the first steps towards the accumulation of capital by concentrating landed property in the hands of a few and compelling the former peasants to seek their support through the sale of their labour power. There had, of course, been landless men before the sixteenth-century enclosures, not only in the towns but also in the villages. No doubt throughout Europe people of this sort could be found. Some, it is true, might eventually inherit land or acquire a holding through some form of tenancy. Others existed as a labour reserve both for agriculture and for rural industry. The point is that they were not a numerous class. Most rural dwellers had some land, even though it might not be adequate to support themselves and their families. On the whole it was the penetration of commercial relations into the villages as much or more than the use of force against the peasants by the lords which tended towards differentiation within the peasantry and the appearance of more or less permanent strata of landless and semilandless rural labourers.

Of course, this is a very generalized picture. Every region and every locality showed its own peculiarities, ringing an infinite variety of possible changes on the basic pattern of a peasant society undergoing change as it was drawn into a market economy. The opportunities offered by the growth of demand from the towns encouraged some peasants to farm for the market. Where labour services were commuted for money payments all those subject to them had to obtain money by selling commodities or by working for wages. If the lords took to managing their estates as commercial enterprises they tended to speed up the process by extending their control over the land, leasing land on a contractual basis and employing wage-labour or leasing the land to farmers who did. It was possible, however, that in some cases for the development of farming for the market on the demesne to lead to an intensification of serfdom, as happened in England in the twelfth century. In some areas, therefore, there appeared many of the characteristic features of a capitalist agriculture in which production was no longer for subsistence but for sale in the market. New relations were established between the lords and the land, and the lords and the peasants. There emerged a class of farmers or peasants producing for the market and growing numbers of wage-workers recruited from those who had no land or insufficient to support their families. On the same soil, too, grew the conditions for the development of the putting-out system as entrepreneurs tapped the reservoir of surplus rural labour constituted by people who needed to supplement their money income by some form of wage-work. This process can be seen at work in different countries at widely separated points in time. In England it is already apparent by the later Middle Ages, in France it is becoming pronounced by the eighteenth century, in parts of Germany about the same time, in eastern Europe and Russia it does not assume real importance until the latter part of the nineteenth century. What is being indicated, in fact, are the different rates of development of capitalism which in turn determined to what extent, and at what period, the areas concerned would become ripe for industrialization.

It is not incorrect to regard the way in which these conditions were prepared in Britain as the classic case. But in no other place were these conditions precisely reproduced. Agrarian development took place on many and varied lines. It showed, in a variety of combinations, the effect of commercial or other motives working on the lords, the penetration of commercial relations into the countryside, the inertias derived from custom and tradition and the influence of state policies. In England the transformation of feudalism began early and conditions rapidly became favourable for the strengthening of the forces of the market and of individual possessiveness. Partly owing to the changes which the feudal class underwent through its internecine conflicts and its ability to strengthen its powers in relation to the Crown, it adapted itself to the commercial possibilities which opened up in the sixteenth century. The disintegration of the peasant community began early and its position steadily weakened while the lords were extending their control over their estates and viewing them increasingly as a commercial proposition. In other parts of Europe the evolution was on the whole distinctly different. For one thing the political role of the lords tended to weaken; many became courtiers and absentees. The product of their estates continued to be the material basis for their existence but it was still syphoned off in the old forms, through compulsory labour services and the payments in money or in kind or the other servitudes exacted from the peasantry. Although money played a role in these transactions, perhaps an increasing one, it did not supersede custom and tradition as the basis of agrarian relations. Substantially the lords' position, and their income, arose from their monopoly of the coercive powers in society. The peasants were kept in subjection as serfs or at least as only semi-free men. On the other hand, if their status seemed inferior to that of their counterparts in England and they paid away so much of the product (or the methods of husbandry were so inferior) that their material lot was worse, through the village community they maintained a certain resistance to the lords' pretensions. The latter, for their part, were mainly interested in drawing the maximum income in the old forms. Where payments had been fixed in terms of money and prices rose they might try to protect themselves by new exactions. On the whole, however, they were not concerned with estate management. The operations of husbandry remained in the hands of peasants; precisely because they did the rate of agricultural progress was slow.

There were, of course, some exceptions to these general principles. In some places the rise of a market, in the towns or in the export trade, led to development on capitalist lines: peasants farming for the market or tenants leasing land from the lords and producing a surplus for sale. In others the lords used serf labour to work the demesne and organized their estate as a grain-producing enterprise. Examples of the former were to be found in the more densely populated and prosperous areas of north-west Europe. The serf cultivated estate was to be found in East Germany and parts of Russia and eastern Europe. There were other variations to be found in southern Europe on the great estates known as latifundia. Barring such cases as these, the pattern sketched above was the most typical. It also had evident defects from the point of view of its effects on economic growth.

Where the peasants retained control of agriculture, preserved the open field system and the old communal type of agriculture and continued to furnish a substantial part of their labour-time or produce to the lords, a brake was imposed upon the rate of economic progress. For one thing it meant that agricultural methods, though they might change a little as a result of empirical experience, tended to remain static from one generation to the next. There was no sharp incentive to make use of improved techniques which, in any case, illiterate and tradition-bound peasants would either not hear about or be suspicious of. But the fact that the bulk of the surplus was paid away to the lords meant that they had little possibility of undertaking improvements for lack of means. As for the use which the lords made of the surplus it went for the most part in conspicuous consumption, in the support of retainers and gave sustenance to industries directed to serving their cultivated tastes. Expressed in another way, it can be said that the European nobility was primarily a parasitic consuming class, it only invested its surplus productively to a very limited extent. Compare this with the situation in England. Involved in estate management, dealing more strictly in rational accounting terms, the landowners not only drew income out of the estate to maintain themselves in the state to which they were accustomed, building stately homes and the like, but they also financed improvements, of which enclosure was the most important, and saw to it, where possible, that the estate was farmed by men able to pay an economic rent.

The European system tended towards the perpetuation of the peasantry, whether in a free or an unfree status. The English system had begun early to undermine the position of the peasantry and a combination of economic forces and institutional pressures weakened the village community and loosened the peasants' hold on the land. The apparent power of the continental nobility and their ability to go on exacting a high proportion of the product of the peasants' labour concealed a real weakness. It still had to contend with the consolidated power of the village community: its ability to reorganize the agrarian system, even if it wanted to, was thus strictly limited. The Crown and the Church had an interest in the existing agrarian set-up, since taxes levied on the peasants and tithes—as well as direct holdings of land—provided a substantial part of their income. The Church, as the weaker party, generally lost out and in one country after another was dispossessed of lands and privileges, generally to the advantage of the Crown. The dynastic governments of the seventeenth and eighteenth centuries were reluctant to interfere in the agrarian sphere. Most of them, although dependent on noble support, sought to curtail the privileges, tax exemptions and so on of the nobility as a means of strengthening the powers of the dynasty and modernizing its administration. While in England the landowners controlled the government and were thus able to carry through an agrarian change from above, in their own interests and to establish the full rights of private landed property in a way which destroyed for good the prospects of the village community, in Europe, generally speaking, they remained passive. They lacked the will and the means to carry through an agrarian revolution from above. On the other hand, governments which sought to diminish the powers of the nobility could make concessions to the peasantry, and did so the more eagerly if this resulted in increasing the taxable capacity of the rural population. They feared, however, the consequences of carrying out a thorough agrarian reform which would include the substitution of enclosure for the open fields, even when the advantages of such a solution had been shown in England. Such change as did take place by conscious action before the French Revolution came from above and did little more than ease the burden of serfdom on the peasantry; in fact, in the other countries of Western Europe, it was not until after 1800 that peasant emancipation from above was carried through. In central Europe it came almost half a century later and in Russia not until 1861. Even then, not only did the peasant often have to repurchase his freedom, but the customary agricultural arrangements were not dealt with.

The whole course of evolution in English agriculture from the late Middle Ages therefore was favourable to the development of capitalism. At the same time the peasantry as a class was steadily weakened and virtually disappeared by the end of the eighteenth century. The old distinction between freedom and unfreedom was replaced by another between the owners and non-owners. Landed property took on a new form and was concentrated in the hands of a comparatively small number of families, leaving the great majority without property. On the whole this was in appearance an evolutionary process, but in fact a decisive turning point came in the revolutions of the seventeenth century. The outcome of these revolutions decided the supremacy of the new forms of property, recognized the legal paramountcy of individual ownership and signed the death warrant of the English peasantry. In the next century, at their convenience, the English landlords were able to take full advantage of these legal possibilities to consolidate their estates and integrate them into the structure of capitalism. Because of its concentrated nature, because of the ancient lineage of many of the landowning families and because of the extensive administrative and juridical powers which landowners conserved, landownership retained a kind of feudal shell even when it had been thoroughly transformed on lines entirely congruous with capitalism. It was not the only form of landownership consistent with the preparation of conditions for industrialization, but its consequences turned out to be particularly propitious.

As a precondition for the industrialization of any society some reshaping of agrarian relations appears to be absolutely indispensable. The British case was exceptional because it took place so completely and apparently fitted in so well with the needs of an industrializing society. The same reasons which favoured the agrarian transition in England also prepared the conditions for industrialization from a date much earlier than the eighteenth century. Agrarian change was in the main a response to what was going on outside agriculture, namely the growth of markets for food and industrial raw materials. It seems that it was the pressure of demand, and thus the possibilities of making profit by satisfying it, not anything happening in rural society, which prompted agrarian change. On the other hand, it is true that continued development of towns and the rise of markets would not have been possible had not a supply of raw materials and foodstuffs been made available. In that sense agrarian and industrial change, linked through the spread of market transactions and the development of the home market, acted in a close reciprocal relationship. If agrarian change was necessary for industrialization, then, it did not precede in time the preparation of the conditions, namely the extension of capitalist relations, but was an indispensable part of that process. Once it was under way changes in industry could stimulate technical improvement or reorganization in the agrarian sphere. At the same time, the introduction of new crops, the spread of technical skills or the availability of new aids to cultivation such as better tools and machines or artificial fertilizers, enabled agriculture to make a contribution of its own to economic growth. But there had to be a market for the increasing output, and some of these improvements required the attainment of a certain level of technical proficiency in industry or the expansion of trade, so that reciprocity is again established.

Approaching the problem from another direction, a predominantly agrarian society will show little potential for growth, whatever its form of social organization, assuming that the quantity of land is limited. At best it could keep pace with a moderate rate of population increase. To raise incomes requires a transfer of resources from activities subject at an early stage to diminishing returns to more productive activities which, over a longer range, are subject to increasing returns. Any growth in incomes in such a predominantly agrarian society would consist of food and raw materials. This surplus could be used to enable specialized production of manufactures to be carried on and various services to be purveyed, making a more than proportionate net addition to the income of the society as a whole. The beginning of this transfer obviously antedates industrialization by the whole span of known civilization; its extent suffices to establish a rough classification on a quantitative basis. The growth of European societies took place as a result of a quickening of this transfer and was conditioned, in each country or region, by the extent to which it took place. In England it began relatively early and took place fairly rapidly for reasons which have already been seen. Where feudal institutions were preserved or strong vestiges survived the transfer was slowed down. More rapid growth therefore turned upon some modification of the traditional agrarian system and eventually upon its complete supersession. But agrarian reform or revolution could take many forms, of which the English model was but one.

It is not being argued, needless to say, that technical change in agriculture was of no importance. Obviously it was, but the improvement of techniques was also bound to be slow as long as the old structures survived. Even without any fundamental change productivity could be favourably affected by innovation. For example, if a community was able to leave only one-third of its land fallow each year instead of one-half, assuming no falling off in yield, output would be increased by nearly one-third. By the eighteenth century a number of new crops became available in Europe which, like the potato, enabled the food yield of a given amount of land to be greatly increased. No doubt as such improvements took place the effects showed themselves primarily in an increase in population: more people could be kept alive and perhaps an improved diet or a more certain supply increased resistance to disease. Certainly the growth in the population of Europe during the eighteenth century was a significant development involving at first pressure on the land and increasing the numbers of the landless and semi-landless.

Where conditions otherwise favoured a more rapid rate of economic growth the growth in population contributed a further favourable factor. In England, for example, where the agrarian system was already in a process of change, population increase made available further supplies of labour for the farmers and for employment in the putting-out system or migration to the towns. The obstacles to mobility arising both from lack of cheap transport facilities and from the operation of poor laws and settlement laws created pools of surplus labour in the mainly agricultural areas while the rapid development of industry in others brought temporary local scarcities. The addition to the population was to a large extent an addition to the numbers of those wholly or partly dependent upon wages. In continental areas this was not necessarily the case. Population growth taking place through an increase in the number of children kept alive increased the pressure on family income and, where partible inheritance persisted, resulted in the subdivision of holdings. Increase in numbers tended to outstrip the need for labour power and the improvement in methods of production; in some areas, then, living standards tended to decline. There was insufficient employment available for the additional people and, lacking purchasing power, they could not have a favourable effect on the internal market. In such circumstances the rural community became even more precariously balanced and a bad harvest could be a disaster. In so far as production was for the market and wage-labour had appeared the equilibrium became more delicate. Poor harvests meant a lower demand for labour, smaller incomes for the rural producers and higher prices for those who had to buy some or all of their food in the market. Those whose incomes were fixed in kind or in services might be better off. The larger producers and dealers also benefited from the sharp rise in prices and by cornering the market. The mass of the peasantry was sharply hit and the effects of the shortfall in the harvest were communicated to the towns in the shape of higher prices for food, a contracting demand, higher unemployment and the inflow of rural poor in search of work or alms.

The explosive social consequences of such a combination was powerfully demonstrated in the uprising of large parts of the French countryside in the summer of 1789. This great peasant movement had as its instinctive aim the abolition of feudal dues and services: all sections of the peasantry were united against the exactions of the seigneur. Because the village community had conserved a certain vitality, and because the lords were already socially isolated in all but a few areas, this movement, sparked off by the urban revolution which followed the calling of the States-General, was able to achieve a wide measure of success. It imposed itself on the urban revolutionaries and forced them to adopt an agrarian programme which was no part of their design. In a series of legislative measures the peasants were relieved of feudal dues and services without the need to pay compensation. In other words they were confirmed in the possession of their holdings unencumbered by the payments formerly made to the lords. Nothing could be done, however, to make a change in the open field village, with its strips, its fallow field and its common rights, mandatory upon the peasantry. The French peasantry, because it was able to emancipate itself from below, retained those features of the traditional agricultural set up which it saw no interest in changing. When the lands of the Church, and later of émigrés and suspects, were seized and put on sale, the more prosperous peasants were able to acquire additional land either directly or as the original purchasers sought to realize on their speculative investment by putting land on the market.

Thanks to these revolutionary changes the French peasantry not only survived, but despite other adverse effects of a period of wars and revolutions, it actually increased its income. By the practice of partible inheritance, which the Napoleonic code enshrined in the French law, peasant holdings were divided among the heirs. To counteract the effect of subdivision the prudent peasantry restricted the size of its families. Eventually, then, the revolutionary land settlement exercised an important influence on the demographic as well as the economic history of France. The movement from the land was slowed down because a large proportion of the peasantry had some land, or the prospect of acquiring or renting it. The formation of an urban proletariat was thus hindered. The peasants continued to produce a large proportion of their requirements and, although they had been drawn into a market economy, the amount which they sold remained small and, since they sold relatively little, their consuming power was low. In respect both to the delaying action which it exercised on the recruitment of a labour force for industry and by restricting the growth of the market the revolutionary land settlement tended to place a brake on the pace and extent of French industrialization.

On the whole this was the case wherever agrarian revolution or reform permitted the peasantry to acquire full legal title to all or most of the land which it tilled. The most propitious sort of reform for accelerated economic growth was one which exposed the peasantry to the full blast of market forces on the English model. The French case, on the other hand, was at the other extreme. The peasant emerged from the revolutionary stress and storm, if he was lucky, as a full proprietor, sheltered from the market and its exigencies by a legal code which, in other respects, was fully in accord with the needs of developing capitalism. The English peasantry, as a class, disappeared, to form the labour force for capitalist farmers and the recruiting ground for urban activities. In France the steady erosion of the old rural peasant society by market forces and agrarian individualism went on throughout the nineteenth century until, by its end, the extent of the rural exodus caused widespread concern. The point is that it was a protracted and uneven process which still left a large proportion of the population pinned to an agrarian sector which, because it contained so many small-scale, poorly arranged and capital-starved units, remained backward and inefficient. As a result the *per capita* income of the country was kept below what it might have been.

In France much of the old structure of agriculture survived in an environment which, in other ways, was favourable for industrialization. In other settings the agrarian structure was generally subject to pressures from two directions which brought about a reshaping which left it still, on the whole, nearer the French than the English model. These pressures came, in the first place, as a part of a pattern of modernization which the French Revolution stimulated, either directly as a result of the Napoleonic occupation, or by a desire, by carrying out a reform from above to avoid a revolution from below. In much of Germany, as well as in central and eastern Europe, including Russia, and in Mediterranean Europe, there was no agrarian revolution carried through by the peasantry itself, nor was reform a gift from the middle class. On the whole the changes in the inherited rural structures which did occur represented a process of adaptation by the dynastic state and the old ruling class as an alternative to peasant revolt. Under these conditions at least some consideration had to be given to pressure from below: the peasantry was therefore preserved as an ally of the state and the big agrarians against the commercial and industrial bourgeoisie. Concessions to the peasantry enabled it to survive but not necessarily to prosper, though on terms which also conserved the landlords, estates and social privileges. In other words there was no agrarian revolution and no solution to the agrarian problem. The second source of pressure was the penetration of market relations into the village which produced growing differentiation within peasant society. Many peasants with small holdings and without capital or technical knowledge could only survive on a subsistence basis and by some members of the family working for wages. Rural indebtedness, in the absence of cooperatives and peasant banks, could lead to expropriation and the concentration of landed property. The forces of the market acted slowly and unevenly and the peasant gained some protection because of his value as a political ally of the big agrarians, especially in the agricultural depression of the late nineteenth century. The fact was that over most of Europe the peasantry survived and parts of it prospered as a result of the opportunities which were offered for producing for the market. But if the peasantry survived it was partly at the expense of a higher *per capita* income than was in fact attained.

Meanwhile an increasing range of technical improvements were becoming available for European agriculturalists and, as the transport network thickened, specialization and production for the market became more general. In these ways industrialization made its impact on agriculture and in varying degrees broke down the old rural self-sufficiency and drew the peasant or farmer into the meshes of a market economy. In some cases, such as Denmark, this change was made the basis for a deliberate policy of specialization. In others it was left to chance, and many opportunities were missed. Without some concerted action through cooperatives or with the help of the state the many small peasants could only adjust slowly and on unfavourable terms to new conditions. Agriculture itself was becoming 'industrialized'. Many of its inputs came from an advanced mechanical or chemical industry or were brought to the farm by a highly-capitalized transport system. More attention had to be paid to costs, prices, interest rates and the fluctuations of demand. Consumers required standardized and graded produce, well packed and sent to distant markets in prime condition. In the advanced parts of Europe, therefore, the impact of industrialization on agriculture was stimulating it to become more productive, and giving it the means at the same time as it undermined the surviving vestiges of the traditional order.

However, European agriculture was not adequate to serve the demands of a growing population an increasing proportion of which was living in towns and engaged in activities other than producing its food and raw materials. The development of industry in any case required a range of materials which could not be produced in Europe at all or not in sufficient quantities. Through the European commodity markets the agriculture of the world became linked to the needs of the advanced industrial countries. With continued population growth in the second half of the nineteenth century extra-European supplies of food were required even by countries which protected their own agriculture. The rapid expansion of world output and the lowering of transport costs revealed that many European cereal growers were high-cost producers only kept in arable farming by protective tariffs. While no country sought complete economic autarchy, most defended their agrarian sector from international competition and thus contributed by their policies to the limitation of the extent of industrial development. Whether consciously or not, the debate over free trade and protection, behind which, of course, definite economic interests lined up, was also one over the extent of industrialization. The issue was to some extent obscured by the fact that industry too was protectionist: immediate preoccupation with foreign competition, which brought alliances between the industrialists and the agrarians, meant that measures were taken which slowed down the transfer of resources out of the rural and into the industrial sector. Paradoxically, then, the interests of the industrialists themselves, as they conceived them in the special conditions which prevailed from the 1870s onwards, helped to keep in being an inflated and only partially modernized agriculture. Only in Britain was agriculture 'sacrificed' to the cause of industry and to the involvement of the economy with the international division of labour.

Problems for discussion

1. Examine the way in which the feudal agrarian system was transformed in England, France and Germany respectively.
2. Why was there an enclosure movement in England and not in France?
3. What meaning(s) can be given to the expression 'agrarian revolution'?
4. Examine the relationship between changes in agriculture and the industrialization process.
5. Is it true to say that the survival of the peasantry inhibited economic growth in the nineteenth century?
6. Examine and compare the agrarian policies of the governments of the main European countries in the period before 1914.

3 French Economic Development — a Paradox?

French industrialization in the nineteenth century was profoundly influenced by two circumstances. In the first place the prior establishment of a powerful machine industry producing at low unit cost in Britain and the ability, therefore, of British industry to gain a dominant position in the export markets of the world placed French entrepreneurs at a disadvantage from which they never really recovered. Secondly, the effects of the Revolution and its sequel were detrimental to French economic growth both directly, by diverting resources to non-productive outlets and curtailing trade links with the overseas world and indirectly through a land settlement which, whatever virtues it may have had, tended to retard the growth of an internal market, the creation of an industrial working force and the transfer of resources from the land to industry.

Compared with the other parts of the world France shared with the rest of western Europe features which made it a suitable theatre for the development of industrial capitalism. By the standards of the eighteenth century it was an advanced country relatively wealthy and growing. In fact French culture was dominant; intellectual trends, as well as fashionable standards in dress and stylish living, were set by Frenchmen for the whole of upper-class Europe. The country had a large and growing population, giving it a quantitative weight which its rulers had used to maintain a leading political role on the Continent. Efforts to establish a colonial empire had been less successful and, while retaining the important sugar islands, most French possessions in India and in North America had been lost to England during the Seven Years War. Despite these setbacks a flourishing overseas trade was carried on, while French territory was adjacent to most of the principal commercial regions of Europe, with which intimate connections existed. There were many evident signs of growing wealth in the ports and towns of the eighteenth century including a prosperous middle class engaged in trade, industry and the urban professions. It is hardly possible to explain the French Revolution of 1789 without reference to such signs of economic change.

Looking only at this side of the evidence, therefore, there seem to be ample reasons to expect that France would become an industrial country. However, the beginning of the transition was to be considerably delayed and it was to prove to be a protracted process. Some of the reasons for this are to be found in the prerevolutionary environment and have now to be examined.

As Crouzet has pointed out, during the seventeenth and early eighteenth centuries French society had undergone a crisis which seriously held back development. Despite the existence of concentrations of wealth at the pinnacles of French society the mass of the population existed at something like a bare subsistence level. Moreover the traditional agrarian structure underwent little change before 1789 so that the growth which did take place was mainly on the old lines. Agriculture was almost entirely in the hands of the peasantry, using the old field layouts and customary methods and paying away most of the surplus above subsistence needs to the nobility, the Church and the State. The nobility, as a whole, was interested in its estates as a source of income, but this income was derived from compulsory labour services, dues in money and in kind and various other obligations levied on the peasantry. Few nobles took an active part in farming or estate management. On the other hand the peasants had been able to consolidate their position so that many of them were to all intents and purposes owners of their land, subject only to these dues and services. The village community had been able to conserve its vitality and adapt itself to change. It not only continued to regulate the husbandry of its members, but it was able to resist the encroachments of the lord. If the lot of the peasant was often poor and miserable, at least he retained his land and his rights in the commons more effectively than his English counterpart.

The preservation of this form of agriculture and the essentially feudal land tenure and landlord-peasant relationship had serious

3

adverse effects on economic change. In agriculture the lords, who
received a large part of the surplus, were not interested in investing
in improvement and the peasants had not the means even if they
had the inclination, which was generally not the case. The peasant
household produced a large part of what it consumed. Although it
needed to sell commodities, or its members had to work for wages,
to meet payments fixed in money terms, it bought little in the
market. What the peasants did buy consisted largely of crude
textiles and everyday articles for use in the home or on the land
which could often be obtained from local craftsmen. The purchasing
power which passed to the nobility found its way for the most part
into consumption, principally, that is to say, of luxury articles and
of services. Likewise, the income which accrued to the state passed
into similar channels, plus, of course, the heavy outlays required on
the maintenance of the armed forces and the carrying on of wars.
The Church, like the nobility, engaged in building and, on the
whole, was a consumer of goods and services of a traditional
sort.

As long as this structure prevailed over a considerable part of
the country a qualitative change in the economy was unlikely.
Industry tended to be carried on in a small way by handicraft
methods by artisans and small masters. In a country of large distances and poor transport facilities markets tended to be localized,
so that the small, inefficient productive unit had little to fear from
outside competition. Although there were signs of growth in some
industries, and a beginning was made in the introduction of
machinery during the latter half of the eighteenth century, methods
of production over the field of industry as a whole remained archaic.

A good deal of the stimulus for the introduction of large scale
organization and new methods of production came from the state.
Various forms of financial encouragement and other inducements
were offered to entrepreneurs and inventors as part of a traditional
policy of active intervention in and regulation of industry given
greater coherence during the reign of Louis XIV by Colbert—hence
'Colbertism'. Although the state may thus have assisted in implant-
ing certain industries or in stimulating interest in new methods, the
enterprises which it fostered tended to have the character of hot-
house growths. They were a response not to a spontaneous effort

by entrepreneurs producing to market demand or ready to take a risk that a market would be found, but to a bureaucratic design without a firm economic base. Technical change in French industry, although enough to suggest that French inventors were capable of matching their English rivals in some fields, had only limited application before 1789.

After 1715 a period of comparatively settled internal development permitted some growth of wealth to take place. This found expression in a more prosperous urban life in Paris, in the ports and in a few provincial towns. The expansion of foreign trade brought prosperity to the west coast ports and this trading sector proved to be the most dynamic in the French economy in the eighteenth century. However, the development of overseas trade did not have a profoundly transforming effect on the internal economic structure. In a sense the ports remained peripheral and although they did give some stimulus to industrial production the effect remained localized. Moreover, this trade was subject to fluctuations attributable to wars and the loss of markets which followed them, especially during the Seven Years War and again in the 1770s. If industrial production grew partly as a response to the pull of the foreign market it did not do so on the basis of new commodities produced by now technical methods as was the case with the leap forward in English foreign trade in textiles in the 1780s.

There were in the second half of the eighteenth century increased inducements for members of the nobility to improve their estates and seek to emulate the improving landlords across the Channel. This was never more than a very patchy effort which received only half-hearted government support in a few regions. The government rapidly drew back when it was demonstrated that any attempt to interfere with customary rights was liable to provoke a threat to public order. The examples of individual nobles or of landowners in particular areas turning to more commercial methods remained exceptional. To maintain or increase their incomes many landowners sought merely to increase their exactions on the peasantry by reimposing feudal dues which had fallen into desuetude.

In France of the eighteenth century the old feudal order was in decay and it acted as a shackle on the forces making for development. If it is asked what was lacking to enable France to carry through an industrial revolution similar to that which was beginning in England, not very much help is obtained by comparing rates of growth of output in the main industries. Nor can the answer be given by considering particular missing prerequisites. It is true, of course, that an organized credit network and an embryonic banking system of the sort which existed in England was almost completely absent in France. Large amounts of money capital were raised and handled by bankers and financiers but chiefly to finance the government or to make possible large-scale transactions in currency and goods on the international market. In the internal economy capital and credit were scarce and banks did not exist. However, this reflected the nature of the internal market, which was still limited and localized for reasons already discussed. In the same way, the disparity between France and England can hardly be satisfactorily explained on the grounds that technological change went ahead only in the latter. To do this is to draw attention to an important difference which still has to be explained.

In England a great structural change had been going on for some time whereby a substantial part of the population depended for its material means of existence upon the production and sale of commodities or upon the sale of its labour. There was already before the Industrial Revolution a quite intricate system of division of labour and therefore market relations and the market economy had penetrated deeply into the whole of social life. In France this process was at a much earlier stage of development and it confronted an insurmountable barrier in the deeply rooted and almost universal traditional agrarian relations which meant that a great majority of the population consisted of largely self-sufficient peasant households.

The economic and social structure of prerevolutionary France permitted growth to take place, within certain limits. It also generated serious social strains which accounted for the extent of the explosion after 1789. It was an environment which provided many disincentives to the investment of capital in industrial production without state support. The risks were high, market prospects were doubtful, the rate of return less than that promised in other fields. The privileges and prestige which were the attributes of noble rank not only stemmed the flow of capital and enterprise from the nobility into trade and industry — though not altogether — they also induced men enriched in trade or the professions to seek ennoblement. As a result of its embarrassments the Crown trafficked in offices and thus drew away capital and enterprise from possibly more productive fields. State offices and service, as well as landed property, for long conserved a special attraction for members of the bourgeoisie. Although such tendencies were not absent in England they appear to have been much less potent in their effect, while the inducements to pursue a business career and to become dedicated to accumulation for the family firm were much greater than in France.

What this brief discussion suggests is that while the conditions of the old régime permitted a steady rate of growth and some development of capitalist activity, the institutions and structures with which its survival was bound up precluded anything in the nature of an industrial revolution. To put it another way, it may be suggested that all the necessary economic conditions for such a change could not be brought together without a thorough reshaping of institutions which were inconsistent with capitalism.

If this must necessarily leave many problems unsolved, the nature of the changes brought about by the Revolution creates others. The leaders of the Revolution did not come from the industrial bourgeoisie which, so far as it existed, was small and feeble, much more buffeted by the events of the revolutionary years than in a position to control them. The men who dominated the Revolutionary Assemblies were, it is true, men of property and substance, but they were drawn from the law and the professions rather than from the ranks of businessmen. They reflected the nature of the bourgeoisie in a preindustrial society: its desire to uphold property rights, to do away with hereditary privilege and vested interest and to provide a favourable climate for individual enterprise. They sought to do this through the overthrow of the old régime and the drawing up of new legal codes, the latter task being completed only during the Empire. As it was completed, however, an extremely favourable juridical basis was provided for the full and free development of capitalism. Industry had henceforth a legal environment which permitted it every scope for the operation of individual enterprise. The guilds and corporations had been abolished. The

wage-earner was placed in an inferior position in the wage contract
and forbidden to combine for purposes of bargaining. Internal
barriers to trade had already been thrown down.

Even while it created these favourable conditions for industrial
development the Revolution acted as a disruptive force on the
economy. The cutting off of trade links with overseas areas was a
serious blow to the most prosperous sector of the economy under
the old régime; the ports went into a dramatic decline. Although
continental markets were open to traders and speculators who
followed in the train of the conquering armies of the Revolution
and Napoleon they did not adequately compensate for what was
lost overseas. Moreover, while the needs of war and the dislocating
effects of civil strife, especially in the 1790s, limited the output of
consumer goods, industrialization in Britain continued to go ahead.
Trade embargo and the Continental System were not able to keep
British goods out of Europe or do much to assist French industry.

The sharp swings from inflation to deflation, the lack of confidence which disturbed political conditions engendered, the chronic
scarcities of essential goods and the needs of the government for
war supplies all encouraged speculative activity rather than long-
term investment in production. The sale of the *biens nationaux*
provided further opportunities for rapid enrichment. What tended
to happen, therefore, was that a new moneyed bourgeoisie sprang
into existence. It was composed, not of political idealists, but of men
with their eye on the main chance. It had not contributed much
towards the making of the Revolution – from which, in any case,
some of the older-established bourgeois had been alienated from
an early stage. Mostly its members had already had some property
under the old régime and they used the opportunities presented by
the social flux of the revolutionary period to establish fortunes and
increase their influence. Men of this stamp were the principal beneficiaries of the Revolution and they gave their support to Napoleon,
who promised to guarantee both their gains and the maintenance
of order. The fortunes of the new bourgeois dynasties were still
based to a large extent on landed property: farm and wood lands,
urban sites and houses; partly they consisted of money capital
which could be lent to the government or used in commerce and
finance. The openings for industrial investment and the rate of

return which it promised had only a limited attractiveness and then mainly for the men of lesser fortune.

Meanwhile the agrarian changes of the Revolution, imposed by the peasant revolt, confirmed the peasantry in possession of its holdings and rid it of its obligations to the lords. A certain amount of additional land became available for purchase by the peasants with means, though nothing was done to improve the lot of those who had little or no land. While laws were passed permitting the reallocation of the open fields and the partition of village commons the break-up of the old system of husbandry was not generally desired by the peasants. It was a long time before the forces of agrarian individualism penetrated the countryside. As it was, then, despite the abolition of feudal relations very little else was changed in the agrarian sector. The peasants continued to cultivate much as before the land which was now securely in their legal possession. They gained by the extent to which their former obligations exceeded new taxes or payments which they had to make. Above all they held the land and intended to keep it at all costs.

In historical perspective the peasantry exacted a heavy price from the bourgeoisie for supporting them in the Revolution. It became a force making for social conservation to which all sections of the property-owning classes were obliged to pay attention, especially as the grumblings of social discontent could be heard in the towns. The change in the agrarian system, because it had been brought about from below, prevented the reorganization of agriculture and kept in existence many of the features of the rural economy which had prevailed in the eighteenth century. Hence it was difficult to reduce the weight of agriculture in the economy or to improve the productivity of the land. While it is true that in some places large estates and capitalist farms existed there was not much chance of this sort of agrarian system being extended at the expense of the peasantry.

The revolutionary land settlement discouraged the movement of labour from the land by giving a large proportion of the peasantry access to the land. The limitation of family size was resorted to in an effort to counteract the effects of division on inheritance which, already a peasant custom, had been written into the Napoleonic Code. So pressure of population on the land was, apart from a few regions, kept down. Many rural people owned a plot of land or could obtain it as a tenant or a *métayer* (i.e. a sharecropper). Their sons stayed in the village – or came back to it after a spell of work somewhere else – with the prospect of themselves acquiring land by inheritance or by marriage or being able to rent it. It is true that the already existing differentiation amongst the peasantry went on apace and that there were many who had too little land to support themselves and their families, or none at all. How important such elements were varied very much from place to place and depended on many conditions. Division of land on inheritance tended to increase their humbers. Even so, although the material conditions of a large part of the peasantry were very low the incentives to leave the village permanently were weak and the prospect of getting land on some terms enough to tie many to their place of birth. Such people formed a reservoir of labour for the more prosperous peasants or for work on the putting-out system.

The continued predominance of agriculture in the economy and the weight of the peasantry in the agrarian sector acted as a brake on industrialization. Purchasing power and incomes were kept down, thus limiting the market and discouraging investment in industry. Labour was pinned to the land rather than drained from it and the recruitment of a labour force for industry was thus made more difficult. The peasant household remained largely self-sufficient, concentrating, in most areas, on producing the necessary foods for the support of the family. Partly because of this, partly because of the maintenance of the old methods of husbandry and the continued subdivision of holdings, output grew only slowly in the peasant sector. Land was used wastefully and for purposes for which it was not well-suited: cereals were cultivated on land which would have been better turned over to permanent grass.

The preservation of the old-style agriculture and its continued heavy weight in the economy which limited division of labour and thus the expansion of the internal market meant, then, that the French economy remained until well after 1815 basically of the old, eighteenth-century type. Paradoxically, a revolution which had created near-perfect legal and institutional conditions for the full flowering of capitalist relations had left intact major social barriers to their realization in the industrial field. Under the conditions which prevailed between 1789 and 1815 there had been little incentive or scope for large-scale investment in new methods of production. The encouragement offered by Napoleon to inventors and entrepreneurs had little appreciable effect on the structure of industry as a whole. In any case, industrialization depended on the investment and generation of capital on a large enough scale to effect a structural transformation of the conditions of production in some major industries which, in turn, could speed up the rate of growth in the economy as a whole. There were only a few isolated signs of any change along these lines in the early years of the Restoration.

Meanwhile, such an industrialization process had already made giant strides across the Channel. French entrepreneurs were thus confronted with industrial competitors armed with highly productive techniques which enabled them to manufacture commodities at lower unit costs and already strongly entrenched in the markets of the world. This inferiority was so great that the French market itself was threatened. Fear of British competition generated a protectionist reaction while the home market, for reasons already explored, remained constricted. On the other hand, as latecomers, French entrepreneurs in the major industries—textiles and the metal trades—were able to draw on an available pool of innovation, The changes wrought by the Revolution, although in some ways placing a brake on industrialization, had, nonetheless, released the economy from the straitjacket of the old régime. After 1815 the bourgeoisie consolidated its social influence and its wealth. Agricultural output slowly increased. Without any spectacular departures. industrial growth was made possible and an incentive was offered to make use of the new machines and sources of power developed in Britain. The steady growth of wealth and rising incomes widened the internal market.

Since the French economy was still dominated by its agrarian sector, and much of the growing purchasing power accrued to the middle class, industrial entrepreneurs could not but adapt themselves to this situation. Much industrial production was geared to satisfy the exigent tastes of the wealthier consumers: the emphasis was on quality not low cost production, on skilled craftsmanship rather than on machine technology. Quality products of this sort enjoyed prestige abroad where French tastes and fashions continued

to lead the way so that they could win a place in the export market
or draw money from the purses of tourists. Manufacturers in the
industries where machine methods were available could also follow
a similar course by emphasizing, not cheap quantity production,
but quality and style. Thus enterprising producers in Alsace and
elsewhere aimed at the quality market for machine-made textiles
both in France and further afield. The rise in incomes abroad,
which was partly a result of the Industrial Revolution in England,
could thus become the basis for industrial growth. At the same
time, other manufacturers adapted themselves to the demand for
cheap goods from the low-income consumers, peasants and the
labouring people in the towns. But much industrial production
continued to consist of the transformation of local materials and
agricultural products by traditional village craftsmen and small-
town artisans for a mainly local market. Even the iron industry
was largely oriented towards the production of tools and implements for the use of peasants and artisans; the small forge using
local ores and charcoal thus sufficed.

In its early stages, therefore, industrialization proceeded in a
way characteristically different from that in England. Large-scale
investment in modern plant for mass production remained exceptional and there were few big industrial concentrations. Instead, the
new techniques were adopted on a piecemeal basis without necessarily bringing about great change in the traditional structure.
The textile industry continued to make considerable use of peasant
labour through the putting-out system. Even mines and ironworks,
established in a rural setting, drew on the peasantry for their labour
supply. The lack of coal, whatever its more far-reaching effects on
French economic growth, certainly meant, in the early stages of
industrialization, that heavy industry played a modest role. In the
meantime the dominant form of industrial capitalism, primarily in
textiles, was the family firm dependent, like its English counterpart, mainly on accumulated profits for its expansion. Progressive
and enterprising in some cases, notably in Alsace where not only
was considerable use made of machinery on the English pattern
but further technical innovations were made, especially in textile
printing; in others, such as Normandy, many of the traits of the old
rural putting-out system were conserved.

By the 1830s an industrial sector of growing weight had emerged within a still predominantly agrarian economy. Its main strength lay in textiles and it was concentrated geographically in a few areas which had an industrial tradition going back into the eighteenth century or earlier. The market expanded only slowly as a result partly of its composition, partly because transport facilities remained inadequate. Technical improvements were absorbed slowly and selectively over a protracted period. Some entrepreneurs responded dynamically to the situation of French industrial inferiority by making a bid for the higher quality market, others were satisfied with routine production for rather stable markets behind tariff walls.

Well into the nineteenth century the property interests of the bourgeoisie continued to be mainly concentrated on land and buildings. Loans to the state offered a further secure outlet. Banking facilities remained limited and the investment habit had still to be created. The confluence of a number of factors began to make for a change during the 1830s and 1840s. Continued steady growth of income and demand favoured the expansion of textiles. Complementary investment was therefore called for elsewhere, in transport, in commerce, in raw materials and finished goods, in the production of machinery and fuel. In and around the textile areas the symptoms of an industrial revolution began to become visible. A stimulus was given to a search for coal and ores. Finally the railway became available and required large amounts of capital and further fired the demand for the products of heavy industry.

These developments prepared the way for a new-style capitalism for which bank finance, associated capital and large-scale business organization were indispensable. Still at a pace conditioned by the resistances imposed by the traditional environment, the nature of the economy began to change or, more specifically, alongside the traditional agrarian sector and the family capitalism of small-scale industry a more modern and dynamic sector was introduced. To build railways and establish enterprises in heavy industry large amounts of capital were required. Somehow it was necessary to tap existing accumulations which had arisen in the circuit of exchange of a still predominantly land-oriented economy or in commerce. Up to then France was poorly endowed with banks. Credit and capital were hard to come by and were expensive. True, had there been more banks the financing of industrial expansion would have been facilitated and the whole course of development might have been different. There was not the intricate web of commercial credit which existed already in England by the early eighteenth century, because there was not the need for it. Thus specialized institutions handling commercial paper and note-issuing banks serving the needs of the commercial community either did not exist or were rare, still being innovations in the 1820s and 1830s. Credit there was locally at usurious rates for the peasants and artisans, or loans on mortgage arranged by notaries on behalf of bourgeois seeking a placement for their money. On the whole, however, there was a pressing shortage of money and credit. Wealth was locked up in land and specie and was not easily tempted into more productive outlets.

The belated development of banking was not so much a causative factor accounting for the slow appearance of modern industry as a reflection, in origin, of a lack of need. It was the growing demand for investment capital and the chronic need of business for short-term credit which encouraged new ventures in the banking field. Even so, the change was slow in coming. Banking was still dominated by a small number of powerful firms, *la haute banque*, concentrated in Paris. During the reign of Louis Philippe they appeared to have great social and political influence but they played little creative role in the development of industrial capitalism at this stage. However, the coming of the railway offered opportunities from which they were willing to profit and the early lines could hardly have been undertaken without their participation.

Railway promotion was largely seen as a financial speculation in which the leading role was played by Parisian and British finance. There was less local initiative than in England and it was more difficult to induce the rentier capitalist to participate in railways finance. It was accepted that the government should concern itself actively with this new form of public works, but it was subject to many contradictory pressures and railway construction made little headway before 1842. The law of that year provided for the construction of a number of main lines for which the government was to supply the land and the infrastructure. The permanent structures were then leased to private operating companies which provided the rolling stock and equipment. Part of the cost of building the lines fell squarely on the general revenue. Attracted by what appeared to be favourable conditions the Rothschilds and other major financial houses, French and foreign, came in as backers of the new projects with a good deal of the share capital being raised in the 1840s in England. Conflicts of interests continued to hold back the rate of new construction.

Thus, despite government backing, railway building proceeded slowly and at the time of the outbreak of the 1848 revolution only about 1,800 kilometres of track were in operation and a number of the lines had encountered major financial difficulties. Certainly the railways were beginning to change the habits of the investing class and the transactions on the Bourse increased in scale. Railway demand, as well as the wider market opened up by improved transport facilities, was just what the lagging heavy industries required. The elimination of small-scale iron producers clinging to charcoal fuel and routine methods took place more rapidly. The more modern large-scale units were the main beneficiaries.

It would be an exaggeration to claim that railway development sparked off a revolution in industry before 1848. Its pace was too leisurely and its spatial effects too limited to do that. However, a start had been made. Neither in the 1840s nor later is there quantitative evidence that France experienced a 'take off' in Rostow's sense. What seems to be happening is the maintenance of a steady rate of growth, going back to the early eighteenth century, which partly reflected, in one sphere after another, some kind of qualitative breakthrough which over time represented a shift towards industry. France was not, taken as a whole, economically stagnant; indeed wealth was growing and assuming new forms as well as the traditional ones of real property and specie. The main beneficiaries of this growth in wealth were the prosperous bourgeois families which had consolidated their position during the Revolution. But all property owners participated and one of the distinguishing features of French society was that there was a wide distribution as well as a concentration of property. Rural France was dotted with small towns in which resided numbers of traders, dealers in agricultural produce, small industrial employers and the usual quota of professional men. Together with the bourgeoisie, large and small, of the cities, they made up a substantial and influential part of the population. From the ranks of this class came the local notables, from it were recruited the civil servants and the politicians who, regardless of the form of government, carried on the administration of the country. Ensconced in the state and already sure of material security, this class perhaps proved a less fertile recruiting ground for industrial entrepreneurs than its counterparts in other countries. It was only from the time of the Second Empire that industralists began to receive full public recognition. For a long period after that there is some case for saying that businessmen enjoyed less esteem than they did in other industrializing countries. Moreover, entrepreneurs seem to have been influenced by the existing environment and to have absorbed its prevailing ethos: they preferred, it is frequently argued, security to risk-taking, they clung too long to obsolete methods, they looked to the government to protect them from foreign competition and retired early to live on their *rentes*.

If this provides an unflattering but reliable portrait of many French industrialists there are also many exceptions. There were throughout the nineteenth and in the present century dynamic sectors and enterprising industrial path-breakers in every field from department stores to aviation. The characteristics of nineteenth-century development can hardly be explained from the character of the businessman, rather does the businessman reflect by his behaviour environmental conditions to which not only the actions of himself and his fellows but also those of other members of the society contribute. It is to the structure as a whole that main attention has to be directed by those wishing to understand the distinguishing characteristics of French industrialization.

After the interruption of the agrarian, financial, industrial and political crisis of the years 1846 to 1851 the trends which had begun to become dominant in the 1830s and 1840s began to reassert themselves. In a favourable international conjuncture industrialization continued and the weight of the state was thrown behind a programme of railway building and other public works. As part of this, large amounts of capital had to be raised which required the establishment of new financial institutions and the adoption of new banking methods. The most spectacular departure was the rise of the *Credit Mobilier* which raised money from the public for direct investment in business concerns. The established banking houses adopted similar practices which were in line with the needs of the new forms of capitalism. The funds of the property-owning classes were now tapped on a greater scale than ever before. The investment habit spread and, with growing prosperity, more and more funds became available. A whole apparatus of credit grew up which made Paris the leading continental financial centre and funds were mobilized which pushed forward the building of railways and the opening up of resources all over Europe.

In Europe, as well as in France, the creation of an infrastructure – transport facilities, public works, ports, harbours and buildings – had to take place some way ahead of the application of capital to the transformation of industry. The vast outlays required could only be raised through an organized capital market and with the help of the banks. Through these means existing accumulations could be tapped and a new flow of credit created to vitalize the economy and permit the financing of large-scale constructional projects. The confidence of the moneyed middle class in the Second Empire, especially in its early years, and all the evidences of growing material prosperity generated an atmosphere of euphoria in which there was every temptation for financiers to take chances. Capital was tied up in projects which could only be expected to yield a return over a long period. Share prices were expected to go on rising and new funds to be available to cover obligations. Such conditions could not, however, prevail indefinitely. The financial crisis of 1857 was the first shock which the new structure of credit had to sustain. At the same time it showed that the economy was becoming more dependent upon fluctuations generated by the business cycle than by vagaries of the harvest.

The main factor in the boom of the 'fifties was railway building. Pushed ahead by the state and under favourable conditions for companies ties in closely with the old established merchant banks as well as the *Credit Mobilier*, France was at last endowed with the main lines of a railway system. Railways were, in fact, a privileged form of capitalism, constructed partly at state expense and with the state shouldering the risks. The new régime guaranteed new lines a 4 per cent return on capital and it was on this basis that the companies confidently raised loan capital to meet a large part of their construction costs. By a process of amalgamation control was concentrated in a small number of large concerns, a foretaste of the type of organization and scale of operation which advancing capitalism demanded.

Stimulated by railway building investment was also encouraged in heavy industry. A greater emphasis was thereby given to the newer forms of industrial capitalism. However, the transforming effects of the railway on the economy as a whole should not be overestimated. Despite the increased rate of construction many parts of France were still untouched by the new means of communication; for them rural isolation and the tendency for markets to be regional or local rather than national still prevailed. The choice of Paris as the great central point of the entire network was inevitable at the time in view of the pronounced centralization which was already a feature of the administration and had profoundly affected the distribution of economic activities. Moreover, the capital market upon which the railways were dependent was also highly centralized. The reconstruction of the Haussmann era further underlined the dominance of Paris, the boundaries of the city were extended and a new industrial belt came into being. The shaping of the railway network tended, therefore, to confirm and intensify the centralization of economic as well as administrative activity and existing economic configurations. Even more than before, capital, enterprise and talent tended to be drawn away from the provinces to the capital.

In the meantime, by a process of accretion rather than by leaps and bounds, industry was coming to play an increasing role in the economy. While the older forms of artisan and decentralized production preserved considerable vitality in many fields, in others the factory had fully established itself. In heavy industry there were a number of giant enterprises which had few equals even in Britain. The industrial structure was extremely variegated and included firms of many sizes and of very unequal levels of efficiency even in the same industry. Safe behind tariff walls and with all sorts of market imperfections there was perhaps a tendency on the part of the more efficient entrepreneurs to pursue a policy of live-and-let-live rather than driving out their weaker rivals by keen price competition.

This situation was materially altered as a result of the Anglo-French Commercial Treaty of 1860 and the other treaties which followed it. Under these treaties France's partners had access to the French market for their goods at tariff rates not exceeding 25 per cent, which marked a big reduction on the high or prohibitive rates which had previously prevailed. This 'industrial *coup d'état*' was extremely repugnant to most French industrialists who continued to oppose it bitterly. As some compensation they were granted loans from the state to facilitate modernization and re-equipment to face the increased competition which was expected. Although the amount of the loans was not large enough to exercise a decisive influence on the level of industrial efficiency, there is reason to believe that the total effect of the liberalizing of trade and this piece of government assistance to industry was to permit an all-round increase in efficiency and some lowering of production costs. It is, of course, difficult to disentangle the effects of the treaties from all the other factors which affected industry at this time: the American Civil War, bad harvests, the recession of 1866-7, for example. On the whole the stronger firms were strengthened, the less competitive went to the wall.

What advantages did French industry reap from the reciprocal lowering of tariffs by her treaty partners? The main stimulus seems to have been received by the traditional industries in which there was already some export strength — the better quality textile products and the products of the soil. The metallurgical and mechanical industries were able to conserve their home market but did not emerge as considerable exporters in the years after 1860. This was probably an accurate reflection of their competitive position. The remaining duties, plus the transport costs of moving the products of heavy industry, left enough protection to enable them to set their house in order. They still remained too weak to do battle with British or Belgian producers in other markets.

The 1860s saw other important changes taking place in the structure of French capitalism. In 1863 the state at last abandoned its control over the formation of joint stock companies; in 1867 limited liability was conceded as a general right and certain administrative controls over the operations of companies were discontinued. It is true that these measures had no immediate revolutionizing effect but they were in line with a tendency towards the concentration of capital and the opening up of new prospects for 'blind' investment characteristic of advanced capitalism. The development of a system of deposit banking extending into the provinces also began, the real breakthrough coming with the formation of the *Credit Lyonnais* in 1863. However, the banking habit spread slowly and discount facilities of the sort which were available in English provincial towns, as well as London, scarcely existed. From the point of view of financial institutions French capitalism was still lagging behind. The French bourgeois remained a cautious investor, still holding much of his wealth in the form of real estate. The rise of new financial institutions and the development of the joint stock company only slowly changed his habits. Industry in particular still depended to a large extent on the old forms of investment represented by family capitalism, though the increased weight of heavy industry was introducing more advanced financial practices on a wider scale.

French industry and French trade participated in the general economic upsurge of the middle decades of the nineteenth century. The building of railways throughout the Continent and the opening up of new industrial areas offered opportunities for investment of which French financiers took full advantage. The growth in incomes abroad extended the export trade to the benefit of merchants and manufacturers. Until the process of rapid catching up starting in Germany from about the 1840s bore fruit, France remained the leading industrial country on the Continent, and the wealthiest.

The many indications of continued growth and change had not fundamentally altered the balance of the economy or eliminated certain inherited weaknesses. Agriculture remained on the whole unprogressive if not actually backward. Disparities between the areas which were experiencing an industrial revolution and those which remained primarily agrarian tended to grow. Over large parts of industry old methods and forms of organization held their own. Entrepreneurs tended to have higher costs for fuel and transport than their foreign rivals. Many were reluctant to push ahead with mechanization or lacked capital to do so. Internal demand was still held back by the preservation of a large agrarian sector and the demographic trend towards a slowing down of the rate of growth probably had unfavourable repercussions on industry. Capitalism in France had taken on a distinctive character which, despite continued modification and the injection of more advanced features, it was to conserve into the twentieth century.

In the last quarter of the nineteenth century and in the years leading up to the First World War, however, France began to take on the contours of a modern industrial country. This period saw a great development of banking and financial institutions participating in industrial investment and in foreign lending. The iron and steel industry was established on modern lines and great new plants were built, especially on the Lorraine orefield. On the coalfields of northern France the familiar, ugly landscape of an industrial society took shape. Important strides were made in engineering and the newer industries. The steady switch towards urban living encouraged more standardized production of articles of common use and brought the usual changes in the distributive system. The more spectacular transformation which took place in Germany and the rise of industrial America overshadowed the transition in which French society was involved. Indeed, so much of the old order was conserved and so many unfavourable comparisons could be made between France and these industrial newcomers that the oversight is perhaps not surprising. For economic historians the problem has seemed to be one of French retardation: why was the economy not industrialized more rapidly and more completely when so many factors seemed to favour it?

In dealing with this problem, as with others, there has been a temptation to seek a single or main cause for the defects in the economy. The French businessman has been held to have been insufficiently enterprising, preferring security behind tariff walls and seeking support from the state rather than investing in modern techniques and pushing into new markets. The stereotype which is thus apt to be created, while it has some veracity when applied to the traditional sectors and small-scale firms, can obviously not account for the real growth and technological advance which took place in modern, large-scale industry. France had its notable entrepreneurs and innovators who won a leading place in the late nineteenth and early twentieth century in steel, engineering, motor cars and aircraft. Firms like Schneider, Peugeot, Michelin and

Renault were in the vanguard of innovation. A major weakness of French industry in the nineteenth century was that it lacked great and expansive export markets for cheap mass produced goods because in such fields it could not compete effectively with the entrenched British firms. On the other hand, entrepreneurs adapted themselves surprisingly well to the opportunities which were available. Still, it was a question of adaptation and the lack of a large expanded export trade, coupled with the nature of the internal market, tended to encourage the traits from which the stereotype is composed.

French industry could have done with more and better directed investment. Here again, entrepreneurs obeyed the laws of the market and their choices are difficult to criticize in view of the environment in which they moved. It is true that the banking system always lagged a good deal behind what was desirable from the point of view of increasing the rate of industrial investment, but here again bankers adapted themselves to the needs and conditions of the market, having to contend with established investment habits which were not easy to change and with the given demand for loanable funds. Bankers were also in business to make money, not to promote growth for its own sake. The view they took of their business indeed inclined them to seek a few large borrowers and to collect the proceeds on large promotions for whose bonds they then sought to find a market. Hence, through the intermediary of the banks and other financial institutions a large part of the savings of the cautious and thrifty middle class found their way into foreign loans. Urged on by government pressure, Tzarist Russia became a principal outlet for French foreign lending with eventually disastrous results for the investors.

Rather than one or two causes, a whole complex of institutional and structural conditions gave French capitalism its peculiar physiognomy and its characteristic weaknesses. Its different parts were closely bonded together and one weakness could not have been removed without a succession of changes in other fields. It seems useless, therefore, to blame the entrepreneur, the banking system, the state, the tariff, lack of cheap coking coal or the bourgeoisie as a whole. All we can really say is that in this particular inherited environment the forces of the market led to responses by the active economic agents which added up to the observable characteristics and trends of French capitalist development. As an explanation it may be unsatisfactory; but a more thorough examination of the social, political and cultural conditions in which these economic forces operated is required to explain the situation fully.

A basic characteristic of the economy was the continued heavy weight of the agrarian sector and the survival of the peasantry. It is true that during the period of depression in the last quarter of the nineteenth century the rural exodus assumed the dimensions of a social problem. It was significant that a large body of opinion deplored the drift from the land as though it were economically and morally debilitating. National self-sufficiency in the basic foods and a balance between industry and agriculture were believed to have special virtues. The peasantry was a factor in social stability and was courted as an ally by the politicians. In fact, little was done to assist peasant agriculture to raise its standards during the period. Instead, the big agrarians who were dependent upon the sale of grain in the home market, agitated for tariff protection. In doing so they tended to exaggerate the effects of the price slide which did not much affect those peasants who sold little or no grain in the market and benefited from lower prices for manufactured goods. However, the industrialists were anxious to take revenge for 1860: they campaigned for the repeal of the trade treaties and for higher tariffs and were glad to find allies in the electoral big battalions of the rural areas. The upshot was the Méline tariff of 1892 which gave agriculture protection. Whether there was a risk of massive inflows of cheap grain is doubtful. As it was the price of the main grains rose by just about the amount of the tariff. The main beneficiaries were the larger farmers and peasants; the national costs are difficult to estimate but the tariff probably did something to put a brake on the drift from the rural areas, helping to preserve the structure of agriculture and thus the inefficiencies and archaisms which went with it. Agriculture certainly experienced difficult times in the latter part of the century, when the production of raw silk and of wine were seriously disrupted by disease. Production in the agrarian sector tended to stagnate, only moving upwards appreciably again in the years preceding 1914.

In the last few years of peace some 55 per cent of the population continued to live in the rural areas and agriculture accounted for over 40 per cent of the active population. Agriculture thus had considerably less weight in the economy than in Russia, eastern Europe or even the most advanced of the Mediterranean countries, Italy. On the other hand it appears grossly inflated compared with Britain, and was higher than in Germany as well as being less productive. A large part of the peasantry continued to experience very low material conditions of life and to have little pull on the market. Despite the recovery of agriculture the 1900s show a remarkable fall in agriculture's proportionate contribution to the national product and increasing emphasis on secondary and tertiary activities. From the point of view of economic growth this was all to the good. Self-sufficiency in basic foods was bought at the expense of more rapid modernization of the economy as a whole. Not a little of the competitive weakness of French industry arose from the nature of its home market, still composed in large part of low-income peasant households. Thus did the effects of the revolutionary land settlement continue to make themselves felt.

Under the Third Republic, despite the continued and even remarkable expansion of the modern sector of the economy, much of the old social structure of the earlier period of petty capitalism was conserved. In fact it fought hard for its survival through its political weight as it was to continue to do after the war. Thus government support for those who had an established position in the economy tended to slow down adaptation to changes in technique and organization.

French industry retained its place in the quality and luxury field. Its exports consisted of sophisticated manufactured goods which appealed to consumers in the higher income brackets. The many visitors to France also bought readily the many specialities for which it was noted, products more likely to come from the small workshop than the large factory. On the other hand, French industry failed to exploit the growing markets in new countries except where colonial policy gave it a sheltered market. On the international market, therefore, French industry appeared to be inferior to that of Britain and Germany. In the international division of labour French imports of primary products had to be paid for from the proceeds of finished goods sold to the advanced countries. Despite the large population engaged in agriculture and excellent physical conditions, French products, with the exception of wine and luxury goods, found little place in the markets of the industrial countries of western Europe.

To some extent this trading pattern can be defended as a rational adaptation to market conditions. On the other hand it accentuated traits in French industry which had their roots in the past and tended to make for high production costs and routine methods of manufacture. The failure to develop agricultural exports also showed a policy weakness since the initiative for improvements in production and marketing could hardly be expected to come from the peasants themselves. The way shown by Denmark could have been followed more closely in Normandy and perhaps other areas but the government kept aloof from positive intervention in agriculture and private capital was not interested.

Weaknesses which appear in retrospect to be significant in explaining the economic and political vicissitudes which France has suffered in more recent decades were not necessarily apparent to contemporaries. In the years before 1914 the immediate signs were of expansion and prosperity. In aggregate terms France retained her position behind Germany on the European continent. Industrialization continued and there were multiplying signs of the transition to urban living. Incomes were rising and wealth was accumulating. The pattern of society remained little disturbed. Despite frequent government changes the locus of power remained unaffected. Monetary stability gave confidence to savers; the franc seemed to be a unit as fixed as the metre or the gramme. The range of government activities remained small, financial policy was extremely orthodox and there was not even a progressive income tax. The challenge of the working class at times broke out in violent collisions between strikers and the police. However, the growing prosperity of the economy made it possible for concessions to be made and for the claims of the working class to find expression through parliamentary channels. In any case the wage-earners remained a minority of the total population and only a relatively small number belonged to trade unions.

Another index of stability was the slow growth in the size of the population. Since France's closest economic and political rivals were still adding to their numbers at an appreciable rate this trend caused some concern. Was there a connection between this demographic pattern and the lack of adaptation to modern requirements of parts of the economic and social structure? The slowing down in the rate of population increase seems to have its origin in the response of the peasantry in many parts of the country to the combination of landownership with partible inheritance. By limiting the number of children in his family the peasant could do something to prevent the division of the land he owned. A similar trend towards a small family size found its way into the middle class. Much of the property of the bourgeoisie continued to consist of real estate and fixed interest investment: it was only caught up to a limited extent with the dynamic possibilities of growing industry. Accumulating wealth seemed therefore to be a question of thrift and parsimony, incompatible with having a large progeny. Those already rich and desiring to lead a stylish urban life also found children an encumbrance. For traditional France the family was bound up with the conservation of a patrimony and its transmission through arranged marriages, dowries and inheritance which legally required a large measure of division among the heirs. The family had not yet become adjusted to the realities of advanced urban society. While on the one side the nuclear family tended to be small, with the emphasis on giving one or two children a start in life which would enable them to rise higher in the scale of income and wealth than their parents, on the other it tended to preserve a multitude of kinship ties which brought it nearer to the type found in peasant societies. Indeed, a large part of the French bourgeoisie was still made up of, or being recruited from, successful peasants or their sons and daughters, nephews and nieces.

By the end of the nineteenth century the wage-earners were also beginning to aspire to a petty bourgeois mode of existence. In the factory and mining areas higher wage levels and greater stability of employment had enabled many workers to rise out of the depths of brutalized poverty characteristic of the first stages of industrialization. Recruitment to the wage-earners' ranks from the peasantry mainly took place on a piecemeal, individual basis and was looked upon by many as a means of self-improvement. Going to towns without large-scale industries, many of the recruits to the labour force continued to be employed in small units and had not yet reconciled themselves to the permanency of their condition. Through taking a small shop, or finding state employment for themselves or their offspring they hoped to climb out of the working class. On the whole, then, the new generations of wage-earners regulated the size of their families just as the peasants and the bourgeois had been doing.

The acceptance of a pattern of small family size seems, therefore, to have been a response to the individual possessiveness which permeated French society after the Revolution. This was a society in which wealth grew steadily and the individual was encouraged to seek his self-advancement without either taking excessive risks or burdening himself with unnecessary obligations. The 'Malthusian' restriction of family size resulted in a pattern of population growth which represented a rational adaptation to the specific features of economic and social development found in the country and helped to reinforce them. The same prudent concern for self-interest and for a future expected, with a due measure of progress, to mirror the present, which found expression in the most intimate concerns of personal life were paralleled in the decisions of businessmen and investors. For the comfortable bourgeois, and even for the aspiring social climber, there was no strong inducement to break from this mould. The watchword was cautious advance without sharp breaks with the past, respect for progress as long as it did not threaten to provoke radical change.

The long-drawn-out and piecemeal character of French industrialization, which brought a steady growth in wealth and income while leaving large areas of the country predominantly rural, helped to perpetuate these traits. Entrepreneurs adapted to the situation which they confronted on the basis of their interpretation of self-interest, which included considerations upon which no market valuation could be placed. Over a large part of the country, away from the influence of the large cities and industrial areas, it was the capitalism of the small town which prevailed. In a way little had changed since the eighteenth century. The town was still the market centre for the peasants in the surrounding countryside with its shops and local industries and services. It was the home of a small-town middle class of traders and professional men, men of property on a modest scale who owned houses and land and sought safe outlets for their money capital. The penetration of advanced business methods into such a milieu was extremely slow. On the other hand, the general prosperity of the country, even the building of railways and improvements in communications, tended to give the small town bourgeoisie a new lease of life. It was still indispensable as a purveyor of goods from the outside world and as a supplier of professional services. As long as agriculture continued to flourish —and to resist changes in its structure—these microcosms of the old-style capitalism would continue, by their sheer weight, to influence the character of the economy as a whole.

In a way, then, there is a temptation to come back to what may be thought of as stereoptype. This time, however, the emphasis is not on the entrepreneur, or, indeed, on one or a number of missing factors which could have made for faster growth or a more profound economic transformation. Rather is it on the distinguishing characteristics of a society as a special historical product to which a whole complex of interacting factors had contributed. Thus industrialization in France was distinctly different from its expression in the other historical and geographical conditions examined in this work. To explain this taxes our comprehension of complex historical phenomena but we need not admit defeat because there are no simple or monocausal answers.

The paradox of French economic development in the period between 1789 and 1914 was primarily that all the potentialities for growth were not realized. Of course, *all* the potentialities were not realized anywhere; it is a question of degree. Who or what was responsible for this? The answer which has been given can be restated in the following way. The institutions of capitalism operated in this particular historically conditioned environment in such a way as to prevent a major breakthrough favourable to a more rapid and thorough industrial transformation. The very favourable legal foundations which were laid for capitalist development by the Revolution preceded the coming together of the necessary conditions for rapid industrial change. This gave an advantage to the small-scale (even preindustrial) forms of capitalism associated with the commercialization of agricultural products and petty production. The opportunities which the Revolution offered for self-advancement favoured speculation and the acquisition of land by the middle class. By their influence in the state, moreover, bourgeois talents were drawn into politics and administration which might have gone into business. Further, the land settlement favourable to the peasantry and permitting it to survive operated in a number of ways to limit the scope for industrial change. Combined with these influences were the repercussions of Britain's head start in industrialization and the preemption of a large share of the world market by British entrepreneurs. Although France was already behind Britain before 1789 it was this effect of the Revolution which made it difficult, in the course of the nineteenth century, to close the gap. In particular, throughout that period, French industry lacked the stimulus of a large and growing export market and was never able to overcome the initial drawback under which it laboured as a result. On the other hand, accepting these limitations, many industrialists certainly showed enterprise and resource by developing an external market for products of higher finish and quality. Throughout, moreover, the nature of the internal market, with its large rural sector, remained a built-in obstacle to more rapid industrialization.

Problems for discussion

1. How did the revolutionary land settlement of the 1790s influence the rate and character of French economic growth in the nineteenth century?
2. Can the entrepreneur be blamed for the alleged retardation of the French economy?
3. Did France experience either an 'Industrial Revolution' or a 'take-off' in the nineteenth century?
4. Account for the survival of the small town and its importance in French social life.
5. Examine the demographic pattern of nineteenth-century France. What influence is it plausible to suppose that it had on the character of economic development?
6. Did protection hold back economic change in France? What were the consequences of the Anglo-French Commercial Treaty of 1860?

7. Why was there so little emigration from France in the period before 1914?

8. What were the major signs before 1914 that the bases had been laid for the development of a modern industrial economy in France?

4 The Rise of Industrial Germany

Within the space of a generation Germany was transformed from a
collection of economically backward states forming a political
patchwork in Central Europe into a unified empire driven forward
by a rapidly expanding industry on an advanced technological base.
This transformation, accompanied as it was by the deliberate resort
to military force as an instrument of national policy and an atmosphere of exacerbated nationalism, represented an event of major
historical significance. Politically a new era had opened for Europe
which was to lead into the two great wars of the twentieth century.
Economically it raised up a new industrial monster able to take the
lead on the continent of Europe and to challenge Britain's position
in the markets of the world.

The conditions which prevailed before and during Germany's
industrial emergence gave capitalism in that country its special
character. This comprised, in short, a high concentration of
economic power in the advanced industries, a close association
between industry and the banks and the combination of an archaic,
traditional institutional framework with the most developed forms
of capitalism. It was a dynamic, not to say explosive, mixture. In
this chapter some attempt will be made to trace out and explain
its formation. The emphasis will therefore be on the peculiarities
of German economic development.

The first problem concerns the retarding forces in preindustrial
Germany. This is not an ordinary case of outlining the conditions
of underdevelopment; eighteenth-century Germany was not an
underdeveloped country in the modern sense. Germany had for
long made contributions to the stock of European technology. Her
ports, trading cities and merchant bankers had at one time played
a relatively important part in the economic development of Europe.

The demands of the Reformation had been first formulated by Germans. The intellectual tradition which it initiated still flourished; German contributions to philosophy, literature and music were of impressive weight and quality. Yet there was no doubt that Germany was economically retarded by comparison with the trading centres of north-west Europe. In fact only a few parts of Germany near enough to feel the stimulus of these growing points showed any signs of breaking away from tradition and routine.

No doubt the virtual economic standstill which Germany experienced as a result of the Thirty Years War, and even more the political divisions which the Peace of Westphalia (1648) consecrated, account in large measure for the growing lag between Germany and neighbouring regions in western Europe. In respect of social structure and political régime the German states in the eighteenth century stood nearer to Tsarist Russia than they did to the West. Within the autocratically governed states of kings, princes and dukes social relations remained feudal or semifeudal in character. This was most evident in the Hohenzollern lands of eastern Germany where the estates of the military landowning caste, the *Junkers*, were cultivated with the compulsory labour services of peasant serfs. In the west, and much of the centre, serfdom in this clearcut form had, by the late eighteenth century, all but disappeared. Nevertheless, although the peasants' obligations had been commuted into payments in money or in kind the social and legal powers of the lords still remained extensive. In practice, moreover, the source of the lords' revenue remained the surplus which they exacted from the underlying agrarian population. The fact that small and medium sized peasant holdings had been established on a hereditary basis did, however, represent an important social advance compared with the bondage of the peasants in the east.

Without dwelling on regional differences and special cases, it is true to say that peasant agriculture was carried on at a low productive level. Part of the peasants' surplus above mere subsistence was paid away to their social superiors, thus reducing the possibility of investment in improved methods of husbandry. The collective servitude of the village community also prevailed to curtail individual initiative and prevent the growth of farming for the market.

Where an estate was farmed by the lord with serf labour organization of agriculture might be more rational. The lords were, on the whole, not great proprietors on the scale of those in the Habsburg Empire or in Britain. They turned to estate farming in order to maintain their revenue and became, where they were competent and able, agricultural entrepreneurs selling surplus crops on the market—to the towns, to the army or for export—or even turning them into marketable commodities on the estate.

Prussian landlords were fortunate in finding a market as well as in having a docile labour force at their disposal. Their interests lay, however, not in the further development of a market economy but rather in preserving existing social relations. They formed an exclusive caste which dominated the state and the army and thus provided the social basis for the Hohenzollern monarchy. None of the changes introduced by Frederick the Great could encroach upon its privileges and he too was conservative in outlook. For both, economic enterprise was to be geared to political needs, the needs of a traditional ruling class. Just as the more enlightened of the *Junkers* sought to run their estates on rational lines to maximize their revenues, so Frederick regarded the country as an estate to be administered as his royal domain. In economic policy he followed the established mercantilist practices, encouraging those activities which seemed to be useful to the state: to supply its needs in times of war, to reduce its dependence on foreign imports or to export to obtain specie. Industry and trade were subject to as wide a measure of bureaucratic direction and control as administrative techniques and the zeal (often more apparent than real) of the officials of the Crown made possible.

The state, it is true, did initiate some industrial enterprises and its officials acted as entrepreneurs in default of private initiative. Under Frederick's guidance, the bureaucracy kept an eye on private business efforts. Advances of money were made to industries which it was thought desirable to encourage and some enterprises were rescued from financial disaster in this way. In some fields, such as mining, public and private enterprise existed side by side. Certainly a tradition of state intervention in the economy was carried on which was to have significance when the first steps in industrialization began to be made in the following century. At the time, however, the policies of Frederick and his officials were not intended to industrialize the country but to serve the interests of the monarchy. The net effect of a policy which involved heavy taxation, high protective duties and the preservation of serfdom, and which was dominated by the needs of the army and war or its preparation, was hardly favourable to industrial development.

The Prussian experience down to 1848 gives little indication that the state bureaucracy desired to promote economic growth either to increase the incomes and welfare of its subjects or to enhance the power of the state. Although some of the high officials were men of the enlightenment, receptive to the ideas of economic liberalism, they behaved empirically, taking from the liberal programme what suited the needs of administrative convenience. At the same time, their attachment to a dynastic monarchy and links with the landed nobility meant that they were conservatively inclined. It was in a spirit of conservatism that the state managed and supported industrial and mining enterprises. Although members of the bureaucracy performed entrepreneurial functions, acting, on occasions, as innovators, they did so broadly within the traditional pattern of 'mercantilism'. As in other European states at a corresponding stage of development, the intervention of the state in the economy was taken for granted; the really revolutionary path was to leave the economy to the spontaneous interaction of competing and conflicting wills in the market-place. The longevity of the state interest in mining and manufacturing was, in the first half of the nineteenth century, at least, a sign of the belatedness of German development. Such an interest did not indicate a concern with growth. Events were to show that the development of industrial capitalism could take place within an environment in which the state retained a prominent role, that it was not incompatible with the existence of a state sector. Alternatively, state-controlled industry should not be equated with socialism and did nothing to alter the capitalist nature of the economic development which took place.

These remarks are largely based on Prussian experience, but some other German states aspired to a similar policy of economic surveillance with varying degrees of success. However, while Prussia emerged territorially strengthened from the trials of the revolutionary and Napoleonic period and with its administration intact and able to reassert itself very quickly, other states disappeared or reappeared much changed by the experience. French occupation had brought revolutionary influences and the Napoleonic codes into Western Germany. The experience helped to break up the old order, to strengthen the business elements and give a taste for greater freedom in the economic sphere. The régimes which survived the torment were less able than their predecessors to continue with the old policies and to preserve the medieval heritage. Prussia herself, after the shock of the defeat at Jena (1806), also went through a renovating process: a controlled agrarian reform 'from above' and the beginning of a more liberal economic policy.

Although this was not part of its intention, the emancipation of the serfs helped to clear the ground for industrialization. The basis was laid for the growth of a free labour force and for the integration of the peasant farm as well as the landlord estate into a market economy. The personal mobility, division of labour and emphasis on individual achievement which capitalism requires would have been impossible without a reform of the old agrarian system.

In the eighteenth century two principal forms of agrarian feudalism existed in Germany. In the west the land was cultivated mainly by the peasants, the lord merely extracting dues in money or in kind. Compulsory labour services and the legal forms of serfdom had died out or had been abolished from above by rulers interested in increasing the taxable capacity of the peasants and weakening the power of the lords. The old field layout and methods of husbandry characteristic of medieval Europe continued to survive. French occupation of these areas during the revolutionary period completed the destruction of feudal survivals, but there was no major redistribution of land and the landlord continued to derive a money rent from his tenants. In the east agrarian development took a different form. Here a good deal of the land was cultivated under the control of the estate owner employing the unfree labour of his tenants and producing a surplus for sale in the market. The lords were, at the same time, socially powerful and the principal support of the Hohenzollern monarchy.

Within this broad division there were many local and regional

4

variations. In the north-west, for instance, serfdom had been abandoned centuries before and the peasants had become hereditary tenants. In the west and south serfdom lasted much longer and only gradually disappeared. In the centre, while peasant farming predominated, there were some estate farms similar to those found in Prussian territory. It was in the east, where the soil was poor, the population scattered and the only market far away, that the estate farmed with servile labour became typical. Here the position of the peasant deteriorated after the Thirty Years War. Many peasants had only small plots of land in which they had lost all hereditary right. Lacking the protection of a strong village community, the Prussian peasant was in some respects worse off than the Russian serf. There were, nevertheless, even in east Germany some hereditary peasants, having land in the open fields and owning draught animals. It was in the western areas, however, that local variations were most pronounced, with peasant ownership, tenant farming and share-cropping all to be found. In general, peasant emancipation had been going on for a long time and all that happened in the nineteenth century was that the remaining traces of feudalism were cleared away.

Where peasant agriculture existed the land was generally held in open fields, though there were, in some places, individually owned and separated holdings. Even where a form of serfdom prevailed the peasant under the old order enjoyed some kind of security, at least from the pressures of the market. The process of agrarian reform tended generally to expose the peasant to market forces and to introduce a new instability into rural life. Before long German agriculture was thrown into a crisis of underproduction as a result of which many peasants in the east as well as in the west left the soil to migrate to the cities or to the New World.

The overrunning of Germany by the Napoleonic armies and the shattering defeat of the Prussian army at Jena opened the way for extensive agrarian changes. In the west existing trends towards an individualist peasant agriculture dependent on the market were accelerated. In the east, where the Hohenzollern monarchy remained in control, the shock of defeat led to a series of reforms intended to 'modernize' Prussian society without disturbing its existing balance. On the territories of the Crown serf emancipation had already taken place at the end of the eighteenth century and the peasants had been permitted to purchase their land. Such lands comprised only about one-fifth of the total area. No inroads could be made into the prerogatives of the *Junkers* upon whose military and political support the monarchy depended. The challenge from Napoleonic France suggested agrarian reform as a first priority in order to release individual energies and patriotic devotion impossible from browbeaten serf, and forestall a revolution from below after the French pattern.

The Stein-Hardenberg reform of Prussian agrarian relations began in 1807 with the abolition of personal serfdom to be effective from 1810, and made it possible for noble estates to be broken up and sold more easily. The serf and his children were no longer bound to the lords' service. It took rather longer to decide what should be done about the peasants' land, which was presumed to belong to the lord and to be held in return for dues and labour services. Clearly the landowners not only required compensation but, since they depended on the peasants' labour to farm their estates, they were concerned lest their labour force would evaporate. Some means had thus to be found of keeping a supply of labour on the land.

Any thought which Stein may have had of protecting the peasantry was lost to sight in the way in which agrarian reform was continued under his successor Hardenberg. By edicts of 1811, 1816 and 1821 provision was made whereby peasants might retain part of their holdings as private property in return for surrendering part to the lord. For those with hereditable plots one-third had to be given up, but for the majority of non-hereditary peasants the amount was two-thirds. The hereditary peasants might, alternatively, acquire their holdings by paying twenty-five years' rent. Such provisions benefited a minority of peasants with larger holdings, draught animals or a little capital. But for many a peasant on the poorer level this 'emancipation' was little short of disastrous. He now had far too little land to support himself and his family or even to bargain at all effectively with his employer. If he remained on the land he had to work for low wages, exposed to the full rigours of an uncertain and fluctuating labour market.

For the lords, on the other hand, the reform was a painless and advantageous operation. Additional arable land accrued to the large estates. The lords also gained from the partition of pasture and common lands, as did the stronger peasants. By the edict of 1816 peasants without holdings in the village fields were excluded from the reform: they remained bound to their place of settlement, forming a labour reserve for the estate owners and richer peasants, and they lost the little security which common rights had previously afforded them. The balance of social forces in East Germany was thus preserved. The *Junker* continued to tower over the rural scene. Having now a larger acreage at his disposal and assured of a supply of labour, at least for a time, he was able to operate increasingly as a large-scale cereal producer and rural entrepreneur. The peasants, if no longer serfs, paid dearly for their freedom. Estimates of the land they lost vary: the figure of 2.5 million acres is often cited. Many holdings simply disappeared, others shrank so that the rest could be retained and much peasant land was sold because the allocations – without pasture and common rights – were inadequate for the peasant's needs.

These changes undoubtedly laid the foundations for a more efficient agriculture in the east by strengthening the large estate and favouring the strong peasant able to turn to farming for the market. Both were able to make untrammelled use of improved agricultural techniques and to take advantage of the opportunities offered by the expansion of the market. The large estate continued to retain a dominant position in the economy and in the nineteenth century could depend upon the constant solicitude of the Prussian government. Entails were encouraged and large estates grew in number and in size. Wage labour was provided by the peasants who had formerly worked as serfs; then, as many left the land, many of the big estates, whose owners were firm believers in German racial superiority, became dependent on immigrant Polish labour. The fact that a class of substantial peasants was created at the same time provided an additional support for the East German social structure dominated by the *Junkers*.

Expansion of demand for agricultural produce, both within Germany and abroad, in the period after 1815 enabled the reorganized agrarian system to prosper. Peace and settled government, the extension of medical knowledge and more hygienic habits, the declining effectiveness of old restrictions on early marriage, the cultivation of the potato and other productive crops brought a demographic revolution to Germany. In the east population density increased with a growth in the numbers of smallholders, rural wage-earners and artisans. A labour reserve was created for industry but population pressure was not acute. Rather was it in the western regions where peasant agriculture prevailed that population growth in the first half of the nineteenth century created intense pressure on the land and on the food supply.

The agrarian crisis in western Germany reflected the deficiencies of peasant agriculture carried on in the old way and the too slow shift of labour and resources into the non-agrarian sector. In the peasant community population growth threw increased burdens on to systems of cultivation which were still enmeshed in the past. This was particularly so, of course, where the open field village continued to exist. Where partible inheritance was the custom holdings tended to become more fragmented; if only the eldest son inherited, more landless men were looking for occupations which rural society did not offer, and which industrialization was only beginning to provide.

By the 1840s this crisis had reached an acute form in western Germany. For many, emigration seemed the only solution and a considerable movement across the Atlantic took place. Since the voyage required funds which the poorest rural strata did not possess, the migrants came mostly from the better off peasants who sold their land and possessions, seeing greater prospects for advancement in the New World than in their native land. Those who stayed behind were gripped, in the later 'forties, by the food crisis which affected the whole of Europe.

While the mass of the rural population in western Germany had some land the peasant farm tended to shrink in size so that the material conditions of the peasantry deteriorated. It is difficult to explain why the German peasants did not seek to combat *morcellement* by limiting the size of their families as their French counterparts did. Perhaps the hold of religion had something to do with it, especially in the Catholic areas of western Germany where the problem of dwarf holdings seems to have been most acute. In any case, the peasant everywhere became increasingly dependent

on the forces of the market as his relationship to the landlord became
a purely monetary one, for not only had emancipation in the west
left the peasant in some places with money payments to make in
lieu of his former dues or services, but land hunger meant that
many peasants had to rent land from the landowners on a purely
contractual basis.

Peasant despair and resentment were expressed in many parts of
Germany in the early stages of the Revolution of 1848. The peasant
sought relief from the monetary burdens of rent, interest and
mortgage payments. He was not revolting so much against feudalism, which had all but disappeared, as against the legal and con-
tractural burdens which had taken its place. In places he demanded
the breaking up of the big estates. Where feudal and manorial
payments and seigneurial privileges still subsisted he sought their
extinction too. The peasant in 1848 was thus not interested in
constitutional forms but in agrarian change. Most of the revolutionaries neither sought nor desired the support of peasants whose
claims threatened established contracts and property rights. What
they failed to give the alarmed conservatives ceded more willingly.
The concessions which the peasants won in 1848 were therefore
granted by the governments of the states under pressure from a
rural revolt which remained largely separate from the revolution
in the towns. The liberals lost the opportunity of an alliance with
the peasants to expropriate the nobility and thus undermine the
social basis of the monarchical states through their own legalism,
respect for property rights and timidity. The peasants rapidly became disillusioned with the liberals, grasped the small gains wrung
from the conservatives and withdrew from the political arena. In
the post-revolutionary years, therefore, the completion of agrarian
reform was carried through by the forces of the old order. Despite
themselves the reactionaries were obliged to uproot the remaining vestiges of feudalism and manorialism and clear the way for
the further victories of the market economy. In west Germany
this meant that the nobility continued as rent receivers and absentee
landlords while the peasant became an outright owner of his hereditary holding. In the east the emancipation was completed by ending
the dues which many of the peasants had continued to pay, either
by the cession of land or by a money payment to the lord.

The long-drawn-out process of agrarian reform, which took many varied forms in the regions of Germany, exposed both the peasant and the landowner to the rigours of the market economy. Adaptations were forced on the rural population which different sections and different individuals made in their own ways. In all strata there were those who lost: peasants who became wage labourers or who migrated to the cities or crossed the ocean, landowners who became increasingly indebted and finally had to sell their property to pay their debts. On the other hand, there were peasants who, as owners or tenants, stayed on the land and achieved a modest prosperity as producers for the market. If there were *Junker* landlords who, through misfortune or incompetence, fell steadily into debt and had to sell up, the *Junkers* as a whole survived. Newly enriched businessmen acquired the estates which the impoverished scions of noble lineage had to relinquish. Through their influence in the state they were able to retain a privileged status and, when threatened by foreign competition, falling prices, labour scarcity or lack of credit, it was to the government that they turned to shield them from the operation of market forces. By the 'seventies the *Junkers* could only survive economically by making an alliance with the business interests which they had once spurned.

The *Junker* solution to the agrarian question was thus no solution at all. It rested on a supply of cheap labour which eventually came, to a large extent, from non-German sources. It conserved a class which embodied the authoritarian and militarist traditions of Prussia and combined it with the new dynamic of industrial power which also tended towards national exclusiveness and added to it a need for external markets.

The changes in agriculture loosened up the ties of many peasants with the land. Together with the population increase with which they were related, and the transport improvements which followed, a supply of labour was made available for the growing towns and population was redistributed according to the changing industrial pattern. Despite pressure from below, the agrarian changes took place as a process controlled from above; the gains which the peasant made were thus seen as the gift of conservative régimes and not associated with revolution or political liberalism. The traditional-minded peasants, accustomed to manorial discipline and a frugal standard of living, thus moved into the city as an adaptable and relatively easily disciplined working force for the mines and factories.

The great unevenness of economic development in politically divided Germany has to be insisted upon. Even after 1815 there remained over thirty separate political administrations each with their systems of laws, currencies, weights and measures and customs frontiers. In addition, there were the usual variations in topography and soil fertility to be expected in such a large geographical area. The new industrialism was based principally on a few raw materials: coal, iron and cotton. Germany was well provided with the first two, but her reserves were found in a few main areas on the periphery. Cotton and other imported raw materials were most economically obtained in the west, particularly on the Rhine. In some regions a quickening of the economic pulse was perceptible before the French Revolution and in the western cities particularly there had been an uninterrupted commercial tradition. Over much of Germany, however, the eighteenth and early nineteenth century saw little change. Many towns had not outgrown their medieval walls and in them life had changed but little. Artisan industry prevailed, still dominated by the guilds. Production was for exchange with the surrounding countryside or to meet the needs of the local court, nobility and patrician middle class. Lack of transport facilities perpetuated the isolation of these small, sleepy towns. Institutions remained steeped in the traditions of status; the crust of custom was unbroken.

Until the French Revolution exerted its effects only a few commercial centres were exceptions to this rule. The influence of French occupation was to quicken the pace of change, especially in the Rhineland. Much land changed hands and became a marketable asset for the first time. Fortunes could be made in land speculation, in contracting for the occupying forces or in the new trade possibilities which the links with a larger market area now offered. Commercial life was expanded under a more favourable legal dispensation. The business class thus prospered in a freer environment than it had known before. As a result the disparities between the west and the rest of Germany tended to widen. Then, after

1815, to create a permanent barrier to future French ambitions, what was the most advanced economic area of Germany passed under the control of Prussia. Despite the post-1806 reforms the Hohenzollern monarchy remained a conservative autocracy of the old régime. The monarchy rested upon the support of a militarist and landowning nobility which, in turn, maintained its social dominance with the help of a hierarchical bureaucracy. While the business elements of the west were thus drawn towards liberalism, asserted the rights of the individual to settle his affairs through the market, and tended to emulate the economic practices of adjacent countries, the tradition and influence of the Prussian administration were towards regulation and intervention in the economy to preserve the existing order.

From what has been said so far it is clear that there was as yet no question of a national economy in Germany. Political fragmentation, local loyalties and the overwhelming predominance of a peasant and small artisan economy, together with the lack of transport facilities, greatly limited the size of the market. Germany was rather a collection of small local economies each more or less isolated from the rest. The vested interests of landowners, rulers, officials and guild masters were distinctly opposed to change. The commercial revolution of the seventeenth and eighteenth centuries had virtually passed Germany by. Some trade had been kept alive in the northern ports and there was a flow of colonial produce down the Rhine but participation in the world market was small compared with that of Britain, France or Holland. The states of Germany were too weak or too immersed in the political quarrels of Central Europe to establish a claim for colonies. The stimulating and invigorating effects of large and growing foreign trade were therefore absent. Economically Germany was closed in on itself.

Under these conditions the retarding influences of the medieval heritage were able to retain their force into the nineteenth century. As would be expected there was a scarcity of entrepreneurs and managers and, apart from a few special areas, there was little in the way of an independent middle class engaged in trade and industry. Merchants and guild masters of the traditional type accepted their position within a stable order, dependent on the favours of the local court or lord and upholders of the existing regulations. The urban middle class was weak because towns were few in number and small in size, administrative centres with some commerce and a little industrial production rather than economic growing points. The middle class in towns of this type had its centre of gravity in the professions and in the service of the state; it therefore lacked the independence and self-consciousness of its counterpart in France or Britain. Its continuing weakness was displayed when in 1848 it attempted to assert its claims for the first time.

A society of this type will produce little investment capital. The accumulations from overseas trade, important in Britain and France, were denied it. Much of the land was poor in quality and what little surplus it produced passed into the hands of landowners who had little interest in investment. The lack of purchasing power on the part of the population at large discouraged investment in increasing the scale of manufacturing industry. The needs of the wealthier sections could be met by industries organized on guild lines or on the putting-out system. So far as the peasants were drawn into a market economy it was also through domestic industries.

If Germany was chronically short of investment capital the supply of labour for industry was also restricted. Of course, levels of living were low and population was increasing. On the other hand, the labour market was limited by the immobility of the peasant population. East of the Elbe serfdom prevented free movement and after its abolition legislation regarding settlement and poor relief tended to act in the same direction. Elsewhere, since the peasants had land or the prospect of obtaining a holding they were normally reluctant to move. Rather did merchant industrialists tap this reservoir of labour power through the putting-out system. As pressure on the land did increase, however, the tendency was for part of the overflow to emigrate. It is true that many of the emigrants were drawn from the better-off peasants but it may be suggested that emigration in the nineteenth century was evidence that the limiting factor in economic growth was not labour supply but is to be found on the demand side in the rate of capital accumulation.

The main reason for Germany's lag can be brought down to

the lack of capital and of opportunities and incentive for its investment in a social environment which was still cluttered up with
many feudal remnants. How, then, did the barriers to growth
come to be removed? No simple answer is possible, but it seems
safe to put forward a hypothesis which takes account of the coming
together of a number of favourable preliminary conditions for
change.

Most decisive, perhaps, was the influence and pressure exerted
within Germany by the changes which were taking place in other
countries. The effect of the French occupation on the Rhineland
has been mentioned and, in a more general way, the influence of
the French Revolution did begin to prepare the ground for change.
At the same time, there was the effect of industrialization in Britain
which operated in complex ways: by bringing manufactured goods
into the German market, by opening up markets for German
products, by exciting interest and a desire to make use of the new
technologies and by the import of capital and enterprise from
Britain. The presence in Germany of accessible supplies of coal
and iron ore was obviously a factor of great importance, in the
first instance by drawing in foreign capital and businessmen.

Changes in Germany itself were to begin with less directly
economic in character, but did tend to make the conditions for
enterprise and capital investment more favourable. The initiative
here came from the Prussian bureaucracy whose policies, after
1815, were determined principally by administrative convenience
rather than a desire to promote economic growth. It was in this
spirit that it tackled the problems imposed by the acquisition of
new territories in the west and the existence of sprawling possessions of the monarchy across Germany to the eastern frontiers. The
first response was to impose some uniformity of administration,
including the levying of customs duties. In the tariff of 1818 a
standard, mildly protectionist, tariff schedule was adopted for all
Prussian territories. This still left Prussia with many hundreds of
miles of customs frontier shared with the other German states,
a circumstance which impeded the free flow of trade and was an
invitation to the smuggler. Administrative convenience suggested
that tariff agreements should be concluded with neighbouring
states, to bring them into the Prussian customs system. From the

point of view of revenue collection such arrangements proved to be mutually satisfactory. The final logical step, once suspicions of Prussian intentions were overcome, was a wider customs union which would enable goods to circulate freely within Germany and levy duties only on those goods which came from foreign countries.

When, in 1834, the *Zollverein* came into effect most of Germany was brought into a single free trade area. This was an arrangement between states which for historical and cultural reasons already had much in common and were loosely associated through the German Confederation set up in 1815. However, while in the Confederation the influence of Austria remained paramount, the *Zollverein* was a Prussian creation which the bureaucracy intended to keep under its control. The territorial and political weight of Prussia was here decisive. Alternative customs unions for parts of Germany without Prussia were not viable, while a customs union without Austria was. And once Austria was excluded the new material ties which developed within the framework of the tariff-free area drew the populations of the member states closer together and created a new distinction between them and Austria. The way was thus being prepared, unconsciously, for the eventual political hegemony of Prussia and a solution of the German question which excluded Austria.

Formed initially for administrative reasons, the *Zollverein* proved to be a major factor in the promotion of German economic development. It widened the legal limits of the market and made possible the free movement of goods. By strengthening trade links between one area and another it tended to break down old particularisms and local differences. It established vested interests in the further consolidation of this preliminary unity and reinforced cultural nationalism, which mainly interested the middle-class intelligentsia, with a new economic nationalism which inspired the developing business groups.

To enable the full potentialities of the *Zollverein* to be realized internal transport would have to be improved. Road transport over long distances was expensive. River transport, especially on the Rhine, although it developed tremendously and could be supplemented by canals, had definite geographical limitations. That is why the availability of the railway at this stage was of such decisive importance. The railway was the product of advanced industrial technology, but it could be introduced into relatively under-developed countries, such as Germany, directly as a going concern, financed from abroad, using imported materials as well as engineers. In this sense Germany was able to leap over stages.

The early reception of the railway by the Prussian and other state governments was not encouraging. Only its disadvantages were seen and the early lines were hedged around with many restrictions; speculative excesses were especially feared. This conservative opposition to novelty began to weaken in the course of the 1840s when the estate owners began to realize that the new form of transport could expand the market for their crops and thus increase their revenues. At about the same time the military men began to understand the strategic significance of the railway. In the years following the restrictive Prussian railway law of 1838, the attitude of the state became much more encouraging and trunk lines were built with a state guarantee of interest.

In the 1840s railway building went ahead rapidly in many parts of the country. This great effort required considerable injections of external finance and state support which in some cases produced state lines, in others some kind of financial guarantee to encourage rentier capital. In the nature of things, German railway development brought the economy into more intimate contact with more advanced foreign countries from which much of the capital came. This capital was drawn into Germany because of the potentialities of the area, particularly the existence of mineral resources which were the basis of the iron and engineering industries which railway building directly stimulated. Furthermore, only with the kind of cheap long-distance transport which the railway provided was it worth while to make the heavy capital outlays on modern equipment to develop deep mining and establish a large-scale metallurgical industry. Such investment could only justify itself on the basis of a great extension of the market which only the railway could provide, the *Zollverein* having already removed the artificial barriers.

It is difficult to see any other force which could have impelled the Germany economy forward at this time. The textile industries

had been changing slowly and some branches had begun moving
into the factories as early as the 1780s, but they were in no position
to lead the way in a general economic transformation. The dominant position of British textiles in the world market excluded the
possibility of rapid growth on the basis of exports and there was
no independent change in the home market which could have
brought rapid growth. For the same reasons no other consumer
goods industry could have taken the lead. The railway was a condition for the opening of the home market for these sectors, as
well as for the mining and metallurgical branches. No other form
of investment at this time could have drawn in the foreign capital —
and it was above all capital which Germany lacked — and at the
same time have received comparable support from the states.
Similarly, the railway opened up entirely new investment opportunities and introduced a new factor of change into German life:
as railway links were established interregional contact and mobility
took the place of particularism and stagnation.

From the 'forties, in the wake of the railways, the economic
awakening of Germany began. Once an initiating force had appeared
many of the former barriers to change lost their force and what had
appeared to be the missing prerequisites for growth were rapidly
assembled. However, the new growth sectors had little or no effect
on many areas of German economic life which continued basically
unchanged in their old patterns. In Germany, as elsewhere, industrialization was an uneven process. The very rapidity of the building
up of the modern sector enhanced the differences between it and
those sectors which still conserved their old attributes. Above all,
the political framework, although it changed in important ways,
retained its old autocratic and conservative character.

The basic reason for this is to be found in the failure of the
liberal middle class in 1848 to establish a unified constitutional
state. At this stage social development was still too backward to
inspire the middle-class leaders of the revolution with either the
self-confidence or the social basis in the country which were
required for success. Consequently, the old traditional forces were
able to re-establish themselves with the help of the military power
of which they had never lost grip, at least in Prussia. After a little
over a decade, in which Austrian influence in the Confederation

remained unchallenged, Prussia under Bismarck staked out a claim for political hegemony in Germany and established it at Austria's expense on the battlefield. Then, with the defeat of the Second Empire of Napoleon III the new German Empire became the most powerful state on the continent of Europe. This new state, for all its acceptance of universal suffrage and a national parliament, remained an autocracy ruled by the Hohenzollern dynasty, which still rested on the support of the traditional landed nobility of eastern Germany. It incorporated the bureaucratic and militarist traditions of the old Prussia and the conservative forces were given a new lease of life by the way in which unification had taken place.

Since 1848 Germany had undergone profound social changes. The growth of the economy had brought into being a larger middle class with its balance now shifted towards business. Its goals were to be found in material success and accommodation with the powers that be rather than in the visions of the intellectuals of the 1848 revolution. Its nationalism outweighed its liberalism and had been given a more egotistical character by the manner in which the Second Reich had been formed. Many of the members therefore cooperated with the dynastic conservatists and accepted the illiberal and militarist traits which the hegemony of Prussia preserved in the new Germany.

A rapidly growing and advanced industry was combined with an archaic political framework and a society still dominated by an agrarian upper class clinging to preindustrial values. The growing economic power of Germany was thus directed by men who belonged to the old régime; the upper middle class, for its part, accepted this situation, indeed its members adapted themselves to it with few regrets. Pursuit of material interests could be carried on more successfully in a powerful and united state than in the old divided Germany. If the bourgeoisie had little share in determining policy and not only had to accept a position of social inferiority but also espoused the ideology of the landed nobility, they at least accumulated wealth on an unprecedented scale and identified their interests with those of the Reich.

The rapid economic change which began in the 'forties, coupled with the unification of the country by force under Prussian leadership, gave German industrial capitalism its special character.

Instead of a slow process of building up of capital by a large number
of individual firms in a competitive environment, the leading
sectors of the economy had leaped ahead on the basis of the advanced
technology and forms of organization already worked out in the
more advanced parts of Europe. Initially part of the capital for the
expanding sectors came from abroad in large amounts. New firms
were organized from the beginning as joint stock companies and
often with the participation of the banks. The lack of either large
fortunes ready to embark on industrial enterprise or a rentier class
made this inevitable. Only the banks could lay their hands on the
large amounts of money capital required to build railways, open
coal mines and establish plants in the heavy industries. Only the
banks could provide credit facilities to finance the vastly increased
scale of monetary transactions which resulted. By making advances
to, or opening credits for, business customers they effectively added
to the volume of purchasing power. Renewal of credits gave some
of this lending a long-term character. In addition, however, bankers,
especially in the Rhineland, which was the most advanced economic
area, played an active role in floating companies. They held blocks
of shares until they could be disposed of to their customers, kept
shares in their own portfolios and sat on the boards of the creditor
companies.

From the initial stages in which existing banks took on such
functions without changing their structure, in the 'fifties, new
joint-stock banks were founded which undertook systematic investment in industry. The new investment banks floated companies,
dealt in industrial shares and provided long-term capital and credit
to industry. Without these efforts by the banks it would have been
impossible to make available the financial means for the building
of the railways and the growth of industry. Unlike the situation
in Britain, where the banks kept clear of long-term investment
not only because it was regarded as unsound but also because
established entrepreneurs were able to obtain all the capital they
required from past profits, close and intimate relations existed
between bankers and industry from an early stage. Again, while in
Britain the joint stock company was little used for industrial investment, in Germany it was often the only way in which sufficient
capital could be obtained to launch a new enterprise or to expand

an existing one. This, of course, is not the whole story. In the consumer goods industry no doubt the picture would not differ greatly in the two countries. In Germany, however, it was heavy industry which took the lead; in fact, an industrial breakthrough was probably impossible in any other way. The investment required in railways and in heavy industry had to be made in large blocks and carried enormous risks: it could not have been provided at all without the participation of bank finance and the use of the company form of organization. A close tie-up between financial institutions and industry thus existed from the start of German industrialization.

The resources of Germany, the potentialities of a market with a large and growing population, the existence of an abundant labour supply, had by the 'forties become attractive to foreign business. Much of the initial development in Ruhr mining and the metal industry therefore took place not only on foreign models but with the participation of foreign capital and enterprise. Once the stimulus was given, however, the rapid growth which followed soon reduced the role of foreign business. There was only a narrow gap, after all, between the teachers and the taught. The lessons taught by foreign entrepreneurs, managers and engineers were rapidly learned. German businessmen had in any case been observing for a long time the industrial developments taking place in Britain and other countries. Educationally the German middle class, and even the general population, was not inferior to its counterparts in other countries. It was simply that the opportunities in industry and trade had been restricted by the whole nature of the society: talents were turned towards the professions or the civil service which only from the 'forties began to find an increasing outlet in business. Moreover, it was soon evident to German governments that economic inferiority could be redressed by an effort in the field of education. Within a short time, therefore, secondary and technical education had been built up to a level second to none in Europe and a stream of scientifically and technically qualified men poured out who were to make it possible, with great speed, to overcome Germany's earlier inferiority in industry and to permit the lead to be taken in some of the science-based industries which were becoming of increasing importance.

Once an impetus had been given to development, and it seems that this came decisively from the railway, the ability of Germany to begin to narrow the gap between herself and the earlier starters, and even to overhaul them, was no miracle. There were many latent forces which could be enlisted to make the transformation: an existing banking and commercial framework, an industrial tradition, natural resources of just the right sort for the existing technology, a receptive population, a dynamic nationalism seeking expression. Certainly there were obstacles to be broken down, but from the end of the eighteenth century they had steadily been losing strength. Even the traditional forces, the agrarian interests of the east, the bureaucracy and the militarists, adapted themselves to the industrialization process. Those who suffered most were the old-style artisans and guild-masters, whose status, if not material conditions, deteriorated, and sections of the peasantry forced by agrarian change to leave the land for the factories or mines or a place on the emigrant ships.

The stimulus provided by railway construction, as well as the widening of the market which the new transport facilities made possible, encouraged investment in coal-mining and the metallurgical industries which were to provide the basis for German industrialization. In these fields an advanced technology was available which could be transplanted into areas of abundant coal resources. Large-scale investment was necessary to enable the new techniques to be used at all. There was no question of beginning in a small way and advancing by slow stages. Large amounts of capital were required initially. Part came from foreign sources. Bank capital played an important part and joint stock companies were formed from an early stage. From the start German industrialism assumed a form which was a product of the technical and financial conditions under which it began.

Foreign influence in German industry dropped into the background as industrialization proceeded and adequate supplies of capital and managerial and entrepreneurial skills became available from native sources. From the ranks of the middle class men were rapidly forthcoming who were able to assimilate all that the foreigner could teach and were soon able to contribute innovations of their own. The overcoming of the financial problem by resort to bank credit was one of them. Realization of the economies of large-scale and integrated production, an emphasis on scientific education and technical and trade training were others. The existing environment had prepared the way, by the middle of the century, for rapid adaptation of this sort. The defeat of the middle class in 1848, followed by a period of reaction which effectively excluded it from politics, perhaps contributed to direct energies into the business field. A growing emphasis on the pursuit of wealth was coupled with national pride and ambition. It was realized that German inferiority in industry could only be overcome by consciously applied effort, especially in the educational field, and by the mastery of scientific method as applied to industrial processes and organization. There was no time to advance by trial-and-error. It was clear that time was not on the side of the German businessman; he had to push forward with the utmost speed and energy to overcome his initial disadvantages. For its own reasons, the administration, particularly in Prussia, encouraged the development of scientific and technical education and helped to provide an environment steadily becoming more favourable for the pursuit of wealth.

In the political sphere, by the 'sixties, the problem of German unification had become ripe for solution. The failure of the liberals in 1848, the inability of Austria to capitalize on its post-revolutionary successes and the lack of any other force able to take the leadership in Germany placed the Hohenzollern monarchy in a position where it could take advantage of all the trends and currents making for unity. These were now no longer of a vague and sentimental kind, drawing strength from echoes of the past and romantic idealizations; rather did they stem from the very real material ties between Germans in the different states made possible by the growth of trade and industry. The business middle class did not mind so much how unification was to be achieved, or under whose auspices, as long as they could depend upon stable and orderly government at home and backing for their enterprise abroad. They were thus ready to accept the hegemony of Prussia and the Hohenzollern monarchy. In any case, the existence of the *Zollverein* and the economic strength of Prussia, in which the growing industrial areas were mainly situated, made it the logical head of Germany. As accomplished by Bismarck unification, of course, meant the preservation both of the monarchy and the East German landlord class with which its existence was bound up. The rise of German industrial power thus took place within an archaic framework of autocracy, traditionalism and militarism antithetical to liberalism and democratic institutions.

During the 'sixties, however, economic liberalism suited the interests of Bismarck as well as of the business middle classes. Externally this meant moderate protectionism and commercial treaties making possible a free exchange of goods with other countries. Internally, within the *Zollverein*, it meant the legal establishment of the full liberal programme relating to economic life. The privileges of the guilds and corporations were swept away. Trades and professions were thrown open to those capable of practising them. A new mining law made minerals in the subsoil more readily accessible to capitalist enterprise. Greater uniformity in commercial and civil law, as well as in weights and measures, improved the conditions for business enterprise. The way was clear for the full and free operation of market forces within an autocratic and bureaucratically controlled political framework.

German business thus accepted the march to unity on Bismarck's terms because of the obvious material advantages. The *Junker* aristocracy, although sections proved unable to adapt to changing economic conditions, remained socially predominant as a class. The new Reich, established after the defeat of France in 1870–71, contained both a powerful industrial sector, with its main base in coal and iron, and an influential agrarian aristocracy. In the 'seventies both sections faced new economic pressures which stemmed from the new conditions of international rivalry on the world market and the price slide which resulted. The liberal foreign trade policy adopted in the 'sixties soon became a casualty. Heavy industry sought protection against British competition in the German home market. The big landowners required defence against cheap Russian or American grain. The tacit alliance thus became closer and more formal and was sealed in the tariff of 1879.

Behind the tariff wall existing traits in German industrial capitalism worked themselves out more fully. The competitive strain in heavy industry, already inherently weak, gave way to a process of cartellization and vertical and horizontal combination. The already close relations between industry and the banks were extended, producing great concentrations of economic power able to gain concessions from the government. Besides the tariff, the railways, which became increasingly a state system after 1871, offered rates which kept down the cost of moving exports to the frontiers or the ports while deterring the penetration of imports into the hinterland. The development of industrial capacity made the economy increasingly dependent on exports for its prosperity, while the growth of population outstripped the productive capacity of German agriculture. The problem of the external relations of Imperial Germany was thus posed from the 'eighties in a sharpened form.

The industrialists, particularly in heavy industry, wanted assured markets for their increasing productive capacity. Protection of the home market was not in itself enough; there also had to be access to assured markets in other countries. Industrialists thus became interested in a forward foreign policy and in colonial expansion. The growth of German foreign trade, in an internationally competitive situation, and the first ventures into the colonial sphere brought the demand for the creation of a high seas fleet. Naval armament, like military equipment, could be an outlet for the surplus capacity of heavy industry. The agrarians were interested in protection and closely linked with the traditionally militaristic upper class. All these interests tended to favour an active foreign and colonial policy backed up by military and naval power. An alliance between them meant that the policy of continental hegemony inherited from Bismarck was combined with a policy of world power of which a powerful navy was a necessary instrument. If the European pretensions of Germany were bound to be opposed by France and Russia, increase in naval armaments and aspirations for colonial expansion were bound to awaken fear and suspicion in Britain.

The economic history of Germany cannot be separated from the politics of power. An industrially powerful Germany in which the old forces of autocracy and militarism were preserved could not fail to develop political ambitions which conflicted with the positions already held by Britain, France and Russia. Economic forces created the conditions out of which the tensions and eventual military conflict arose, but the ultimately deciding factors were to be found at the political level, in relations between states and the behaviour of the men who controlled their destinies.

From an economic point of view German industrialization may appear to have been an unqualified success. Compressed into a comparatively short period of time it soon endowed the country with a highly concentrated and technologically advanced heavy industry. The emphasis in this typical latecomer on education, scientific expertise and organization paid off in the development of new branches of production, among which chemicals and electricity were outstanding, and contributed to give the industrial structure a highly modern appearance. When comparison is made with Britain, the pioneer and slow developer in which many of the early industrial traits were conserved into the twentieth century, German success seems even more impressive. The rapid growth of the export trade and German successes in competition with British goods in the world market apparently underlines the contrast between the progressive newcomer and the less adaptable, older-established industrial country.

While a picture of this kind presents one aspect of the truth it would be inadequate without laying some stress on the incompleteness of the German transition to an industrial society in the years before 1914. The rapidity of German industrial growth had left almost untouched some parts of the preindustrial society. This was true on a geographical basis as there were large areas of Germany which were not yet ripe for industrial development and therefore conserved an old-world charm. As has been seen, also, the traditional ruling class had retained its position in control of the state, and the army and continued to impress its own values on society. The newly enriched middle layers grew into the established system of precedence and deference, accepting to a marked extent that business pursuits lacked something in dignity and prestige as compared with leisure class activities, army life and the honorific professions. Such an outlook by no means inhibited the search for wealth even on the part of the nobility and was based, of course, on self-deception and illusion. In any case, for the time being the German industrialist or merchant knew that he could not afford to relax if he were to establish a place for his products in the market.

He was therefore more rather than less dedicated to acquisition than his British or French counterpart; he simply left political affairs, and the establishment of social trends, more readily to the traditional ruling class.

Another feature of German social development which tended to limit the extent of industrialization was the survival of the peasantry. Although there had been some clearing of the estates in the east even there some prosperous peasants continued to exist. In the rest of Germany, despite the vicissitudes of agriculture in the 'forties and again during the Great Depression, the peasantry continued to be a substantial social force. Pressure on the land which accompanied the growth in population was alleviated by large-scale emigration as well as by the steady drift to the towns. In addition, of course, agriculture became more productive as more modern methods of cultivation spread and the potato and the cabbage were added to rye or wheat as basic elements in the diet. Until the 'seventies Germany remained a net exporter of food, but even the preservation of a large agrarian sector could not prevent growing dependence on imports from then onwards. The adoption of protection and other measures to sustain agriculture and preserve both the large grain-producing estate and the peasant farm from the full pressure of market forces brought doubtful benefits to the German economy and had a perhaps baneful effect on social development.

The conservation of an agrarian sector larger than could have existed without 'artificial' supports raised the costs of home-produced food and raw materials and was only possible on the basis of all-round tariff protection. Presumably it tended to place a brake on industrial development and to keep average *per capita* income below what it might otherwise have been. In the debate between the traditionalists, who wished to conserve a large farm population, and the advocates of the industrial state neither side scored a clearcut victory which found expression in policy. Instead, by means of the tariff, a compromise was worked out which could only be productive of tensions and contradictions. The home market for German industry grew more slowly than it might have done had the agrarian sector contracted to a greater extent. At the same time its growing productive capacity forced it to seek outlets in the world market but, although German imports increased, despite the tariff, the market for foreign goods in Germany was kept below what it might have been. By the time that Germany became an advanced capitalist country it might have been expected that its balance of payments would have shown a larger import surplus than was in fact the case.

Although autarchy was never pursued as a deliberate policy and, in the Caprivi period a policy of tariff reduction by agreement was put into effect, the protectionist policy did distort the German economy's relationship to the world economy, limiting its involvement in some respects. As a result industry sought assured markets at home and abroad and the weight of heavy industry in the economy as a whole continued to be excessive. It was heavy industry which sought an alliance with the big agrarian interests, which favoured an active foreign and colonial policy, and advocated large expenditures on the army and then the building of a high seas fleet. This accorded well with the outlook of the traditional and conservative forces in the bureaucracy and the ruling class and still further cemented the alliance between coal and steel, and rye and wheat. Doubtless Germany paid for this, not only in a risky foreign policy which antagonized Britain as well as Russia and France, but also in a lower standard of living before 1914 than might have been possible.

Those who gained, apart from the magnates of heavy industry, the big banks and the stockholders in these firms, were presumably the East German estate owners who were now effectively subsidized, and the peasantry who, as a class, survived. For the latter, however, survival was not always easy and if many peasants were spared being thrown into the factory cauldron they did not escape the vicissitudes of the small producer in a market economy. Many peasants were thus crippled by mortgage and other debts, despite the efforts of credit banks and cooperatives, and saw their living standards outstripped by the urban petty bourgeoisie and working class. Resentment among the poorer sections of the peasantry could become support for political reaction, for the *Volkisch* sentiments which were widespread in Germany and which tended towards racialism and antisemitism.

German industrialization proved to be compatible with the

existence of a firmly entrenched agrarian ruling class and a dynastic state of a conservative and militaristic stamp. It took place without the destruction of the peasantry as a class and gave opportunities for the emergence of prosperous peasant strata producing for the market. Indeed, the survival and prosperity of the peasantry, or of substantial sections of it, seemed to contradict expectations of capitalist development which Marxists and others had derived from English experience. In the light of the peculiarities of German social and economic development it was perhaps not so surprising. The full and free operation of market forces had not been permitted because of the survival in places of political power of an agrarian-based ruling class. This ruling class did, in East Germany, carry out an agrarian reform from above and as a result many former peasants were forced to leave the land. On the other hand, it had no interest in attacking those more prosperous peasants who already existed or who established themselves in the period after abolition of serfdom. Nor, in other parts of Germany, had the landlord interested himself in estate management or farming to the same extent as his English counterpart. The peasants were thus able to retain their control over the land as well as over agricultural opera-tions, and stood in no risk of being dispossessed except under the pressure of market forces. In some places, it is true, there were estates parcelled out into fairly large farms, but even here family farms and peasant holdings predominated. The changes which the peasantry experienced in the wake of industrialization resulted from market forces as restricted and modified by rulers who were interested not in speeding up the disappearance of the peasantry but in preserving it for social as well as economic reasons.

If the old ruling class and the peasantry survived into the indus-trial era, so did a substantial number of craftsmen and artisans of the old type and small entrepreneurs and traders whose activities had little to do with machine industry and might be threatened by it. Guild control of handicraft occupations continued until the 1860s, that is long after it had disappeared in Britain, France and other parts of western Europe. The new laws governing the right of entry to these occupations and other professions only demolished the compulsory powers of the guilds, which continued to exist as voluntary and still influential bodies. As in other countries, industrialization was a piecemeal process both on a geographical basis and because only certain activities were, to begin with, affected by mechanization and large-scale organization. Over large areas of the country life went on much as before, with market towns servicing the surrounding regions and still harbouring their quota of crafts-men and artisans. Growing national prosperity meant, in some instances, that the small producer could flourish, enter new fields and become more numerous. In short, to a much greater extent than in England Germany continued to display, into the twentieth century, some of the features of a dual economy.

The survival of the artisan was, of course, also bound up with the preservation of a rural and peasant society. It was in the small town in mainly rural areas that he held his own best. It was in the vicinity of new industrial areas that many former artisans, or workers whose position had closely approximated to them, found themselves ousted or threatened by factory methods. At least some part of the developing working class in the second and third quarter of the nineteenth century would have been former artisans (using the term in a broad sense) who, although their earnings may have been higher in the factory, felt that their skill had been degraded and suffered a sense of deprivation. This kind of former artisan resentment contributed to the foundation of a labour movement, particularly of the Lassallian sort. Those artisans who continued in the old trades, and whose numbers continued to be well main-tained, sought other outlets for their feeling of insecurity. While the proletariat became resigned to the growth of large-scale industry, the artisans tried to arrest it; they looked backwards to an idyllic past and found spokesmen among romantic intellectuals or con-servatives who also thought that industrialization was destroying something precious in the old Germany.

To a certain extent, then, there was opposition to industrialism among the old agrarian ruling class, the peasantry and the artisans and a tendency for them to converge in the advocacy of restrictive and conservative policies. From these preindustrial strata came similar hostility towards many of the manifestations of industrial capitalism; a search for status in a society increasingly dominated by the cash nexus, an emphasis on community rather than market relations, distrust of the towns and especially of the banker and the

Jew. Such sentiments found a wide echo in middle-class society, more particularly among small businessmen, in professional circles in provincial Germany, in the army and the universities. They converged to form a broad groundwork of nationalist and vaguely anticapitalist sentiment, inconsistent and contradictory, irrational and reactionary which provided a somewhat incongruous ideological background to Germany's rise to world power. It remained hostile or unreconciled to the Weimar Republic and provided the grass roots for National Socialism.

Despite the great conquests which industrialization made in Germany, therefore, its ability to reshape society was considerably more limited than in Britain. It carried along with it many pre-industrial survivals which began to take on new forms as they were combined with a market economy and industrial power. After the formation of the Reich, the role of the state, still dominated by dynastic and upper class agrarian interests which entered, how-ever, into closer alliance with the new aristocracy of business, began once again to become important. The contribution which the state (i.e. of Prussia) made to the preparation of conditions for an early growth of industry in Germany may easily be exaggerated. Until the 1840s its influence in such fields as money and banking, company and commercial law, transport and railway building was generally conservative, in the preindustrial eighteenth-century tradi-tion. After that its principal contribution was in the direction of liberalization: internal free trade through the *Zollverein*, moderate tariffs and commercial treaties, the virtual enactment in com-mercial matters of the programme of the Manchester School. The trend back towards interventionism was a product of the Great Depression of the 'seventies which brought an industrial slump together with the collapse of agricultural prices.

With the cementing of the agrarian-industrial alliance by the Tariff Law of 1879 the way was clear for a policy of state inter-vention on new lines. As conceived initially by Bismarck this was an adaptation of the old structures to changing conditions which enabled the ruling class and dynasty to survive in new times. Industry, and the industrial bourgeoisie, which might have become a serious rival to the agrarians, now needed the support of the government to defend its home market against intensified British competition. It had therefore to accept a policy of agrarian protection, now advocated by the once free trade *Junkers*, as a corollary to their own demands. For Bismarck the tariff gave him the financial independence required to prevent a repetition of the constitutional crisis which had brought him to power in the early 'sixties. His policy now included a firm defence of private property by outlawing the Social Democratic Party and an attempt to ensure the loyalty of the working class to the Reich by a state-sponsored system of social security. In the meantime the state steadily extended its control over the railway system and was thus able to manipulate railway rates in order to defend the home market while stimulating exports.

The inspiration of German industrial and social policy at the end of the nineteenth century must be sought in a continuing tradition of state paternalism which now sought to accommodate itself to the new problems raised by industrialization. However, there were serious divisions of opinion about whether the state should intervene to preserve as much as possible of the old social forms or should accept Germany's commitment to industrialism. Legislation thus assumed a contradictory character. Despite the alliance between the agrarian nobility and the lords of heavy industry policy often seemed to swing more towards one set of interests than to the other. The state, responsive to contrary pressures had, at the same time to play an arbitrating role. At times it seemed to favour the peasants against the great producers of cereals or the artisans and small businessmen against big business. Real or seeming concessions were necessary as a result of the social and electoral pressure which these middle layers could bring to bear, but there is no doubt that the main lines of policy were determined by the powerful agrarian and industrial interests. But the alliance cemented in 1879 remained subject to strains as the economic balance swung in favour of industry and as Germany became inevitably dependent upon imported grain. Despite this fact, and the probable advantages of allowing the agrarian sector to decline more rapidly than it did despite protection and other supports, industrial Germany still retained, down to 1914, a considerable proportion of its active population on the land. In other words, in the compromises which went on over matters of economic policy the agrarians were able to maintain a strong position.

The German state was a pioneer in the promotion of compulsory social insurance for the working population. The only partially realized aim was to draw the working class away from Social Democracy by diminishing the insecurity which went with the extension of market relations and growing urbanization. If this policy did not succeed in diminishing the political influence of the Social Democratic Party, it did, together with the industrial expansion which was resumed in the 'nineties, blunt its revolutionary edge and make it increasingly, in practice, a loyal reformist opposition. This policy was pursued in a context which was still reactionary. The dynastic state remained in being and there was no effective parliamentary control over the autocratic powers which it legally possessed. The landed nobility, and the bureaucracy with which it was interlaced, retained its privileges and its social prestige and, through its influence on state policy, retarded the reduction in the weight of agriculture in the economy which industrialization demanded. Behind the state, too, other sections of the old economic order took shelter and prolonged their life artificially into the twentieth century.

German industrial and social policy was still bent on adapting old institutions to new requirements; it was still not fully attuned to the needs of an industrial society. And yet, despite the preservation of much which was archaic industry advanced with rapid strides, thereby increasing the strains and tensions. Industry pushed with growing aggressiveness into foreign markets. It sought the support of the state for its expansionist schemes. Colonial and naval policy won a wide measure of support. The incompleteness of the internal transformation made the search for foreign outlets, a 'place in the sun', more imperative. On national aims, however dangerous, a wide measure of consensus could be attained. The armaments which a forward foreign policy made necessary meant orders for heavy industry and contributed to the general prosperity, feeding still more the growing nationalist fervour and ambition.

Within this framework German industrial capitalism carried forward and developed to a higher stage traits which had been with it from its first steps. The leading role played by heavy industry and the need, in the absence of already existing accumulations available for investment, to resort at an early stage to the joint stock company and bank lending produced a highly concentrated industrial structure. Over the main fields of advanced industry cartels and combines had practically extinguished competition and there was a close interrelationship between industrial firms and banking institutions. The need to acquire and assimilate technical know-how with great rapidity and the recognition of the importance of scientific and technical education had made it impossible for German industry to permit technological change to take place on the same piecemeal basis as in Britain. Much greater emphasis was therefore placed upon formal training for industry and greater use was made of men educated in fundamental and applied science, while industrial leaders themselves were more frequently trained in science or technology. This emphasis, which arose from the relative lateness of industrialization in Germany, established habits and practices which conformed with the needs of an increasingly technological age. It enabled the lead to be taken in fields such as chemicals and electricity which depended on applied science. Greater advantage could be taken of the new processes in metallurgy which required scientific control. The laboratory became an integral part of the large industrial concern, invention an organized activity and the patenting of new methods part of the business.

In ways such as these, without much conscious planning or purpose, German industry realized the advantages of the latecomer. Entrepreneurs were placed in a position where they could hardly establish a business or expand it without adopting the sort of methods which came to characterize German industry. The conditions were simply not present for a reproduction of British experience in ownership and finance, organization, on the job training and dependence on the practical man and trial-and-error methods. What was perhaps impressive was that, despite the previous industrial backwardness of Germany, many entrepreneurs came forward, with great rapidity, to seize the new opportunities which opened up from about the 1840s. There was evidently a reserve of entrepreneurial talent in the German middle class which had already acquired a certain level of education but whose opportunities for social and material advancement were greatly restricted in preindustrial times. Awareness of development abroad, sharpened by national feelings, obviously played a part. The closing up of political channels for the ambitious and the enterprising after the fiasco of the 1848 Revolution left the middle class with only business activities as a medium for expressing their restless energies. In politics, in the bureaucracy, in the army the higher positions were virtually monopolized by comparatively narrow circles, an élite of birth and rank closely tied to the landowning class which only a few outsiders could penetrate. Once the middle class had decided, after the failure of its bid for power in 1848, to accept this situation it was free to throw itself into the battle for material enrichment with all the more determination. If business did not succeed in throwing off the stigma which attached to it in a society which, until the twentieth century, was still strongly permeated with the status values of the old ruling class, there was simply no other field in which the middle class man could expect to succeed so rapidly and completely.

Thus the German middle class remained without the political influence which its counterparts in France and Britain acquired. In France the tendency was for the bourgeoisie to be so firmly ensconced in the state that its ambitious young men were diverted into its service (or into the professions) and away from business. In Britain the very power of the commercial and industrial middle class enabled it to influence policy and permeate institutions without a sharp and open confrontation with a traditional ruling class with which it tended to coalesce and which retained its position only by a series of tactical withdrawals from untenable positions. Both in France and in Britain the business middle class found outlets for its young and ambitious men in politics, state service, colonial service and other fields of public life which were largely closed to it in Germany. In Germany, it may be suggested, these alternatives were much narrower, and perhaps not so highly sought after. As a result, despite the somewhat inferior status of money-making it drew off a larger reservoir of talent and perhaps inspired a more assiduous devotion and dedication than where alternatives were available. As business grew in size and became more heavily bureaucratized, so it offered positions for the educated men of more average talents who found there a satisfying niche. The comparative quiescence and conservatism of the educated middle class in

Germany may thus be contrasted with the endemic discontent and revolutionary proclivities of the Russian intelligentsia. Yet, in real political terms, the middle class had scarcely more power than it had in Russia.

Harnessed single-mindedly to business pursuits, accepting a social system which condemned it in fact to second class status and yet nourished on a militant patriotism which made it proud of Germany's steadily increasing power to which it made a major contribution, the middle class remained largely unaware of the dangerous international position into which the country was being led. Business was obliged to seek abroad ever larger markets for the output of an industry which, built up behind tariff walls, greatly exceeded the absorptive capacity of the home market. This one-sidedness was, in part, a consequence of the compromises which it had been obliged to make with the agrarian interest rather than a simple reflection of Germany's participation in an international division of labour. In the world conditions of the time trade expansion was bound to have a competitive edge. German merchants thrust into markets which brought them into especially sharp competition with their British rivals. Industry and finance sought privileged spheres of influence. The alliance between big industry, agrarians, the supporters of a high seas fleet and a forward world policy had brought Germany onto the international political scene in a manner which evoked a nervous response elsewhere. The naval and military arms race which ensued brought closer a war between the major industrial powers. Certainly the events which preceded the eventual conflict were of a political character and the decisions were made in the cabinet room and not by businessmen. Behind the politics of the powers, however, can be discerned the compelling motive forces of advanced capitalism which were contained uneasily within the framework of the national state. The rise of industrial Germany, a latecomer excluded from the earlier phases of colonial expansion and with the peculiar combination of internal political and social forces already noted, gave the contest between the powers in the late nineteenth century and early twentieth a peculiarly tense and dangerous character. By combining a drive for European hegemony, which antagonized France and Russia, with aspirations for world power which brought her into collision with established British interests, Germany's rulers headed for disaster. Such a policy combination would have been unthinkable as well as unnecessary without the enormous industrial power built up in the previous decades.

It is difficult to avoid the conclusion that the industrialization of Germany, in the form in which it took place and under the prevailing international conditions, was bound to lead to a drive for external expansion which may be accurately described as 'imperialist'. It was just as inevitable that this should bring about a head-on collision with the established powers. Capitalism developed within the political forms of the national state in a very uneven way. The pressures which it contributed by its inner nature aggravated rivalry between states through which the bourgeoisie, in each country, whether or not in alliance with the traditional ruling class, sought the expression of its interests. This process was accompanied by a growing trade between the industrial rivals themselves which expressed, as it were, the rationality of the market and the international division of labour. In the whole process of development at this stage, however, this was not the predominant influence. National exclusiveness and protectionism, a contest of rival capitalist groups operating from a national base, the imperatives of industries and financial institutions built up by the bourgeoisie in separate countries, harnessed the dynamic of capitalist expansionism to the chariots of the nation state.

In this context, the responsibility of Germany – of its bourgeoisie or ruling class, or of its rulers in the narrower political sense – for the crisis of capitalist civilization in the twentieth century was no greater than that of Britain, France or Russia. Diplomacy could influence the timing of events or the posture of states at a given time and could show greater or lesser skill, could permit reason or unreason to prevail when particular matters came up for decision, but the deeper underlying forces were beyond its command. The way in which industrialization had developed, the forms which it had taken within the existing European states system produced all the elements for a collision between the great capitalist powers which no conceivable diplomatic intervention could have averted. Industrial capitalism as it actually developed as part of the system of national states (and it could hardly have appeared in any other

5

way) provided the motive force, as well as the means, for wars of greater scale and intensity than anything known before in human history. The scope for attributing responsibility to individuals or nations for the occurrence of such wars is, it would seem, therefore strictly limited. Perhaps more than anything else the rise of industrial Germany, in the particular way in which it took place, made a war of some sort, and at some time, against the other industrial capitalist countries inevitable.

Problems for discussion

1. Account for Germany's belated start on the road to industrialization.
2. Examine the course of agrarian change in Germany in the first half of the nineteenth century with particular reference to its effects on preparing the way for industrial advance.
3. Discuss the *Zollverein* and the railways as instruments of German economic unification.
4. Why did the investment banks play such a prominent role in German industrialization?
5. 'What Bismarck attempted to do was to compress the political economy of an age of mass production into the outmoded framework of a society adopted to promote a pre-industrial national life' (R. A. Brady). Discuss this view.
6. What was the significance of the tariff law of 1879?
7. Why was the German dye-stuffs industry able to gain such a dominant position in world markets before 1914?
8. Account for the rapidity of German industrialization, note its limitations and consider to what extent Germany benefited from the advantages of the latecomer.

5 The Modernization of Tsarist Russia

A comparison between the character of the economy of Tsarist Russia and that of other parts of Europe made in the middle of the eighteenth century would not have revealed striking differences with any but the most advanced areas of the West. A century later a profound contrast was beginning to emerge between those countries which had undergone some industrialization and whose institutions had been remodelled in accordance with the aspirations of the liberal middle class and those whose social and economic development had been virtually standing still. It was, then, during this period that 'backwardness' became a notable characteristic of the Russian economy, a product, in comparative terms, of the spread of industry and awakening to consciousness of the middle class in the more advanced parts of Europe.

The economic growth of western Europe and the spread of industry into central Europe from the mid-century exposed crucial weaknesses in the Russian state to the gaze of its own rulers as well as to foreigners. The Crimean War (1854–56) underlined the fact that without an effort at modernization the international influence of Russia would go into irrevocable decline and the power of tsarism come under increasing internal challenge.

If in many ways Russian society and the Russian economy had much in common with other parts of Europe in the eighteenth century, there were evidently some built-in barriers to change which had special force. The widening gap has to be explained, at least in part, from pre-existing conditions: the lack of the dynamic elements for change which existed elsewhere, combined with the great strength of those parts of the old order which inhibited change.

In the eighteenth century Russia was the most populous European country and an expansive power. The frontiers of the Tsarist

Empire were being extended at the expense of the old Polish kingdom in the west and at the expense of the Ottoman Empire in the south while a great power vacuum lay before it in the land masses of central Asia. At this period sheer size and the ability to raise large armies were major factors in the political standing of states. Confronted by a fragmented Germany and the slowly decaying empire of the Turks Russia was able to assume a crucial political role which she continued to play until changes in transport and technology revolutionized the methods of warfare and exposed her backwardness.

The economic structure of eighteenth-century Russia had in common with most of the rest of Europe its overwhelmingly agrarian character. Its peculiarities were provided by a combination of physical, cultural and historical features. Of the natural conditions, over much of the country life was profoundly marked by the length and depth of the winter which made for a short growing season and curtailed activity during the cold weather. Again, while there were marked local differences, it is true to say that much of the soil was difficult to cultivate and the area was not bountifully endowed with raw materials which could be extracted and made use of with the techniques then available. In addition, Russia was a land of vast distances and scattered natural resources. This made for isolation of the village communities and greatly restricted the growth of anything like a national market for large-scale industry.

To these factors must be added the geographical situation of the Tsarist Empire, standing at a great distance from those areas of Europe which had felt the stimulus of the New World and lacking outlets to the sea. As a continental land mass Russia tended to be drawn in upon itself, not to be fertilized by the new currents which were sweeping the rest of the civilized world.

The social structure of Russia was broadly feudal in character: the ruling class was a landowning nobility which extracted a surplus from the underlying peasantry. While in Europe the old feudal ties had disappeared or were being slackened, in Russia a probably once free peasantry had been subjected to increasingly severe forms of serfdom from about the sixteenth century. Serfdom is always difficult to define because while at one end it shades into the contractual status of free wage labour, at the other it approaches chattel slavery. In addition, in Russia there were various sorts of serf: those who were settled on lands which belonged to the state, the Imperial family or the Church, and who, for the most part, paid a quit rent; and those who belonged to the lords and who owed dues in money, kind or compulsory labour services. On the whole the serfs of the nobility were the worst off; many could be sold, given away or won or lost at the gambling tables and their owners assumed powers of life or death over them. In the worst case the serf had no more protection than the slave and might be separated from the land he tilled or from his family. Many serfs worked as domestic servants and some became the spoiled favourites of their masters or mistresses, able to learn skills or even display their talents in artistic performance. Such serfs did not generally have land or cottages, but the great majority were indeed peasants living in village communities whether under the jurisdiction of the state or of the lord. State peasants might find themselves transferred to a lord by royal whim and, since the social weight of the lords in relation to the absolutism of the monarch was slighter than in most parts of Europe, the reverse process was possible. It is with the stable majority of state or gentry owned peasants that we shall mainly be concerned.

Within the peasant mass which made up the great majority of the Russian population there were already some important differences which arose from the nature and severity of the servile bonds upon which they were dependent. In addition there were those which arose from differences in the fertility of the soil or proximity to centres of trade and population or means of communication. There were the differences between the old, settled areas of traditional Russia and the newly developing frontier regions in which peasant-soldiers and their families were settled by the state. Almost everywhere, however, the peasants were grouped in families as part of a village community which controlled the distribution and use of the peasant lands and through which the peasants' obligations in dues, services, taxes, military service and so on were met. The *mir* or *obshchina*, which was to play so important a part in nineteenth-century controveries about the Russian way to economic development, was by no means unique, since similar institutions are found in peasant societies all over the world. However, while in the developed parts of Europe the village community had disappeared or was breaking up, in Russia it was favoured by the state and appeared to flourish.

It was perhaps less the tenacity of the *mir* than the weakness of forces capable of disintegrating peasant life which was characteristic of Russia at this period. The conditions already described left little scope for the operations of merchant capital or specialized industry producing for the market. The peasants acquitted themselves of their obligations to a large extent in kind or in labour services. They had little produce left over to sell and what they did not produce within the household they could obtain by local exchange. Likewise, although the nobility had need of money it constituted a market for only a limited range of luxury or semiluxury goods. The converse of this was the small size and lack of social weight of the middle strata of merchants, traders and industrial entrepreneurs. The Russian social structure was thus simpler than that of the developing areas of western Europe; it lacked an individualist, independent middle class based on the possession of mobile property. Entrepreneurs and merchants tended to be of lowly status, and might even be serfs, dependent on the bestowal of rights or protection by the state.

Russia was therefore the least likely country for a revolution of the type which broke out in France in 1789. She had had her mass peasant revolts, indeed had experienced, little more than a decade before, the great rising led by Pugachev. So far as the ruling class had fears for its security it was from a renewal of a rising of this type and not from an urban revolt of bourgeois and artisans that they stemmed. But though this made for a kind of political solidity which enabled Russia to play a prominent role in the defeat of Napoleon and then act as the gendarme of Europe for a generation, it was also a reflection of what was increasingly being revealed as her economic backwardness. A society with a narrow privileged stratum of landowners and a mass of serf peasants and little or nothing between lacks all the vital stimuli for growth and change. Even more than in Germany and eastern Europe the numerical weakness and lack of independence of the bourgeoisie were to have crucial effects on the course of Russian economic history in the nineteenth century. It was from this class, whose existence testified to the beginnings of growth, that enterprise, inventiveness and the capital to finance innovations generally came. Without its appearance as a spontaneous process the speeding up of growth would require support from the state, and the development which took place would display structural peculiarities proper to it.

The economic development of Russia cannot be seen apart from the international political role which her rulers sought to play and thus from the developments in other countries which continually changed her relative weight in European politics.

The overriding consideration here was the failure of Russia, in the first half of the nineteenth century, to participate in the process of industrial change which was steadily changing the face of western Europe. The innovations in machinery and metallurgy gave countries which had adopted them the basis for increasing their wealth and equipping armies and navies with more formidable weapons than in the past. It was no longer sufficient to be able to mobilize massive armies, cumbersome and lightly equipped, and deploy them slowly over many weeks. Such armies, of the preindustrial type, had been the foundation of Russian power; their last effective use came in repressing the Hungarian Revolution in 1849. To engage the armies of the industrializing countries was a different matter. Russia's lack of internal communications, weaknesses in the commissariat and inferior equipment resulted in failure to repel the Anglo-French invaders of the Crimea who were operating thousands of miles from their home bases in unfamiliar territory. From this time it became evident, if it had not been so before, that Russia's great power status and the cherished international aims of the régime would be imperilled unless some renovation of the economic and social structure took place.

The close interweaving of political considerations with economic developments was thus inherent in the Russian situation. The autocracy intended to remain in command and many of its supporters feared the consequences of pursuing a path which would mean the growth of new strata of the population who might be carriers of disorder and subversive ideas. But the conservation of traditional Russia and of the powers of the autocracy could not be ensured at all without some imitation of the West. The Tsar and his advisers were not converted to belief in economic change as a desirable thing for Russia, far less did they project a programme of industrialization. Their actions were governed by necessities which, considered in isolation, were political in nature. However, they were, at the same time, by implication, seeking to conserve the old order and its economic basis: that is to say, the privileged position of the landowners and their continued prerogative to extract a surplus from the dependent peasantry.

All the reforms and changes which went to make up the modernization of Russia from the middle of the century to 1914 were in the grip of a profound contradiction. Intended to maintain absolutism and the social structure upon which it depended and to enable tsarism to play an independent power role on the international scene, this process set in train forces which tended towards quite opposite results. Every step to modernize Russia brought into play influences which acted corrosively on what the autocracy sought to preserve and revealed its incompatibility with industrial capitalism. At the same time, these efforts, far from enabling Russia to play an independent role in foreign affairs made her increasingly dependent on foreign capital and military alliances.

At the time of the Crimean War Russia was virtually unique in Europe in that a great majority of the peasant population was still in a servile condition. The bonds of serfdom, which had been drawn tighter in the course of the eighteenth century, had shown little signs of relaxation in the first half of the nineteenth. It is true that in the non-black earth areas compulsory labour services were on the decline and many peasants were performing wage work. However, they were still subject to the proprietary rights of the lords to whom part of their earnings were paid. It is true that there was a record of peasant discontent which tended to become more dangerous and to reawaken fears of a general revolt and the abolition of serfdom 'from below' as in the French Revolution. The inefficiencies of serf labour were well known to industrial employers and the newer forms of industrial enterprise employed free hired labour wherever possible.

It is doubtless true that without the abolition of serfdom the economy could not grow and in growing be transformed. Frequently the existence of serfdom is seen as the principal brake upon more rapid development and the cause of Russia's backwardness. This does not mean, however, that it was the only one. Professor Baykov, for example, has argued that the persistence of serfdom was of less importance than the scattered distribution of Russia's natural resources, which awaited a modern transport system before large-scale industrial development could begin, in particular through the bringing together of the iron ore of Krivoi Rog and the coking coal in the Donetz Basin. He probably overstates his case by trying to prove that since there were 32 million people, or 42.3 per cent of the population, free of serf status, there were available supplies of labour and a market if the other factors favourable for growth had been present. In reply to this it may be pointed out that besides including those who were already working for wages and the miscellaneous population of the pre-industrial towns it comprised non-Russian territories in which serfdom had never existed or had disappeared. These 32 million must not be seen as a homogeneous mass from which a large supply of wage labour could have been extracted; it was scattered over the vast territories of the empire and was often as immobile and unresponsive to monetary incentives (supposing that they had been offered) as the serfs.

However, when this has been said, it is well to bear in mind that it was not the institution of serfdom alone, but the whole institutional structure with which it was bound up which was, if not the unique cause, at least an outstanding symptom of the backwardness of the country. Thus, as we shall see, since the abolition of serfdom was carried out in a way which was compatible with the maintenance of the essentials of the old society of which it had been a part, it did not lead the way immediately towards a new era of rapid economic growth.

Gerschenkron insists on the political nature of the decision to abolish serfdom and rejects the view that it was in some way the response to the working out of economic forces. It is unlikely that the landowners would have emancipated their serfs on economic grounds, because, however inefficient serf labour may have been, the cost-output ratio was still a good deal lower than with hired labour. Also many serfs were simply a source of cash income to the lords which they would not voluntarily forego. And a large proportion of the serfs paid quit rents to the state so that any decision about their future was bound to be directly political. As already pointed out, however, the political nature of the decision reflected the desire to conserve particular social relationships and income flows. As for whether advancing capitalism tended to undermine serfdom, the evidence is meagre and in some cases, for example, on fertile grain-producing lands, it may have worked in the opposite direction. The growth of market relations, of money economy, certainly emptied the serf–lord relationship of its old content where it had become merely a money payment for a piece of land extracted on the basis of extra-economic compulsion. That is to say, the peasant remained a serf in legal status, unable to disentangle himself from his obligations or to leave the land without his lord's permission and subject to his judicial and police powers. The test of abolition would be how it dealt with all these aspects of serfdom and what sort of settlement it put in its place.

Serfdom was thus part of a complex of forces which tended to ossify the existing mode of economic life. With primitive means an ignorant peasantry spent its forces in extracting what it could from a particularly harsh environment. Most of what it produced over bare subsistence was drawn off by the nobility and the state. It lacked even elemental physical security under conditions of serfdom and there was little chance that extra effort would result in material improvement. What security there was came from the peasant community; this was in one regard a protection against the exactions of lord and official. It was through the community that the peasants regulated their husbandry, to whom they were responsible but through which a kind of collective responsibility was exercised. In many cases there were periodical redistributions of the village land to take into account changes in family size and circumstance. Security was bought at the cost of individual incentive. Just as in western Europe before enclosures, the land was divided into strips allocated amongst the peasant families. There were commons and pastures or meadowland whose use was regulated by the community. All this was the antithesis of the agrarian individualism which was to make possible great increases in production and productivity in the West. But it also meant that the peasant was kept securely on the land, or that if he left it he only

did so with permission and on condition that his obligations would
be fulfilled. Some serfs did abscond, to the towns or to the frontier
zones, but the majority stayed, discontented often, at times reveng-
ing themselves on an oppressive lord or official or taking part in a
wider but still futile uprising. Fears of a *Pugachevshchina* remained
alive until serfdom was abolished.

From an economic point of view the agrarian system was wasteful
and unproductive, giving little scope for improvement and providing
the peasant mass with little above the barest minimum necessary
for existence. The surplus extracted from the peasantry went to
support a nobility not interested in improving the productivity of
the land and essentially a parastitic consuming class. The state
likewise, though needing to promote some forms of industry for its
own purposes, was not concerned to carry through any changes in
the agrarian sector which would disturb the social equilibrium with
which its own existence was bound up. For both the lords and the
state maintenance of their position appeared to enjoin the preservation of serfdom as the only means of extracting a surplus from the
peasantry.

Some significant differences had already shown themselves in
the way in which this surplus was extracted. Dependence on compulsory labour services, or *barshchina*, was most complete in the
great black soil belt which straddled across the southern part of
Russia. A relatively fertile area for cereals and other crops, it lent
itself to estate farming by the lords themselves or by large tenants.
Here peasant lands tended to be meagre in extent since the serf-
holders wished to assure themselves of a ready labour force. At
the same time, serfs could be recruited to work in the mines, forests
or industrial enterprises. The surplus product was appropriated
directly and sold to the state, in the towns or for export. The
developing market thus tended to rivet serfdom more securely on
the peasantry.

In the more northerly areas of Russia where the soil was less
fertile and the climate harsher the major part of the serfs' dues was
furnished in money, or perhaps in kind, through the quit rent
known as *obrok*. This left on the peasant the onus of finding the
means to meet his obligations: by selling produce in the market,
by working for wages in agriculture or in industry or by carrying

on some kind of manufacture in his own cottage or workshop. It was in this area, therefore, that market forces began to exert an influence for change and growth. Relationships were established between the towns and the villages and part of the product of agriculture was turned into money in the course of exchange. At the same time, to meet his *obrok*, the peasant, or a member of his household, might have to work for wages whether in the village or in the town. Where conditions were favourable he might, in addition, become a small commodity producer turning out consumer goods for the market and perhaps becoming dependent on a merchant to market his product and sometimes to provide the raw material as well. Parallel with this went the growth of a peasant market for various goods which could not be produced inside the home, or for which special techniques and organization were required. As this kind of development took place opportunities arose for the trader and the putter-out to accumulate capital and extend the range of their operations.

There are signs, therefore, especially in the *obrok* regions, that conditions were being prepared for a spontaneous development of industry. However, this was taking place in a slow and patchy way much hampered by the circumstances already described. In short, these precursive signs of capitalist development were combined with the continuation of the old patriarchal and serf relations in the villages and with a political and social order which restricted their scope. Thus to a large extent industry grew out of and adapted itself to the serf economy. This was particularly clear in the case of the 'possessional' factories, usually large workshops set up, under government direction and using serf labour. Such enterprises, while offering some scope for private capital, were turned essentially towards satisfying the needs of the state for naval and military supplies. They were in direct line from the plants set up by Peter the Great and formed part of a tradition of state-aided and privileged industry which was to continue through the nineteenth century. Some workshops were set up on their estates by the landowners to process agricultural produce for sale in the market. Here again serf labour predominated, with the peasants working out their *barshchina* and no doubt with little incentive to work hard or well.

On the whole there was little future in enterprises of this kind which fitted into the prevailing economic landscape without difficulty. More important was the development of putting out methods in the *kustar* industries carried on in the homes of the peasantry in the *obrok* areas. Here the peasants worked because they needed money to meet their obligations and to buy what they needed in the market. The merchants who organized production themselves came from the serf peasantry; there was nothing to stop a serf getting rich if his lord permitted. In the first thirty or forty years of the nineteenth century such industry remained largely of a handicraft character. It was the spread of the English inventions in textile spinning and the introduction of the steam engine which brought the first examples of a fully capitalist machine industry in Russia. After a period in which imported machine-made yarns were woven by cottage workers, spinning factories were established in the 1840's and a distinct cotton textile industrial area made its appearance. The new factory industry was introduced on too small a scale by comparison with the dimensions of the Russian economy to be seen as an industrial revolution. But still it did introduce the first elements of an industrial capitalist economy to Russia using free hired labour and owing nothing to government privileges or promotion. Given the narrow basis of the home market and the stability of the agrarian economy, however, its sphere was bound to remain restricted.

If the year of the abolition of serfdom, 1861, marks a date in Russian economic history, it is almost as much for what it failed to do as for what it did. The nature of the reform, as an edict of the Tsar, based on several years of discussion and enquiry by a government which represented the owners of land and serfs, provides the reason. Because it left so much of the old institutional structure unchanged the agrarian problem remained unresolved, with many sequels and vestiges of serfdom remaining to dominate Russian economic development down to the fall of tsardom and even beyond.

Emancipation was conceived as a means of safeguarding the social order. Speaking to an audience of Moscow nobles in 1856, Alexander II had said: 'It is better to destroy serfdom from above, than to wait until that time when it begins to destroy itself from below.' No decision taken from above could go against the interests of the nobility, though concern with public order made it impossible to satisfy its more extreme claims. Emancipation, if carried out from below, or in the interests of the peasantry, would have recognized the peasants' claim to all the land which they tilled and cancelled payments to the lords for the village lands. In the provincial commissions the landowners fought to keep the allocations of land to the serfs as low as possible. This was particularly the case where the estates were being cultivated by serf labour since the lords feared that if the former serfs obtained enough land to live on their labour force would disappear. However, it had to be recognized generally that the serfs could not be emancipated without land if violence was to be averted. In fact, such a change could not be seriously considered. Since the lords' revenues were drawn from their ownership of land and the payments they exacted from the serfs the state had to make provision for its main social supports and did so by compensating them with state bonds carrying interest.

The fact that emancipation took place at such a late date was a testimony to the slow rate of economic progress in Russia, and its form signified, too, that economic forces alone had been unable to bring about the downfall of this institution. In a sense serfdom still 'flourished' until it was ended by governmental edict. The long-drawn-out winding up process after 1861 also testified to the relative weakness of the economic forces which, in a developing economy, would be expected to erode such feudal survivals. But for the long aftermath the way in which emancipation took place was partly responsible.

By the edict the peasant gained personal freedom in the sense that he was able to do many things which had previously required the permission of the serf-holder or had been practised only on sufferance. However, the former serf had to pay for his new freedom because the value of his redemption exceeded the market value of the land which he obtained. But the peasants had regarded the land as theirs, a view which the emancipation procedure rejected since the peasant could only acquire full title to the land he used by paying for it over a period of years. Moreover, peasant title was only recognized to what in general represented the arable strips in the open fields. The other parts of the village lands, which formed an indispensable part of the economy of the community, were considered to be the property of the lords. In addition, the way in which the emancipation was worked out in certain regions enabled the lords to regain some peasant lands over a certain maximum per household. It was also possible for peasants to avoid the redemption payments by surrendering three-quarters of their land. In short, the peasantry as a whole held less land after emancipation than before and had lost the use of much forest and common land. Whether on the state lands or the landlord estates, the former serfs continued to make payments which absorbed much of the revenue from the land which they retained; in some cases the payments amounted to more than the land yielded. The lands which were reckoned as peasant lands left some three-quarters of the rural households with under 25 acres. The losses of land referred to applied only to the landlords' serfs, but the state serfs, though perhaps more fortunate in some ways, had little more land on the average than the former.

Thus the peasantry was, in a sense, confirmed in its title to land. It continued to be tied to the village because the *mir* was the chosen instrument through which the redemption payments were exacted and the peasant had an obligation to meet his share whether he wanted to or not. The *mir* was given a new lease of life as an administrative organ. At the same time, peasant husbandry continued to be carried on as before the reform and the practices of the village community continued to impede agrarian individualism and labour mobility. Household serfs were freed without lands, thus becoming hired servants or being free to move to where they might find work. Apart from these the peasants could only move by surrendering their land in the course of the redemption procedure.

The details of redemption were complex, varied from one region to another and were brought into operation by stages over a number of years. An enormous task of dividing up and valuing the lands of rural Russia had to be carried out. As it took place the landowners were granted state bonds to the amount of 80 per cent of the valuation of the land which carried interest at 5 per cent. The peasants then became liable to repay the advance from the government at the annual rate of 6 per cent over a period of forty-nine years and to meet the other 20 per cent on whatever terms had been arranged with the landlord. On the whole it is true to say that the land was overvalued and that the peasants had to purchase their personal freedom as well as the land which they traditionally considered as being rightfully their own. It seems likely that the peasants did not have to pay out more than before; they received a title to their land and would, in time, no longer have any payments to make. Many peasants, and those who sympathized with their claims, had expected more; for them, therefore the emancipation proved to be a deception.

From the economic standpoint very little was altered when emancipation came into effect. The majority of peasant households had insufficient land allotted to them to enable them to meet their payments and have enough left over to live reasonably and constitute a market for consumer goods. Movement from the land was still difficult if not impossible for the former serfs so that as population increase took place the villages became overpopulated and living standards fell. The former serf-owners retained their lands and their social power. The land-hungry peasants thus had to rent land from the landlords if the latter were willing to let it. Those who could bought land which, in some areas, the landlords were only too willing to sell. Where large estate farming was carried on the peasants had to work for wages or on contracts which involved the performance of labour in return for the use of land on terms which resembled serfdom. The mass of the peasants thus remained in poverty which emancipation did nothing to relieve. They still had to pay away a disproportionate part of their incomes to the landlords or to the state which, as it were, acted on their behalf. The conditions of agriculture were not directly changed. In the immediate post-emancipation period an increased labour force was not made available to industry; indeed, serfs working in the towns to meet their *obrok* or in 'possessional' factories returned to the villages in quite large numbers.

Most historians agree that without the abolition of serfdom there could have been no industrialization, that it contributed, at least in the long run, to the formation of a free labour force and greater mobility of labour. In the most general sense this is no doubt a truism: to give it more concrete meaning is, however, difficult.

Had serfdom survived it would have become a barrier to subsequent economic growth by rendering the recruitment of a labour force even more difficult than it proved to be. It does not seem possible to prove that it already was a barrier in the 1850s and that it was this which motivated the emancipation. It was really as the village community began to break up under the pressure of developing market forces that the absence of serfdom can be said to have enabled them to take their course. Even so, the way in which emancipation was carried through left many obstacles to more rapid economic change deeply embedded in the structure of rural Russia.

Emancipation was the most important of a series of reforms carried out during the reign of Alexander II which included the establishment of a system of local government, improvements in the judiciary and in education. The role of the public services was extended and employment opportunities were opened up to educated and trained people in various directions. The autocracy had already evolved a large and comprehensive hierarchy of officials and policemen to administer its territories and regulate the underlying population. The importance of this bureaucracy which carried the influence of the autocracy into every cranny of social life was strengthened by the weakness of the middle classes and by the acceptance of state intervention in the economy. In a way the bureaucracy was a middle class of a special sort dependent on the monarchy. In its upper reaches it was necessarily closely connected with the nobility, though as a special body its agents might have to act in ways which particular interests or individuals in this class disliked. At the same time, as Russia modernized, albeit slowly, and became more exposed to outside influences, critical tendencies took root among the educated minority. The development of the intelligentsia was bound up with these modern tendencies and with the need of the autocracy itself for more trained and educated people, which required the establishment of more and larger high schools and universities. In a backward, overwhelmingly peasant society, the appearance of such an educated stratum creates special problems. Its members stand out rather more sharply from the majority than in a society where literacy is widespread and the

average level of living higher. At the same time, as people concerned with ideas, techniques and professional procedures, as the
most conscious element in the society, they are more likely to develop
liberal and critical tendencies which conflict with the ideology and
practice of the established order. Thus the efforts of Tsardom to
survive, and reform in order to conserve, inevitably increased the
numbers of the educated and potentially critical. At the same time,
the very backwardness of the society invited criticism and efforts
to speed the process of reform or to revolutionize it. But criticism
of the mildest sort was made difficult by censorship and repression
and tended to push the intelligentsia, especially its youthful contingents in the schools and universities, towards revolution.

Of itself the intelligentsia was powerless to bring about changes;
it looked to the people, and especially to the peasantry, to be
inspired by its example and its teaching to bring about the renovation of Russia. But while some thought that this could be done
by building upon the specifically Slavonic elements in the traditional society, of which the *mir* was considered a vital part, others,
the westernizers, wished to see Russia emulate the West and move
forward on the road to liberalism and industrialism. So far as
economic development was concerned these differences sharpened
towards the end of the century in the famous controversy between
the Narodniks and the Marxists. While the former hoped that
Russia could avoid the excesses of capitalism by carrying through
a transition to socialism on the basis of the agrarian commune, the
Marxists thought that the country was moving inevitably into a
phase of capitalist development which, by destroying the vestiges
of the patriarchal order and bringing into existence a modern proletariat, would prepare the way for a socialist society organized on
a modern industrial foundation. This was, perhaps, the first great
conscious discussion about preferable paths to economic growth, and
Russia was to prove to be a great historical laboratory for the testing
of these theories.

Many firmly rooted vestiges of the old, patriarchal order remained
intact after the reforms of the 'sixties and the conditions for a
capitalist type development only gradually came into existence.
The peasants were still, in the main, producing for subsistence and
to meet their obligations to the state and to the lord. The Russian

landowners, as a body, proved incapable of making a transition to capitalist agriculture, and the way in which abolition was carried out did not facilitate such a change. Except where estate farming was already the rule a labour force only came into existence slowly. The lords were not experienced in estate management or familiar with business procedures, nor did they show much inclination in that direction as many of their counterparts did in England or Prussia. Often financially embarrassed owing to the expense of keeping up an establishment or extravagant living the gentry and nobility became increasingly an indebted class. Consequently they rented land to the peasants and steadily sold off the land which they retained under the post-1861 settlement. For some time, and wherever possible, they kept their powers over the peasantry. In any case the peasants were chronically short of land and in places the lords leased land under share-cropping agreements or in return for labour services not unlike those furnished in the days of serfdom.

The penetration of capitalist relations into the countryside was thus a long-drawn-out and uneven process and, as was to be expected in such a large and diverse country, an enormous variety of transitional patterns emerged. The driving forces for change came mainly from outside the rural economy, though the seeds of disintegration were sown by the abolition of serfdom and the growing dependence upon money economy which followed it.

It is, then, mainly to the non-agrarian sectors that we have to look in order to observe the modernization process and to understand the post-emancipation changes in agriculture. However, it should be noted that the ending of serfdom was followed by increased population migration into the less densely populated southern and eastern areas of Russia. The migrants remained engaged in agriculture whether as hired workers or as peasant settlers on newly opened lands. These possibilities of migration, later extended into Siberia, helped to relieve the growing crisis in peasant agriculture and offered an alternative to movement to the cities.

Post-reform development took place in an environment which was still encumbered by many survivals of the traditional patriarchal and feudal order. The autocracy, and its bureaucratic agents, remained profoundly suspicious of the accompaniments of developing

capitalism which it had to accept, or even encourage, in order
to survive. Business enterprise was carried on in an atmosphere
which tended to be stifling and to encourage a search for influence
and privilege as a means of short-circuiting the forces of the market.
The smallness of the middle class, the lack of interest in, or con-
tempt for, business manifest in the gentry and the intelligentsia,
depleted the reservoir for the recruitment of entrepreneurs. As a
result, many came from the ranks of the peasants or the small
producers; they were hard taskmasters able to make a profit from
existing techniques rather than being innovators. New and large-
scale enterprises were often established by foreign entrepreneurs
with managers and capital brought from outside Russia. This was
another enduring characteristic of the economic scene which
reflected the backwardness of the economy. The factors which
caused this could not disappear overnight but remained to
complicate the development of capitalism and give it a peculiar
physiognomy which will be examined later.

In the absence of an adequate supply of entrepreneurs able to
mobilize and build up capital the rate of development in a backward country is bound to be slow. Large-scale projects involving
a high degree of risk are not likely to be carried out at all, yet
such projects, especially in the sphere of transport, may be indispensable to widen the market and stimulate investment in industry
and the mobility of labour. In such circumstances the intervention
of the state, whatever its motivation, may play a vital role in initiating
and speeding up a process which, if left to itself, would have been
spread over a longer period of time and taken a different form.
The state, as it were, substitutes itself for those agents of change
who, in a backward environment, were not coming forward fast
enough or at all. It is able to provide capital and a market. Its
influence is found mainly in the producers' goods sector and takes
the form of the setting up of large-scale modern plants incorporating
the latest technology available. In a sense, therefore, the latecomer
enjoys the advantage of being able to jump over stages. At the
same time, where industrialization takes this form, the consumer
market has little influence on the character of production and the
whole process is dependent upon continued injections of government expenditure. In this form industrialization takes place as

one or a number of big spurts associated with heavy government spending and big investment projects. This, in a somewhat modified form, is the thesis which has been applied to Russia by Professor Gerschenkron.

Between the 1860s and the 1890s such traits only appear in a muted form and they were combined with spontaneous forces which, despite the resistances in the environment, were making for the extension of capitalist relations. Through this period, then, industrial development continued on lines already described. Sections of the textile industry, particularly cotton, had moved into the factory and had tended to concentrate in a few areas of central Russia with some genuine factory towns such as Ivanovo and Shuja. The availability of imported coal and other raw materials favoured the industrial development of St Petersburg. Here and there large mining and metallurgical enterprises were being carried on; to some extent these activities received a stimulus from railway building both in the demand for their products and in the widening of the market which the new system of transport offered. Some large enterprises were also found in the processing of agricultural produce, notably sugar-beet refining and distilleries.

By comparison with western Europe and the United States Russian industry remained very much behind. Its advanced sectors remained outposts in a vast ocean of backward peasant agriculture and small-scale production carried on by hand methods in cottages and small workshops. The preparation for subsequent development took place to a large extent in modest ways: in the spread of the putting-out system, the dependence of many peasants on industrial work and the expansion of the home market for cheap consumer goods manufactured under the control of merchant-entrepreneurs. There was a great variety of industrial forms and as yet the factory was far from typical. What was important was the steady extension of capitalist relations into artisan and small-scale production and the growing dependence of the peasants both on wage work and on the market for the satisfaction of their consumer needs. By its nature this process is difficult to trace out without a mass of detail since it took place gradually and unevenly. Within twenty years of the emancipation edict it had gone far enough to awaken interest and by the 1890s it had sparked off the great controversy between the Narodniks and the Marxists. In his *Development of Capitalism in Russia* Lenin marshalled a mass of evidence to show the existence of capitalist control over artisan and cottage industry and support his case that Russia was already well embarked on the capitalist road.

The impetus from the state found expression in the 'sixties in the first great burst of railway which linked Moscow with a number of provincial cities. Other lines were built into Western Russia and the Ukraine. An unprecedented financial as well as constructional effort was thus involved which greatly increased the scope for modern business activities. The motive for railway building was largely administrative and strategic and the major part of the capital came from the state. An Imperial Bank was founded in 1864 and private joint-stock banks and discount houses followed. Since Russia lacked a machine-making or engineering industry a good deal of the railway material had to be imported. Moreover, the finance of railway construction imposed problems for the Treasury and until 1880, when tighter budgetary control was introduced, inflation was resorted to. As modernization took place Russia was forced into more intimate contact with the world market. Imports of machinery and railway equipment were paid for partly by increased exports of agricultural products, partly by borrowing abroad. Financial policy was determined by the need to retain the confidence of foreign creditors and uphold the country's credit worthiness in foreign capital markets. But debts had to be serviced and to keep the balance of payments healthy a large export of grain was necessary. There thus arose the characteristic paradox that Russia became a leading grain exporter at the very time when *per capita* food consumption among the peasants was low and may have been declining, and when the main grain-producing areas themselves were stricken periodically by terrible famines. The grain 'surpluses' involved in the export trade came partly from the larger estates worked with hired labour, partly from the grain marketed by the peasants to meet their redemption payments and other monetary obligations. The healthy front presented in the budget thus concealed a growing agrarian crisis.

These early steps in industrialization took place, of course, on the agrarian basis left by the emancipation of 1861, which kept intact the *mir* and limited both the mobility and the consuming power of the peasantry. At the same time, to a greater extent than before, the peasant now had to have cash to meet his obligations. He had to sell produce or he, or his family, had to seek work for wages if his holding was not sufficient for their support. On the other hand, the village community continued to give the peasants a minimal security and to limit the scope for individual advancement through improving methods of cultivation, introducing new crops and accumulating capital. As in other countries the communal methods of agriculture acted as an undoubted hindrance to more rapid economic growth and re-enforced the habits of sloth and routine for which the Russian peasant was notorious. The autocracy had not dared to carry out a thoroughgoing agrarian revolution. It could not do so at the noble's expense (as had happened from below in France and other countries) because this would have cut away its own main social support. Nor could it undertake thorough-going measures to enclose the open fields and strengthen the nobles' hold over the land while speeding up the creation of a rural proletariat, because it feared the consequences for public order and because, probably, the lords would have been unable to cope with a situation which would have obliged them to become agricultural entrepreneurs. The preservation of the *mir*, and with it the open fields and the collective servitudes of the traditional husbandry, could not but act as a brake on change outside agriculture as well as within it.

But this was not an absolute check. Change did take place. The *mir* was, though very gradually, being undermined. The extension of capitalist relations, which emancipation had done something to bring about, slowly did its work in corroding the forces of custom and tradition. Agrarian individualism, if not given its head, did begin to find a way to express itself. The peasant community, which was seldom a society of equals, was increasingly subject to a process of differentiation similar to that visible in most similar cases when market exchange begins to play a more important role. Although the practices of the *mir* frequently meant that land holdings were related to the needs of the household, it was not land alone which accounted for the appearances of growing differences within the peasant community. The ownership of draught animals was of greater importance, since they enabled more land to be tilled on a rental basis. Once some such advantage enabled a peasant family to produce a surplus for sale in the market, accumulate money capital and rent or buy additional land from the lord the apparent unity of the *mir* began to be undermined. There came into existence a more prosperous rural stratum, people who in eighteenth-century France have been called *coqs du village* and in Russia became known as *kulaks*. The more prosperous individualist peasants became the employers of their poorer, less enterprising, less thrifty, or unfortunate neighbours. So some of the villagers became a rural labour reserve. Since the *kulaks* made money from their transactions they could also play the role of village usurers as there were always peasants who through some misfortune, or through the costliness of some event such as the marriage of a daughter, had to borrow regardless of the rate of interest exacted.

In the decades after emancipation agriculture was slowly and unevenly penetrated by commercial relations, shedding the vestiges of serfdom and taking on the attributes of a market-oriented activity. To a growing extent relations between the lords and the peasants and differences within the peasantry were attributable to market conditions rather than to tradition and to the settlement of 1861. Where opportunities for production for the market offered themselves possession of capital and business acumen became the key to success or even survival. Those with the means added to the number of their draught animals, bought better implements and machines, and took advantage of improved methods, often encouraged by local officials.

As many of the lords were indebted before serfdom ended and displayed little interest in, or aptitude for, the role of agricultural entrepreneurs it is not surprising that the later decades of the century show them becoming increasingly impoverished. The bonds which they had received in compensation for their serfs depreciated in value and their indebtedness increased. The only resort for a landowner whose estate was mortgaged to the hilt was to sell. On the whole this resulted not in concentration of land-holding but in dispersion either to non-noble capitalists or to the better off section of the peasantry. Consequently the proportion of non-noble and peasant land rose. Thus the development of a market economy seemed to be moving inexorably towards the disappearance of the landowners and towards the creation of a class of peasant proprietors.

This tendency, however, was extremely long-drawn-out and geographically uneven. In the fertile areas where the peasants had little land or opportunity for individual advancement the landlord estate flourished on the basis of the growing market opportunities. Taken as a whole noble lands were relinquished all too slowly by comparison with the land hunger of the peasants among whom continued population growth decreased the average size of the family holding even while their share of the total cultivable land increased. Much peasant land was also mortgaged, of course, and continuing differentiation increased the numbers of the landless and semi-landless. The advance of agrarian individualism therefore intensified the agrarian crisis which gripped Russia in the late nineteenth century.

This crisis was still further aggravated by the fact that there had been no sharp break with the old traditional forms. Survivals of serfdom made themselves felt in many ways, notably in the special status of the peasants and their responsibility for the obligations which emancipation had thrust upon them. The peasant was still generally subject to the *mir* both for his redemption payments and other obligations to the state, and in regard to the traditional practices of open-field husbandry. In appearance the peasant village remained much as it had done before 1861, but the archaic forms were now being acted upon by the dissolvents of a market economy. The peasant produced for sale, not for household consumption only; he thus became dependent on the vagaries of the national and local market as well as upon the harvests. The patriarchal serf-owner was transformed into an estate manager and rent receiver, or into an employer of hired labour, a transition for which many were unprepared and ill-equipped. The formerly isolated village community was drawn into a wider network of relations, feeling the influence of the growth of towns, the railways and the growing demand for primary products on the world market. In turn this permitted crop specialization and the improvement of farming methods. But the modernization of agriculture, which took place very patchily, only intensified its contradictions.

The preservation of the tsarist autocracy and the social structure bound up with it meant that the process of industrialization and agrarian change was beset with strains and crises which threatened the régime itself. And yet, for its own preservation, tsarism was obliged to promote these economic changes; successive officials and ministers grappled with the problem of survival under these conditions until its final downfall. Policy towards the peasants was at first based upon the preservation of the *mir* as an instrument of social conservation although officials influenced by western liberalism had their doubts. After the accession of Alexander III in 1881, following the assassination of his predecessor, some fiscal concessions were made to the peasants. These were followed by the establishment of a new corps of officials, called Land Captains, with wide powers over the peasants, re-enforcing, and if necessary, overruling the *mir* as a disciplinary organ in relation to redemption payments, taxes and other peasant obligations to the state. Although a comparatively small proportion of peasants had extricated themselves from the *mir* by completing their payments ahead of time, the government was so anxious to preserve the village community that as late as 1893 it passed a law preventing a peasant from withdrawing on completion of his payments without a two-thirds vote of the members. At the same time, sale of settlement lands to persons not of peasant status was prohibited.

The rapid industrialization of the 'nineties, coming in a period of low or falling agricultural prices, did nothing to alleviate the position of the mass of the peasants. Population had been growing for decades. There were more families in each village and more mouths to feed in each family. Through lack of means, ignorance or sloth, the methods of husbandry employed by the majority improved little if at all. The more enterprising peasant with draught animals who rented land and farmed for the market was still tied by his membership of the *mir* which, at the same time, limited the supply of labour power to the market. Meanwhile, down to the revolution of 1905, the former serfs were still liable to the unpopular redemption payments, arrears of which mounted year by year. Part of the burden of industrialization fell on the peasantry through the rising level of indirect taxes, while the prices of industrial goods remained high. While the peasant was driven into increasing dependence on the market he was still living to a large extent on the fringes of a market economy. In any case, the poverty of the peasantry prevented it from providing a healthy basis for the expansion of the market for consumer goods.

Peasant discontent was endemic in rural Russia, breaking out in sporadic and localized acts of violence against the landlords and officialdom which were put down by the military. In 1905, in the wake of the war with Japan, it flared up on a much wider scale and was accompanied by a strike wave and open insurrection in the large cities. The series of outbreaks which made up the revolutionary 'dress rehearsal' of that year were followed by severe repression which helped to undermine peasant confidence in the Tsar as the 'little father' who was really on their side but whose will was frustrated by landlords and officials. To grapple with the dangers revealed in 1905 the government made some concessions to the constitutional claims of the middle class; it also adopted a decidedly different approach to the agrarian question.

While the punitive expeditions sent out into the countryside were still doing their work the Tsar issued a manifesto which promised that peasant conditions would be improved. Redemption payments were to cease from 1906: a gesture which meant little to many peasants who were too far behind with their payments ever to be likely to meet them. By another measure a quantity of the lands held by the Imperial family were to be sold on easy terms to the peasantry through the Peasant Bank. This again was merely a palliative of limited effect. Officials concerned with the agrarian question were coming to the conclusion, in the light of the events of 1905, that the faith in the commune as a factor of social stability in the villages which had been almost unswerving since 1861 had been misplaced. Instead, the régime should seek its main rural support in a class of independent peasant proprietors.

The new policy is associated with the name of Stolypin, the former Minister of the Interior who became Prime Minister in 1906, whose experiences in the provinces had convinced him that the village commune was a vicious institution. The reform was embodied in general enactments whose application in detail was left in the hands of the bureaucracy in the following years. It was the product of an emergency and of continued fear of peasant insurrection; for Stolypin at least this motive, and not an understanding that agrarian reform of the type proposed might assist industrialization, was the governing one.

The principle of the Stolypin reform was to permit the individual peasant holding to be taken out of the communal lands as private landed property to be dealt with as its owner thought fit. As Stolypin expressed it: 'The government has placed its wager, not on the needy and the drunken, but on the sturdy and the strong—on the sturdy individual proprietor who is called to play a part in the reconstruction of our Tsardom on strong monarchical foundations.'

It was easier to express such an intention than to translate it into practice. In the early stages of the reform there was little inclination on the part of the peasants to abandon the *mir*. The extrication of individual holdings from the open fields which, in the course of time, had become divided and subdivided posed a tremendous problem in any case. The holdings of each peasant were based on the custom of the *mir* and the delimitation of his scattered bits and pieces depended in the main upon purely verbal agreements with his neighbours, many of whom would resent any alteration in the existing distribution of land. In any case the government lacked the corps of trained and experienced surveyors and lawyers, or even a sufficient number of merely competent officials, to enable such a profound change in the way of life of the peasantry to be carried out quickly and smoothly. It was understood, therefore, that the break up of the open-field village and the constitution of an individualist type agriculture was bound to take many decades.

The first step was to encourage the peasants to come forward to claim full title to the strips which they held. Then the peasant was to be assisted either to sell this land and buy an enclosed plot elsewhere or to make arrangements with the other villagers to bring his land together into a single piece. Encouragement was therefore to be offered to the 'strong' peasant to leave the *mir*, thus undermining it and the weaker peasants who continued to form part of it. They would tend to become increasingly dependent on wage work, perhaps selling or renting their plots to the stronger peasants. In other words, the Stolypin reforms tended to put government support behind the process of differentiation which had been going on as market relations penetrated into the village.

From 1905 onwards a definite weakening of the old communal and traditional ties set in, now favoured by the government. The administrative machinery for carrying through the Stolypin reform was improved and procedures worked out. Experience showed that individual withdrawal from the commune resulted in opposition and dissension and official support swung behind a general redistribution of land for an entire village in which the *mir* was dissolved. The conditions under which the reform operated varied greatly from place to place and many parts of the countryside continued to be in a troubled state down to the outbreak of war. In some places pressure was brought to bear on the peasants to induce them to make the change, in others the initiative seems to have come from themselves. By 1915 about 2.5 million peasants had applied for permanent and separate title to their holdings, though this did not necessarily mean taking the land out of the three-field system. It is estimated that about three-quarters of the hereditary lands remained in strips, still subject to the compulsory crop cycle imposed by the village community.

In 1910 a further Act was passed including a clause which made individual hereditary holdings compulsory in those communes where no repartition had taken place since the allocation of land under the law of 1861; the practical effect of this was, however, very limited. Despite an element of compulsion at the local level, the government moved warily in applying the reform. It could not take the risks involved in imposed enclosure and the destruction of the village community from above. Consequently, in European Russia, the open field village and the *mir* continued to predominate and the peasants remained attached to their tradition. The Stolypin reforms, therefore, by no means solved the agrarian question and the tsarist administration was not to be allowed the time to see how they would work out in the long run. Several courses were open within the general framework which the law provided. The most likely one appeared to be a continued selection process in which a class of large peasant proprietors and tenant farmers emerged alongside large estate farming by the landlords while the majority of the peasantry remained as a landless or semi-landless labour reserve able to leave the villages in response to economic forces. Only a revolution from below could arrest this process and establish agriculture on a different basis, namely that of small peasant holdings with or without state ownership of the land and the redistribution of estate lands.

As Gerschenkron points out, industrialization did begin in Russia without an agrarian reform, or at least without a complete one. However, as has been seen, one of the factors which brought the first great spurt to an end was the limited purchasing power of the peasants who still formed by far the majority of the population. Industrialization would continue to be retarded and distorted until the agrarian structure could be made more consonant with its requirements. The revolution of 1917 enabled the land to be redistributed at the expense of the landlords on the basis of small peasant holdings while still preserving the strip system and the *mir*. The great problem in the 1920s was how the peasants' surplus could be increased and made available to provide for the urban industrial population and whether this could be done without further strengthening the 'strong' peasant, or *kulak*, at the expense of the rural poor. Conciliation of the *kulak* harked back to Stolypin and stimulated rural capitalism which, if allowed to develop un-hindered, would have made planned industrialization impossible. On the other hand, the peasants, who had at last realized their aims in 1917, albeit on a basis of nationalized property, could not easily be won to accept the cooperative or collective farming which was the alternative to capitalist farming. Enforced collectivization, at one brutal stroke, appeared to put an end to the dilemma inherited from tsardom. In practice it did so only at frightful human costs and at the expense of an agrarian crisis of a new sort which besets Soviet policy to this day.

There is no doubt that the preservation of the village community and the difficulty which faced those peasants who sought to disen-tangle themselves from it acted to impede the recruitment of a labour force for the non-agrarian sectors. What is more, the recruits from a peasant background had a low cultural level and were unfamiliar with the exigencies of urban living. If the disciplining of an industrial proletariat proved to be a difficult and lengthy process everywhere it was rendered that much more difficult in Russia by the nature of the rural society from which it came and from the effects of the still recent experience of serfdom. From the point of view of the employers of labour the Russian recruits, although they came cheaply in terms of the average wage, were substandard in every other regard. In other words, labour costs were not necessarily low because the workers were poorly paid by west-European standards. Where skilled and supervisory labour was involved wages, were in any case, probably not much less than, say, in Germany, if only because foreigners had often to be engaged. In a sense, then, labour was relatively scarce and costly and Russian entrepreneurs were thus behaving rationally when they installed capital-intensive methods of production comparable with the most advanced to be found in the industrial countries.

After 1861 serf labour disappeared from the factories and mines and free hired labour took its place though in the meantime some enterprises went into decline or disappeared. Much of the hired labour already in the towns or recruited in the following decades was there on a seasonal or temporary basis. Young men might leave their households to earn money to help the family meet its financial obligations or to enable them to get married and set up house in the village. Others might go into the towns when there was no work to do on their plots but with the intention of returning for the ploughing or sowing. Even those who settled for longer spells did not necessarily regard their stay in the town as permanent. The labour force tended to be composed of temporary migrants who were peasants first and wage workers only by force of circumstance. This, of course, aggravated the problems for the employer. Labour turnover tended to be high and the new recruits were once again raw newcomers from the village. Big employers had to provide dormitories to retain a labour force at all, and for the workers the discomforts they had to put up with while in the towns were less important than whether they could earn enough money to meet their obligations or pay for whatever they needed.

A more permanent labour force was established as men began to bring their wives to the cities and to raise families. Then they needed housing and began to put down roots. Their children grew up in the city streets not the fields and from the start they became prospective proletarians rather than peasants. Even so, because the peasantry had kept its land even those workers who came to the cities on a long-term basis might retain their links with relations in the villages, go back to give a hand at harvest time or find a refuge when they were too sick or old to work, or when there were no jobs available. Some might eventually acquire a holding and return to the village for good. Town life and factory employment held out few inducements and improved only the more slowly because many of the workers were transients. In the factories the workers were subject to a rigorous discipline against which they reacted by sporadic and violent strikes or disturbances. By the 1870s the turbulence of some of the factory districts had caused serious concern to the police department of the tsarist government. It was clear that repression alone could not deal with the problem, which was seen essentially as one of public order. Hence, as industry developed the government sought to deal with its consequences by adopting factory regulation on the English model. The first such measure, to regulate child labour and night work for children, was put into effect in 1882 and was followed by similar laws. However, strikes continued and in 1886 a law was passed which set up a system of rules which employers and workers were to observe covering wages, contracts of employment and the rights and duties of the two parties. The tsarist officials hoped by these means to bring peace to the factories but they failed. Inevitably the law leaned to the side of the employer and worker grievances could not be removed by a police measure of this kind. In fact strikes continued to increase and within a few years the workers had begun to organize into trade unions. Meanwhile attempts at a bureaucratic control of labour relations tended to multiply while the workers' demands were raised as they gained in experience and the permanent worker element grew. The response of the government, in line with its established policy, was towards repression. Trade unions were illegal until after the revolution of 1905. However, another strain in the policy of the bureaucracy was to organize trade unions in order to prevent the thoughts of the workers from turning against the régime. The police and the bureaucracy had no particular sympathy for the employers as individuals. There was a conservative strain hostile to industrialism and many employers were, of course, non-Russians. The policy of the autocracy was far from being a success. As Rimlinger concludes: 'Not only was the government unable to prevent the progressive alienation of the working classes, it failed also to avert the disaffection of the employers. Its methods promoted neither the development of a stable work force nor the creation of a flexible system of industrial discipline.'

With the industrial upswing of the 1890s, which coincided with accelerated differentiation within the peasant community, many new recruits were inevitably added to the urban labour force. In fact every acceleration of growth required a migration of raw, largely illiterate peasant newcomers to the industrial and mining areas. The Russian labour force thus assumed an ever-changing character but always contained a more or less sizeable proportion of new peasant recruits at one extreme and an old-established hereditary proletariat at the other. In the large factories in the metallurgical industry, wherever advanced machine techniques required the presence of skilled workers, the nucleus of a modern proletariat had taken root. It was always accompanied, and generally outnumbered, by the newer and rawer contingents.

The acceleration of the pace of industrial growth becomes evident from the late 1880s and continues to 1900 to be followed by several years of stagnation and crisis which culminate in the war with Japan and the Revolution of 1905. Growth is resumed again at a smart rate from about 1909 and continues down to the First World War. It is necessary, therefore, to examine the reason for what Gerschenkron calls 'the great spurt' and its failure to be sustained and to consider the basis upon which the prewar expansion took place.

As in the 'sixties the role of the state was decisive in the rapid expansion of the 'nineties and once again railway building was the main growth force. The expansion in the 'sixties had been brought to an end by the general European financial crisis of 1873. For over a decade there were marked fluctuations in industry and falling prices in agriculture. The smaller firms were especially hard hit by recurrent periods of depression. By the late 'eighties and early 'nineties the conditions were ripe for a revival. The strength of this revival is mainly attributable to the more positive policy towards industrialization which the state then adopted. After the

6

mild protectionism of the previous decades high tariffs were imposed which ensured industry of command of the home market. Government-supported public works, principally railways, were embarked on at an unprecedented rate; half as much mileage was added in the decade of the 'nineties as in the previous fifty years. About half the capital for the new lines was provided by the government, which also guaranteed private investors their return on the remainder. Foreign investment was encouraged but in the main the great new effort had to be paid for from internal sources. In any case, increased foreign indebtedness made the burden on agriculture still heavier.

Government sponsored outlays on railways opened up a new market for heavy industry and required large additions to the labour force. Private investment opportunities thus widened and confidence was enhanced by the support received from the government. The increased flow of incomes opened the way for expansion over a wide front. In the Ukraine a wholly new industrial region came into existence with the aid of the railway which linked up Donetz coal to the Krivoi Rog iron ore deposits. By comparison the older industrial region of the Urals went into eclipse. The industries of St Petersburg and Moscow continued to expand and, metallurgical and engineering plants, some of them very large, were of special importance. In the central regions, which contained almost a third of the industrial labour force, textiles and consumer goods industries predominated. The growth of the home market favoured further concentration and specialization. Industries were shifting to a factory basis or becoming more highly mechanized. Of course, the industrial pattern was still highly variegated, with many of the old and transitional forms flourishing. The massive weight of a backward peasant agriculture in the economy continued to exert itself, though capitalist relations steadily penetrated the rural economy. In the changing structure the most advanced forms of organization and of technique existed side by side with the primitive and the archaic.

Although Narodnik writers continued to maintain that there was some specifically Russian way of avoiding the capitalist road the industrial upsurge of the 'nineties made their thesis increasingly unreal. The government itself had now shifted definitely towards support for industrialization, though there were still influential conservative voices arguing against it. Sergei Witte was a representative of those modernizers who thought that there was no future for the autocracy unless it sponsored rapid economic development. While ownership and management of enterprise were to remain in private hands, the industrial movement was to proceed under the direction of an enlightened bureaucracy. The state was to encourage capitalists to invest in newly developing areas and especially in the heavy industries associated with railway building. Foreign supplies of capital were indispensable to make good the inadequate supply from domestic sources and to undertake, with the aid of imported technique and management, investment which Russian capitalists were unwilling or unable to make.

In terms of rates of growth Witte's policy in the 'nineties scored some apparently brilliant successes. By means of high protection and state outlays Russia was placed unquestionably on the road to industrialization. However, the policy had serious limitations, it encountered mounting opposition in official circles and it led, not to sustained growth, but to a serious economic depression. Under conditions of private capitalism the state could only partially substitute itself for an entrepreneurial element. The whole programme was handicapped by the relative lack of business talent in Russia and the poor quality of the businessmen. Encouragement of foreign capitalists to set up businesses in Russia only added to the isolation and unpopularity of the class. Witte himself complained bitterly about the entrepreneurs with whom he had to deal; some he regarded as downright scoundrels. Nor did he have at his disposal a trained, efficient and incorruptible bureaucracy able to translate his policy into effect. Few of its members were really convinced that a policy of economic development was desirable or could succeed; it never became a national goal which commanded wide support or was even backed wholeheartedly by those who held the reins of power.

It may be wondered, in any case, whether the autocracy could have long survived a sustained process of industrialization which would have strengthened critical tendencies in the bourgeoisie and added to the ferment among the urban population. Although Witte set out to save the régime his policy led logically to the carrying out of big changes in the central organs of power, which the Tsar and all the reactionary forces in the court and the government would have opposed. When Witte was eventually dismissed in 1903 he was succeeded by men without personality or policy of their own who performed what was, in effect, a holding operation.

Unlike other cases where the state intervened to promote industrialization, the attempt in Russia in the 'nineties was the victim of its own contradictions. Something like a revolution from above would have been required to clear the ground for a sustained process of growth. As it was the state-promoted boom reached its limit within less than a decade. Although the rapid development of the heavy industrial sector was accompanied by a general expansion of the home market this was all the time a subordinate phenomenon. Once investment in heavy industry slackened off or the market for its products narrowed the expansion would come to an end. Initiated by the state, economic growth continued to depend on state outlays. Since the state depended heavily on loans from abroad and had to maintain its credit standing it was necessary to balance the budget and preserve the value of the currency. This could be done only by heavy tax rates, especially by indirect taxes which, by imposing a burden on consumers, in the main peasants, curtailed the market for consumer goods. The internal market for cheap manufactured goods expanded so far as peasants became more dependent on exchange or became more numerous, but a large part of the peasantry was impoverished and increased tax burdens ate directly into *per capita* spending power. Thus if state spending slackened the expansion was in jeopardy, but if it maintained its spending by higher taxation the contraction of market demand would have the same effect.

By 1901 the first great spurt of Russian industrialization was at an end. The incentive for large new capital outlays had petered out; private capital did not take over on an adequate scale where the state left off. No doubt there would have been an industrial recession in any case, but it was intensified by the failure of the home market to grow rapidly enough owing to the poverty of the mass of the people and by the poor harvest which reduced spending power still further. All the weaknesses of the traditional Russian social and economic structure reasserted themselves with force. The first attempt at a revolution from above had failed because it could not be carried far enough in the prevailing conditions. It would be impossible for industrialization to proceed without serious crises and contradictions without a reform of the agrarian system. All Russian problems turned in the last analysis on the agrarian question; yet any fundamental change in agriculture struck at the heart of traditional Russia and the dominant interests in the society and the state.

The conditions did not exist in Russia for a prolonged phase of competitive capitalism. The role of the state, the nature of the market, the scarcity of entrepreneurs and of rentier capital contributed to the high degree of concentration found from an early stage. A number of cartels had been formed in the 'nineties and in the early years of the new century they became more general and increased their scope. The sagging market after the first industrial upsurge favoured the movement. Syndicates were formed in the metal industry of the Ukraine (Prodamet) in 1902, in the production of railway equipment (Prodwagen) in 1904 and in south Russian coal mining (Produgol). The rapidly developing petroleum industry was dominated by three large firms which had foreign connections. The finance of industry became highly dependent on the banks which had developed, under government aegis, ahead of the creation of a capital market and the appearance of a rentier element. As the bourgeoisie became more prosperous it went to the banks as despositors and as borrowers. Industry, too, had perforce to look to the banks, especially since it developed, to a large extent, not by a steady process of growth and the ploughing back of profits but as newly founded enterprises which required heavy capital investment if they were to get off the ground at all.

To some extent the banks took over from the state as a substitute for the individual entrepreneur and rentier capitalist whose roles had been so vital in capitalist development in the West. As a result, Russian capitalism, for all its weaknesses, on the financial and organizational, as well as on the technological side, displayed all the most modern features of the advanced countries. Put in another way this can be seen as a jumping-over-stages process; Russian capitalism followed a distinctive path simply because it began late with state assistance and did not develop in an entirely spontaneous way as in Britain. The fact that foreign capital played a decisive part also contributed to large-scale organization and the association of industry with bank capital.

After the suppression of the revolution of 1905 economic growth was resumed down to the outbreak of the First World War on similar lines to those of the earlier upsurge. The government paid special attention to the railway system; a large part of the existing lines had come under its control and new construction went ahead with a guarantee of interest on loan and share capital. From the point of view of profitability the railways were uneconomic. They represented an enormous investment of capital which was comprised in the state debt or covered by government guarantees and much of it was in foreign ownership. Receipts fell short of the operating expenses and interest payments and the deficit had to be met by the Treasury which involved further indebtedness until 1911. The prosperity of the next few years, together with some skimping on salaries and maintenance, then led to an improved financial position. However, as Margaret Miller points out, the result of the state's activity 'was a railway net which was at one and the same time inadequate for the needs of the country, and far in advance of what the country could economically support'.

Railway construction was a major factor in the development of the mining and metallurgical industries. In these fields large-scale enterprises and advanced techniques were employed with foreign capital, enterprise and management continuing to play a prominent part. State encouragement to industry, large-scale operation, concentration of control, close ties between industry and the banks and the presence of foreign capital gave the Russian economy its distinctive physiognomy at this time. It was a product of the peculiarities of Russia's historical development and it was productive of social strains and economic weaknesses which were to be revealed during the war.

Industry continued to have something of the character of an artificial creation, not integrated into the still predominantly peasant economy. It was localized in a few centres and although with the improvement in transport facilities and technical change new industrial areas were opened up still much of the country had changed little in the preceding century. The fact that many factories, mines and other enterprises were owned and run by foreigners contributed to this impression. New draughts of workers were still recruited from the countryside without breaking their ties with their villages; many moved directly from primitive rural conditions to work in the environment of the most highly developed industry by world standards.

Dependence on foreign capital was marked in the case both of the state and private industry. After the alliance of 1894 France became the principal creditor of the tsarist government; investment in industry came from a wider variety of sources and included substantial amounts of German, British and Belgian capital. Servicing of foreign capital and the maintenance of foreign confidence in the rouble dominated the financial policy of the government. The former required a favourable balance of trade, the latter a balanced state budget and both hinged on the preservation of the gold basis of the currency. Financial strategy was therefore closely circumscribed and depended very much on international economic trends. As an exporter of primary products a great deal hinged on price movements which, in the decade before 1914, were strongly upwards. However, exports, especially those of cereals, were exacted from the peasantry by means of rent and taxes or by their employment at low wages on the large estates. The burden of state-sponsored industrialization was therefore shifted to a very large extent onto the shoulders of the peasantry whose material standards may well have deteriorated in the early twentieth century. This, in turn, limited the rate of expansion of the home market for manufactured goods. It was a complex and in the end disastrous method of financing capital formation; it made the economy a tributary of foreign business and aggravated resentment in the peasantry. To some extent internal sources of capital supply grew as industrialization proceeded but history was not to allow time to show whether domestic capital would be able to take over from the foreigner as had happened in Germany and the USA.

On the eve of the First World War, in a favourable conjunctural situation, the Russian economy was in an expansive phase. But over the period from the early 'eighties the main industrial countries had been growing faster so that the Russian lag was even larger than before. The proportion of the population in the modern sector rose only slowly and the dead weight of the traditional agrarian sector, which the Stolypin reforms could only slowly ease, remained the major symptom of Russia's backwardness. In 1913 about two-thirds of the population still remained attached to agriculture. Yields per man, as well as per acre, were low and bore witness to the unwillingness or inability of the peasantry to adapt to change. On the other hand the foundations of a modern economy had been laid. The industrial sector, although it only employed a small part of the total population, was dominated by large-scale, technologically efficient units. Surrounded by a sea of peasants an industrial pro-letariat of a modern type had come into existence, highly concen-trated round large, often foreign-owned, plants. This combination had shown its explosive potential in 1905 and in the expansive prewar years it was developing to flash point. At the same time there was also in existence an increasingly powerful class of business-men; many were foreigners, but a new type of modern Russian capitalist was also to be found. The middle class, though still relatively weak and lacking in self-confidence, was also growing numerically; in the main it looked to slow improvement on liberal and constitutional lines. Tsarism, however, was hardly prepared to go even half-way to meet these needs and the bourgeoisie was unable to impose its will through the weak Duma and its own organs. Preservation of the traditions of old Russia, not adaptation to the new pressures which its own encouragement of industry had created, was the watchword of the monarchy in its last peace-time years.

Pre-revolutionary Russia was thus a country of immense con-trasts in which the most modern existed uneasily side by side with archaic survivals. In terms of *per capita* income Russia remained well behind the main industrial countries. According to Goldsmith, 'Real income per head . . . was only about one third as high as in the United States or the United Kingdom . . . about one half as high as in Germany. . . . On the other hand, real income per head in Russia was approximately equal to that in Italy, and, of course, was well ahead of the levels prevailing throughout Asia and Africa.' This intermediate position suggests that Russia, although still relatively 'backward', was by no means an 'underdeveloped country' as modern discussions of economic growth generally use the term. It was important that the basic initial steps in industrialization had been taken and that two phases of rapid growth had already been experienced. Russia's involvement with the world market as an exporter of commodities and an importer of capital had become very deep. There was no doubt about the inroads which capitalism had made even into the rural economy. The arguments of the Narodniks had less and less force in the light of these developments. The continued weight of peasant agriculture had not prevented Russia from becoming, in important particulars, a country of advanced industrial capitalism. But the process was far from complete. The way in which this development had taken place showed itself in some outstanding weaknesses: the continued dependence on foreign capital, the need to export agricultural produce wrung from an impoverished peasantry, the lack of sophisticated machine-making and machine-tool industries, the poor foundation which the home market offered for further mechanization in the consumer goods industries and the political and social tensions which followed from the preservation of the institutions bound up with the autocracy. It is probable that the future of Russia would have been at least as stormy as its recent past had not the onset of war greatly speeded up the historical process and concentrated into a few years what might otherwise have required decades.

Problems for discussion

1. In what did the 'backwardness' of Russia consist? How far had it been removed by 1914?
2. Was the survival of serfdom the major reason for the belatedness of Russian growth?
3. Account for the weakness of a middle class in Russia and discuss its relationship to the character of Russian industrial development.
4. What problems were encountered in recruiting a labour force for Russian factory industry and how were they overcome?
5. Discuss the role of the state in Russian economic development before 1914.
6. Examine and explain the degree of concentration found in the

advanced sectors of Russian industry in the late nineteenth and
early twentieth centuries.

7. What was the intention of the Stolypin reforms and how far
were they successful in overcoming the crisis in Russian agriculture?

8. Examine the career of Sergei Witte. To what extent were his
policies applied and could they have succeeded?

6 Italy – the Disadvantaged Latecomer

By the eighteenth century there were few evidences that parts of Italy had once been in the vanguard of European economic development. Despite a few relatively prosperous commercial centres the peninsula as a whole was predominantly agrarian, dominated by an unprogressive agriculture and displaying all the characteristics of underdevelopment. The shift of the balance of economic activity in Europe to the north-west which had followed the opening of the Atlantic trade in the sixteenth century had tended to make the Mediterranean a backwater. Moreover Italy was politically divided and partly governed directly as part of the Habsburg Empire. Although the Napoleonic occupation introduced into Italy more advanced systems of law and administration, and speeded up the acceptance of the idea of unification as the remedy for the country's ills, its immediate economic effects were deleterious. The exactions of the French occupying forces and the cutting off of normal trade links, together with the direct effects of wars and the general disorganization which accompanied them, could do nothing but harm to the Italian economy.

Meanwhile the Industrial Revolution in Britain and its emulation in other parts of north-west Europe opened the gap between Italy and the more advanced areas of the Continent. As it happened the area was poorly supplied with precisely those resources, notably coal and iron ore, upon which the new industrial techniques were based. The growing economic inferiority of Italy coincided with awakening national consciousness on the part of the educated representatives of the small but politically significant urban middle and upper classes. For the nationalists the principal weakness of their country resided in its political disunity and subordination to Austrian influence which had been restored after 1815. Although there were some who saw as early as the 1840s the possible advantages of a customs union, railway building and economic development, the nature of the struggle for national liberation led to the underestimation of the economic factors in Italy's backwardness. From this political emphasis flowed exaggerated hopes of what could be expected from the Risorgimento.

The geographical layout of Italy, a lengthy peninsula with a mountainous spine and a large proportion of the land area unsuitable for cultivation, raised a number of obstacles to economic advance. The great distance, and thus the costliness of transport, from north to south was matched by the mountain barrier to intercourse between the western and eastern coastal plains. Climatic conditions and topography kept down the yield from the land in many areas where it could be cultivated. Apart from the Po valley nature had provided few transport connections. Physically, then, the environment made for regional disparities and localized economies rather than for a homogeneous and compact national market area. Given, too, that for many centuries different parts of the country had been separated politically under régimes of varying degrees of competence which became, in the Kingdom of the Two Sicilies, downright oppression and corruption, it was not surprising that Italy was, in economic as well as political terms, 'a geographical expression'.

It seems, therefore, that the regional disparities which were to loom so large in the history of the nineteenth and twentieth centuries were already built in by a long previous process of separate development. What has to be explained is why such disparities showed no sign of diminishing after economic development had begun. It is unlikely that economic factors alone can explain the deeply rooted and still ineradicable dualism represented by the differential between northern Italy and the Mezzogiorno. Basic physical features and human adjustments to them over a long period of time, which resulted in the appearance of particular cultural and social characteristics in the two regions, a whole historical process extending over centuries, would have to be brought into any full analysis.

It is evident that as industrialization went ahead in western Europe the northern states were bound to be much more closely affected than the south. Commercial and financial ties, which already existed at the opening of the nineteenth century, were extended. Here there were commercial and administrative centres and an urban life exposed to all the material and intellectual influences flowing in from the most advanced areas of Europe. The Italian middle class, although only a small part of the total population, became the social basis for the unification movement. It was, however, as was bound to be the case in a preindustrial country, a middle class in which the professional, intellectual and bureaucratic elements were prominent. The Italian nobility, on the other hand, had also become largely an urban class little interested in its estates or in agriculture, though there were exceptions. There was no great clash between the nobility and the bourgeoisie such as took place in England or France. Political differences were determined by the position taken up on the national question rather than by class origins. This tended to keep social issues in the background and to facilitate combinations based upon common political interests. Moreover, in the period before there was much industrial opportunity, bourgeois property, like that of the nobility, consisted mainly of real estate. If there was a difference it consisted in the greater weight of urban property, and agricultural land leased on a commercial basis, among the land holdings of the bourgeoisie. Land had obvious importance in such a society as a secure, prestige-laden investment. There was, in any case, little incentive to invest in trade and industry and, especially in the less developed areas, a definite prejudice against it. Thus the southern landowners used their incomes neither to improve agriculture nor to invest in industry or commerce, but rather to carry on a leisured class life in the cities.

It must not be thought that there was no drive and enterprise in business; but the opportunities had to be forthcoming, they could not be entirely made by the entrepreneur and investor. Indeed, it was largely the rise of incomes outside Italy which widened the opportunities by making available new technologies and encouraging a certain influx of foreign capital, enterprise and skill. In the decades after the defeat of Napoleon a slow beginning was made in modernizing agriculture in some regions, in introducing a factory industry and improving financial institutions. On the whole such developments were confined to those parts of Italy which were later to be the seats of modern industry and they were far from constituting an economic revolution. Besides the handicap of inadequate raw materials for modern industry the home market remained narrow and grew only slowly while high cost Italian producers could not hope to make much of a mark in the international market.

As in all preindustrial countries the basic problem was the preponderance in the economy of agriculture operating with little capital and at a low level of technique. Consequently the cultivators, most of whom were peasant owners, small tenants or share-croppers, produced little above subsistence needs once rents, taxes, tithes and other payments had been met. What the peasants, who made up the great majority of the population, did not produce within the household they could mostly obtain by exchange within the village or in the nearest local market. For most, in any case, there was little escape from an existence of bare subsistence. There were few areas, therefore, where agriculture was organized on capitalist lines. The home market for cheap, standardized industrial products was consequently limited; thus there was little incentive to invest in this kind of production. In general this was the situation which continued to prevail in the Mezzogiorno and has still not been overcome to this day. In northern Italy, however, a break out of this vicious circle of economic stagnation was made earlier and more completely. Until the 1890s, however, the developments which occurred can hardly be considered more than preparatory.

Before the establishment of the united Kingdom of Italy in 1861 only a few restricted areas displayed signs of economic modernization and they were almost entirely in the north. During this period political disunity and the tariff barriers consequent upon it undoubtedly retarded growth, though it is obviously difficult to say how much weight should be given to these factors. Especially in Piedmont, ideas of economic liberalism as well as nationalism made progress. Cavour and his supporters were aware of the importance of railways and favoured the establishment of trading links with other countries. Some railway lines had been opened before unification as local improvements in the separate states: a mere 1,623 kilometres for which a large part of the material had been imported.

Once Austrian influence over the peninsula had been destroyed with the help of French arms the movement towards unification proved irresistible. The Risorgimento was achieved, as it were, unexpectedly, and in a fashion which neither Cavour nor Garibaldi had sought. It was a result of political and military activity mainly under the control of professionals and to a large extent over the heads of the masses of the population, especially in the south. It brought about no social and economic changes and involved administrative compromises with the ruling officialdom in the states which were incorporated in the new kingdom, and the retention of social power and influence by the existing ruling classes. There was therefore no room for an agrarian reform or revolution or, indeed, wide social changes of any sort.

Given that the Risorgimento took place as it did, as a result of compromises, there was really no question of enacting a social programme; indeed, no such programme existed. Something like 60 per cent of the population at this time was illiterate, made up of peasants eking out a bare subsistence or poverty-stricken labourers and artisans in a few overgrown towns. They had played little part in the liberation movement and remained, as before, without political rights. For the masses, therefore, the Risorgimento meant little and might even have been followed by increased taxation and other burdens.

Whether a social revolution, especially in the countryside, would have advanced Italian economic development is an academic question. Had the peasants made the sort of gains which their French counterparts had won after 1789 it is arguable that economic growth would have been slowed down. But then everything would have been different from what it turned out to be, including the demographic pattern. As it was Italy did not have an agrarian revolution: that may have kept the distribution of incomes favourable to accumulation. At the same time it presumably limited the growth of the home market and thus reduced the incentive to invest in consumer goods industries.

From the economic point of view the Risorgimento had some ambiguous results. Unification within a single tariff system, the establishment of a single civil code and administrative system, unification of the currency, could all be reckoned as of positive value in the creation of a larger and more uniform market area.

As it happened these changes, brought about by a highly centralized and bureaucratic state directed from the north, could not fail to have some deleterious results for the underprivileged regions of Italy. In particular, southern industry was exposed to the full blast of competition from more efficient rivals in the north and tax rates rose as a result of the heavy debt burden which the new state had to assume. From the start, then, the southern question became an inherent part of united Italy.

The new state began with a heavy public debt against which no productive assets had been created and heavy expenditures involved in carrying through the unifying process. Public finance became a central problem and the search for more sources of revenue a main, and grievance-creating, function of government. However, expenditure constantly tended to outrun budgetary income and there was little scope for the state financing of development schemes which might have benefited the country economically. Indeed, education, communications and the infrastructure generally remained sadly neglected in the early decades of unification.

In an attempt to solve the financial problems which it had inherited the government seized and disposed of Church properties not used for religious purposes, sold off part of the state domain and sold the state railway lines to private concerns. The lands involved were not large enough in extent greatly to change the pattern of landowning; in any case existing landowners and the better off peasants were the principal beneficiaries.

The economic crisis of the mid-sixties found the government in an uncomfortable financial posture. Confidence in government securities and Italian banknotes crumbled abroad and this was followed in 1866 by a rush for liquidity in the main financial centres at home. As a result an inconvertible paper currency was established by decree, thus permitting resort to monetary inflation during the period of the *Corso Forzoso* which lasted until 1881. The population became habituated to a paper currency and there was a growth in the use of bank credit. The question of the effect of the *Corso Forzoso* on Italian economic growth remains problematic. At least the greater evils of deflation or runaway inflation were avoided and, while imports or capital investment by foreigners may have been diminished, the devaluation offered a premium to the export trade.

The 'seventies and 'eighties were hardly propitious for economic growth in a mainly agrarian country. The world price slide hit agricultural producers and thus reduced their capacity to consume industrial goods. At the same time the slight industrial development could not absorb the available labour supply of a growing population which ate up the increases in agricultural productivity which took place. The wealthier sections of the population continued, for the most part, to indulge in conspicuous consumption rather than productive investment and to despise entrepreneurial activities. Much of the social surplus, that part at least which arose from work on the land, was in the main not turned into capital but went on some form of consumption, especially services. Existing liabilities made it difficult for the state to spend as much on social and economic projects as the general backwardness of the country warranted. Dependence on indirect and regressive taxes reduced the purchasing power of the poorer consumers. In these circumstances little foreign capital was attracted into the country. In short, the conditions under which unification was achieved, by leaving the existing social and political equilibrium intact and by saddling the country with an expensive administrative apparatus and a large debt made it difficult to break out of the prevailing backwardness.

Had development been left to the unaided forces of the market a slow penetration of capitalist relations into agriculture and the movement of capital and labour into industries producing for consumer needs could have been expected. Such movements did occur, though, as would also be expected, the process was regionally very uneven. The north, exposed to western European influences and stimulated by trade connections with a high income and rapidly growing area, experienced the extension of production for the market in agriculture and the rise of a mechanized textile industry as well as a multiplicity of small-scale industries producing for the market. In this area landowners tended to have a closer contact with trade and to be more ready to invest either in land improvement or in urban enterprise. By and large northern Italy became drawn into the wider movement of European industrialization as one of its main southern outposts.

In southern Italy, however, the forces of tradition proved much more resistant to change. A large part of the population remained enmeshed in a tradition-bound social structure, producing at subsistence level in more or less self-contained and often isolated communities. There was little stimulus received from the outside, even from the more rapidly advancing parts of Italy. The southern landowners were drawn to the towns, the bureaucracy and professions, acting the role of a leisure class to whom commerce was distasteful; they neglected agriculture and took little interest in the new economic stirrings in the rest of the country. There was little capital forthcoming for investment and little incentive to invest it in establishing industry in a region without the prospect of a flourishing market because of the poverty of the mass of the inhabitants. Although some improvement in material conditions was probably taking place, albeit very slowly, the changes which were beginning in the north, by creating a society which in many ways was qualitatively different from southern traditionalism, widened the gap and increased the misunderstanding between the two regions.

Of course, market forces did not work themselves out without the influence of the state. Some reference has been made to its activities in relation to the sale of Church and state lands, the railways, the currency and public finance. All these influenced the course of economic change, though hardly in an unqualifiedly favourable way. At best it could be said that, at great cost, the political framework was being created for the development of a modern economic life. In a more positive way—though this again is not meant to imply that the activities in question were necessarily beneficial in an economic sense—state intervention contributed to the rise of a capital goods industry and a more adequate transport system. The principal instruments of state intervention were financial aid to the railways and mercantile marine, and the tariff. A major formative influence in the development of public policy was the fall in prices during the post-1873 depression.

After 1860 railways were counted on to consolidate the new won unity as well as to assist in economic prosperity. There was, therefore, as Clough puts it, 'an almost frantic effort on the part of the government to get railways built where they did not exist'. A great deal of public money thus went into railway building, placing a heavy burden on the exchequer. In 1865 the railways were sold back to private enterprise, but their subsequent financial vicissitudes caused the state to return to the field as a main purveyor of funds, so that by the 1880s about two-thirds of the railway system was again state-owned. In 1884 a new railway plan consolidated the lines into four major networks in which the state would own the infrastructure and the operating equipment be provided by profit-making companies. This system did not work to the satisfaction of either the companies or the government, and when the convention between them expired in 1905 the bulk of the railway system passed into the hands of the state.

The Italian state, burdened as it was with debt, nevertheless made a substantial financial contribution to the establishment of a railway system. There is no doubt that in view of the layout of the country the improvement of internal means of communication was of great significance. Many of the typical effects of the building and operation of railways duly followed. Most notable, perhaps, was the establishment of a modern, large-scale, iron and steel and engineering industry which would clearly not have come into existence otherwise. A general stimulus was offered to investment in industries and some branches of agriculture producing for wider markets than were accessible in the pre-railway age. No doubt, too, by aiding the easier circulation of ideas and people the railways made a contribution towards diminishing regional differences and making political union more effective. However, when everything possible has been said on behalf of the railway there remains a certain doubt about the effectiveness of this form of investment. As Gerschenkron has pointed out, the construction of the main line railways preceded by a decade or more the first acceleration in Italian economic growth, which he places in the period 1896–1908. They did not, therefore, have as marked an effect as in some other countries in the nineteenth century, and when this first industrial push took place it was weaker than it might have been because the railways had already been built. Apart from this point, it is also arguable that the resources poured into railway building were in part, at least, misdirected and that a greater stimulus to growth would have arisen from other forms of investment, for example in local roads, education, public health, irrigation, land drainage and similar improvements. However, at the time prevailing ideologies made a planned approach to growth unlikely and it is clear that railways did have a captivating effect on the minds of public men, entrepreneurs, bankers and middle-class investors as the form of capital outlay most likely to bring beneficial material results. Furthermore, in the later period capital could search for other outlays with the expenditure on the basic railway network already in the past.

Government intervention in railways may be said to have led artificially to the creation of a heavy industrial sector which would otherwise have been smaller and grown up later. From the point of view of economic nationalism, as well as that of the business interests concerned, this, by reducing dependence on outside sources of supply of basic industrial materials and machines, made the outlays involved unquestionably worth while. On a purely economic reckoning the benefits are not so certain. These high cost industries soon required tariff protection and other forms of assistance to remain in existence. They were also closely bound up with the provision of armaments and, so far as they had political influence, their owners were favourable to the forward policies in the foreign and colonial field which further diverted limited resources into unproductive uses. Thus Italian capitalism came to have a somewhat top-heavy structure. While at the base it still carried along into the twentieth century a high proportion of small-scale, backward industry, together with an agrarian sector which was both excessive in its proportionate size and largely precapitalist in structure, it was represented, too, by a relatively small number of large firms, comparable in scale and methods of organization with those found in the most advanced countries.

The question of state aid to the mercantile marine is still more problematic. By virtue of its geographical position and long sea coast the Italian peninsula could not be developed without a great deal of coastal trade and sea connections with the world market. The vulnerability of the coast to attack also gave the question a strategic aspect upon which the nationalists seized. Further, Italy appeared on the scene as a united country at a time when technical changes were transforming sea transport and making shipbuilding dependent on the possession of an iron, steel and mechanical

engineering industry. The choice seemed to be either to allow the
forces of the market to decide—in which case Italian seaborne
trade would have remained largely in foreign hands and the country
would have remained dependent on the sea power of Britain for
defence of her coasts—or government intervention of the sort which
most countries at a similar stage of economic development have
embarked on. The latter choice was inevitable: the question became
how much and what kind of state support the shipping industry
should receive. Despite a policy of loans and subsidies to shipowners the relative position of Italian shipping deteriorated in the
1870s. Aid was therefore increased and made more systematic and
subsidies were paid for ships constructed in Italian yards, which
were intended to favour those vessels which could be put to war-
time use. A succession of laws involving considerable handouts
from the exchequer kept the Italian flag on the high seas and
enabled the major shipping lines to be equipped with modern
vessels, though even by 1913 under one-third of the steam tonnage
came from national shipyards. On the other hand there seems to
have been much waste both in construction and operation of ships
by firms enjoying government favours which preserved them from
foreign competition. The whole operation had in it a large element
of prestige.

Shipping policy, like that for the railways, gave Italian capitalism
its special character at this period. State aid was called for by the
weakness of the heavy industries and by Italy's backwardness compared with other industrializing countries. Besides benefiting from
the assistance accorded to the transport sector these industries also
obtained high protective tariffs and some other forms of state aid
followed. In heavy industry, which did not begin to grow rapidly
until the 'nineties, as well as in some of the industries based on
new techniques set up in the early twentieth century, bank finance
and promotion played a vital role. Despite handicaps Italian capitalism did produce its share of outstanding entrepreneurs; it grew
rapidly and in a way under hot-house conditions, in a difficult
environment. Instead of the slow organic growth of numerous firms
under competing conditions by the ploughing back of profits, or
resort to the raising of capital from a moneyed middle class used to
the investment habit, Italian business, to get started at all, or to

grow, required large injections of capital which only big financial institutions could provide. The model for such institutions, and for the practice of investment banking had, moreover, already been established, first by the *Credit Mobilier* type of banking in France and then by the German banks. Not only could Italians copy these examples, but foreigners, particularly Germans, were able to apply the experience which they had acquired in their own lands.

The history of banking in this period followed a chequered course. The development of joint stock banking proceeded apace in the period of the *Corso Forzoso*, serving the needs of the growing commercial and industrial middle classes. Many of the new banks overreached themselves in the great boom which came to an end in 1873–74 by becoming too heavily involved in the finance of long-term projects or speculative ventures. However, there was no possibility of the banks avoiding some commitment to long-term finance since the other sources from which it could come were entirely inadequate. In a sense, then, the emulation of French and German rather than British models was forced upon the Italian banks by the similarity of the conditions in which they operated to those of the other latecomers. It was a necessity as much as a virtue, a question of adaptation to circumstances. Thus, despite the unfortunate experiences of the earlier boom and crisis, bankers had to continue to make business by undertaking investments which tended to be few in number, large in scale and inherently risky. In the 'eighties the banks were deeply involved with the major projects of advancing capitalism: public works, railways and heavy industry. It only required some unsuccessful projects, overshooting in one or two cases, or the exposure of over-risky or downright fraudulent activities, to bring down particular banks or to paralyse the whole precarious structure of credit and confidence. Italian banking could thus not escape its failures, its scandals and its crises. Matters came to a head in 1893 with a political scandal concerning the Banca Romana which went bankrupt and brought down with it a series of other banks. Clough is inclined to see some benefit in this episode: 'The nation got its public buildings, some of its railroads, and some industry partly through the losses of the depositors and shareholders of the bankrupt institutions.'

In the following years the banking system was reorganized,

beginning with the note-issuing banks which were reduced to three with the Bank of Italy regarded as pre-eminent. In the 'nineties the German influence and example became more prominent in the establishment, on the remnants of pre-existing banks, of the Banca Commerciale Italiana and the Banca di Credito Italiano. These banks followed German practice of combining the business of commercial banking with the granting of credit against collateral and the holding of industrial investments. Presumably they made a contribution, together with other banks, to the upsurge in economic growth which marked the period 1896–1908. However, the banks' role was not accepted so readily as in Germany and, according to Gerschenkron, their freedom of action was correspondingly less. He does grant them a major role in promoting new firms and helping others to expand, in providing 'entrepreneurial guidance' and in favouring monopolistic compacts. Italian industry, on the other hand, leant even more upon the banks than its German counterpart.

By 1914 Italy had assumed some of the characteristics of an advanced industrial country. Politically, especially in the foreign and colonial arena, her leaders behaved as though she was already the equal of the other great powers. In terms of all the basic industrial statistics, while the growth of Italy since 1860 had been quite impressive, her absolute industrial power and relative standing revealed major weaknesses which had still to be eliminated. The rates of growth achieved in the first great spurt, 6.7 per cent per annum, were not maintained in the following years. The emphasis on heavy industry, favoured by state policy and by the investment activities of the banks, and the inevitable concentration which resulted in this sector made the industrial structure even more top-heavy. The full impact of this rapid development had fallen upon a few sectors and geographical areas, chiefly located in the already more advanced north. While growth proceeded in other parts of Italy, too, there was no sign of the north-south differential disappearing. In fact, because of the absence of any kind of structural change in the Mezzogiorno the characteristics of economic dualism became more pronounced and political debate on its causes more acrimonious. The traditional hegemony of the north was thus reinforced. The failure to transform in the economy as a

whole, the limitations of the home market as a result of the continued predominance of agriculture, much of which was still carried
on on a subsistence basis, bore down in turn upon the rate of
growth. The big spurt had not cut very deeply into the inherited
backwardness of a large part of Italy; a life of hardship and poverty
was still the lot of the vast majority.

Although Italy did begin to take on the attributes of a modern
industrial country, at least in the north, this development, however
important, was combined with evidences of extreme social disorganization and even decay. Provision for higher education for
those who could afford it was good, but the growing numbers of
educated young men in the middle class found inadequate opportunities for their ambitions in a society which remained relatively
under-developed. There was little desire or inducement to go into
business and no strong intellectual conviction of the desirability of
more rapid economic growth. Political life suffered from the disre-
pute of parliamentary combinationism and corruption. Those who
sought security and had the requisite qualifications or influence
found it in the tentacular ramifications of the state bureaucracy.
There remained a large discontented body of educated opinion
generally sceptical and individualist from which support could be
found for nationalism and imperialist adventures. This reflected
the weakness and lack of self-confidence of the Italian middle
class, the domestic difficulties which industrial growth tended to
aggravate and the position in the world of a latecomer whose rulers
considered it to be a 'great power' but which lacked the material
means to play the role with success. For large numbers of peasants
and workers there seemed to be no way out at home and millions
emigrated. The fact of emigration, apart from offering some spurious
justification for the colonial ventures of the politicians, laid a
further burden on the economy. In fact most of the emigrants were
in the prime of their working life: the cost of supporting them in
their unproductive years had fallen upon Italy, subsequently they
contributed to the labour supply of other countries and only their
remittances made a contribution to the economy of their native land.

Just as Italian business took over from an early stage the most
advanced techniques and forms of organization worked out in the
advanced countries, so the working class took over the doctrines

and methods to be found in the international labour movement. From the 'nineties labour history was marked by great turbulence and a ruling class response which, while including some concessions which helped to bring labour conditions in the north up to western European standards, was often repressive. In any case, apart from the ideological divisions in the labour movement, which were characteristic of all countries, the slow and uneven nature of industrialization meant that the working class was a minority, highly concentrated in a few centres and with material levels considerably higher than the great mass of the small peasants and agricultural labourers. The lack of homogeneity and the economic and social divisions, the low level of education, the limited franchise until 1912, the intellectual composition of the socialist leadership, were among the factors which weakened the labour movement in the period before the First World War. On the whole, too, the party combinations at the centre of government which, by a process of compromise, satisfied the different sections of the property-owning classes, were able to find a reservoir of support among the peasantry in the more backward areas (except where clerical feeling was strong) to oppose working-class claims.

It is evident that Italian economic development bequeathed to the twentieth century a complex of unresolved problems, still further tangled by the effects of intervention in the First World War, which prepared the way for the dictatorship of Mussolini. There was, in fact, but a limited foundation for the maintenance of the institutions of bourgeois parliamentarianism from which many elements in the middle class were, in any case, alienated and which large parts of the working class never accepted.

The economic achievements of Italian capitalism before 1914 must be seen within this unsatisfactory and precarious social and political framework which seemed to prepare the ground for authoritarian government. Democratic, or more strictly, parliamentary interventionism made possible only a one-sided sort of development in Italian conditions. It was axiomatic that established interests should be upheld if that was the price for their political support. New interests which could mobilize sufficient pressure were able to secure state benefits. The voteless and voiceless were practically disregarded. There was, as Gerschenkron points out, no powerful ideological commitment to economic growth. Indeed, there were strong traditional tendencies in the educated and propertied sections of society which resisted change and were indifferent or hostile to the new forces of developing capitalism. The way had not been cleared by any deep-going social changes for a more rapid and even economic growth. This was particularly the case in the south which had been incorporated into the kingdom on the understanding that existing property rights and vested interests would be respected.

The argument that the absence of an agrarian revolution favoured the development of Italian capitalism by preserving an income distribution conducive to accumulation does not seem to be sound. In the first place the rate of saving was not high owing to the social tendency towards conspicuous consumption among the wealthy. Secondly, in the leading sectors of development a large part of the capital was provided by the banks and by the state rather than by wealthy individuals or corporations. What has to be judged is the investment policy of these organs: whether, in fact, if social power had been differently distributed, decisions about investment more favourable to growth would have been made. As pointed out earlier, this is very much a hypothetical question, though it might have some meaning for presentday underdeveloped countries. What may be suggested is that insufficient resources were directed into education, agriculture and improvements in the social environment and too many, at certain stages, into transport, heavy industry, armaments, colonial adventures and the state apparatus. This maldistribution reflected a balance of social and political forces which issued from the Risorgimento. It does not follow that if unification had taken place in a different way and had been accompanied by a social revolution economic growth would have been more even or higher or that the north–south differential would have been any the less, but this is not logically excluded. It was not that statesmen and others made wrong choices but that given the situation in which they found themselves they could not be true to their class interests and behave otherwise. We do not therefore have to conclude that all that they did was for the best. On the other hand, to conceive of a different course of development, say an agrarian revolution which strengthened the position of the peasantry and enabled them to retain a larger proportion of the income from agriculture, would involve the assumption that many other aspects of social life also changed. It is impossible to say what might have happened, except as an intellectual exercise on a variety of possible permutations. For example, the peasantry might have saved less than the rent-receivers but their spending pattern would have been different and might have encouraged a more rapid growth of the internal market. More ambitious individuals from the peasantry might have ventured into business as well as farming for the market more efficiently. As it was the Italian way of financing industry from the agrarian surplus seems to have been inefficient; too much was lost on the way.

No doubt controversy will continue about the nature of Italian economic development before 1914 with some emphasizing the achievement in laying the basis for a modern economy in an unpropitious Mediterranean environment while others stress the continued backwardness of much of the country and the comparatively limited extent of industrialization. Any judgment would seem necessarily to be coloured by the view taken of Italy's subsequent development, particularly the lapse into dictatorship in the 1920s and the continued problem of the Mezzogiorno, despite the efforts made in that region during the prosperous 1950s and 1960s. Certainly in Italy many of the problems to be faced by later developing countries were to be prefigured. However, she was already intellectually part of the advanced western world before industrialization began and this in some ways facilitated the catching up process. Northern Italy, moreover, may be considered as definitely part of the industrial belt of western Europe by the end of the nineteenth century, able to make high class technical and other contributions of its own. The heavy weight of the near-African conditions prevailing in the south bore down heavily on national averages of production, income and growth. The existence of poverty and illiteracy on a massive scale in the Mezzogiorno was the most conspicuous failure of the combination of economic liberalism and parliamentary interventionism which made up Italian economic policy in the period.

The Italian economic structure on the eve of the First World War was typically that of a latecomer. As in Russia there was a very advanced and highly concentrated modern sector with its centre of gravity in heavy industry. The large concerns in these industries tended to draw still closer together and to enter into cartel agreements. They could not have existed at all without the supply of investment funds provided by a few large investment banks which therefore held a dominant position in the economy. Despite the declining role of agriculture in total output it was still greatly overrepresented and was still dominated by small-scale, inefficient units with low productivity and low purchasing power. The home market for large-scale modern industry was thus narrowly restricted and it depended very much on government supports in the shape of contracts, especially for military supplies, and tariff protection.

The Italian economy perhaps grew faster than it might otherwise have done as a result of the lop-sidedness of its industrial structure and the concentration of ownership and control through the role played by the banks. In other respects this was a potentially unstable form of development. The home market remained narrow and the business outlets for middle-class enterprise were probably restricted. The dependence of industry on bank finance was paralleled by the fact that the solvency of the banks depended directly on industrial prosperity. In time of crisis the big banks were thus liable to look to the state for assistance. The character of Italian business organization was thus to create a powerful bloc of interests able to influence political decisions. Later, as a recent student, Jon S. Cohen, has pointed out, 'Mussolini was to find this industrial structure an ideal framework for his "Corporative State" '.

In the period before 1914 Italy shared in European prosperity and, at least in the industrial areas, boom conditions prevailed. However, the strong underlying weaknesses have to be noted. Despite growth in exports imports rose still faster to meet the needs of industry for fuel and raw material, and the demands of a growing population for imported food. Invisible payments from tourism and services, especially the earnings of the mercantile marine, thus played an important part in the balance of payments. But the remaining deficit was made up from the remittances sent home by Italians overseas to support relations or to enable them to join them in emigration. It was hardly a sound financial position when the drain of population from a country unable to support all its children provided at the same time the bridging item in its balance of payments.

Before 1914, therefore, despite considerable economic advance, the Italian economy had not been able to overcome its inherited disadvantages. It still reflected in its structure the great regional diversities which the political unification of the country had been unable to overcome. The preservation of the traditional social structure after 1860 and especially the fact that the Risorgimento had not been accompanied by agrarian reforms were, in all probability, and despite some arguments to the contrary, factors which retarded economic change. For example, besides impeding the movement of resources out of agriculture into more productive occupations they were both cause and effect of the weakness of Italian entrepreneurship and the reluctance with which the property-owning classes turned to industrial investment. One result of this was that when industrial development did accelerate it depended heavily on the support of the state and the investment funds provided by the banks. Instead of reproducing the stages through which the earlier industrialized countries had passed, Italy, like Russia, 'jumped over stages', and, while the economy remained largely agrarian and much industrial production was carried on in tiny units and by handicraftsmen, huge enterprises of the most modern form loomed above this traditional base. Indeed, it was in the new industrial giants, and in the already notable beginnings in industries based on the new technologies of the twentieth century, in which Italy's disabilities in resource endowment were little or no handicap, that the modern industrial vocation of the country was prefigured. The war proved to be a great forcing house for the modern industrial sector and resulted in its weight being greatly increased. At the same time, however, all the unresolved contradictions inherited from the manner in which political unification had been achieved also assumed a sharply concentrated form and precipitated a social crisis which opened the way for fascist dictatorship. But the advent of fascism, while it too had been prepared by a lengthy historical process, and while it opened a new era in Italian history, by no means permitted the secular problems of the economy to be overcome; but that is another story which will not be discussed here. However, the summary of Italian economic history presented here should throw some light on the reasons for the coming of an authoritarian dictatorship and make clear the kind of forces which were to operate to shape its character. In the light of Italian history fascism was not at all an aberration but had its social bases in the inability of the institutions of the united Kingdom of Italy which issued from the Risorgimento to contain the new dynamic forces which accompanied the rise of advanced industry.

Problems for discussion

1. What were the principal obstacles to economic development in nineteenth-century Italy?
2. Why did the Risorgimento have so little effect on the economic structure of Italy? Did this impede or favour further growth?
3. Examine the nature of the Italian agrarian system and its regional variations. Why was the weight of the agrarian sector in the economy reduced so slowly?
4. Examine the role of the banks as a factor promoting industrialization.
5. What were the effects on the Italian economy of the high rate of emigration in the late nineteenth and early twentieth centuries?
6. Why did the problem of the Mezzogiorno prove so intractable?
7. Why was the high rate of growth attained in the 1890s not sustained?
8. To what extent had Italy become an advanced industrial country by 1914?

7 Britain 1870-1914: a Pioneer under Pressure

Previous chapters have examined the conditions under which a number of countries carried through the initial phases of industrialization. The main problems have concerned the barriers to growth in a traditional agrarian economy and the way in which the industrial structure was shaped, in each case, by the peculiar combination of dynamic and retarding factors which operated. Instead of building economic models or adopting a monocausal approach some attempt has been made, from a range of historical evidence, both to depict the process in outline and to explain it. However, this has not been done with the degree of ostensible rigour which a more quantitative, or a more abstract, treatment would have permitted. The picture in each case has not been an altogether clear or tidy one. It has been shown that purely economic explanations have not been adequate. In the developing pattern of the economic life of nations all manner of social, cultural and political factors are worked into an intricate ensemble which distinguishes one from another. At the same time, it will be evident to the reader that the basic economic processes of capitalist industrialization impose themselves in each environment and create similar problems and comparable responses. Behind the great variety of conditions to be found, from Britain to Italy or from Russia to Germany, there is at the same time a certain identity imposed by the accumulation of capital, the mobilization of an industrial proletariat, the exigencies of the machine technology and modern industrial organization. In all cases, whatever role the state may have played, the bulk of the significant economic decisions have been made by private individuals responding to market indicators and seeking to make a profit. Into the behaviour of these individuals, the capitalist entrepreneurs, as well as into that of all the other *dramatis personae*, enter many considerations not reducible to quantitative measurement, which have somehow been distilled from the prevailing cultural milieu. We are never dealing, historically, with purely economic men, with perfectly competitive markets or a chemically pure capitalist economy. That is why an historical assessment is bound, in the last resort, to be qualitative and therefore not as precise as some would wish. In fact, there has been no pretence here at arriving at such a spurious accuracy and no sense of discouragement that the explanations offered are by their nature open-ended, provisional and contestable. It is only by revealing problems, offering hypotheses and inviting others to strengthen the argument – or to overthrow it by offering empirical evidence which contradicts it, or an alternative hypothesis which is more convincing or internally more consistent – that historiography can make real advances.

This statement of methodology is appropriate at this concluding stage where we examine a case which is rather different from the others and is attracting more and more interest from economic historians today. So far the subject matter of these case studies has been growth, more or less rapid or successful, in new or young industrial economies. The British economy after 1870, however, had already advanced a considerable way towards becoming a predominantly industrial society. The establishment of its leading industries and of many individual firms went back several generations, even into the preceding century. Its principal railway lines had already been built, its industrial landscape to a large extent determined by a process of urban building and the exploitation of mineral resources extending back over many decades. Its agrarian sector had already contracted in relative weight to an extent never before paralleled, and it was to contract still further in the next half a century. Capitalist relations had an unbroken record over many centuries and the wage-earning class already constituted the majority of the population. As a class the peasantry had, for all practical purposes, disappeared and the agrarian system, although fully capitalist, had developed in such a way as to permit the survival of a class of great landowners with a power in the land, and especially in rural society, which still contained something broadly 'feudal'. But economic power principally resided with a broadly based and self-confident class of bourgeois industrialists, merchants and financiers whose aggregate wealth and economic influence at this time had no equal. Here were the first great beneficiaries of the rise of modern industry whose nature was bound up with the time and conditions under which industrialization in Britain took place. By the normal process of heredity inseparable from a private property system, by intermarriage and a conscious conservation of wealth, a number of great industrial fortunes had come into existence. If many of the firms from which these fortunes were derived seemed small in the coming age of the great business company and the integrated concern, they were, for their age, relatively large. They made, in any case, for rich men and represented a high degree of concentration of productive property in the hands of a few.

As the leading industrial country dominating a world market which the needs of British capitalism had largely called into existence it continued to operate in a highly favourable environment. It is with the enumeration of the advantages it had acquired that the development of its subsequent problems rightly begins.

British entrepreneurs retained a considerable cost advantage over their rivals in the main sorts of manufactured goods which entered into world trade. For the most part, therefore, they were strong and dogmatic supporters of free trade. If foreigners found a market for certain of their manufactured goods in Britain, mostly higher quality specialities or goods in which for special reasons they had a comparative costs advantage, that was not seen as a reason to exclude them. On the whole there was no need to take foreign competition in the staple lines of manufacturing industry with much seriousness. In the recession after 1873 there was more alarm in Europe at intensified British competition than there was in Britain over foreign competition, and the former was a powerful factor in the general return to protection which began to take effect towards the end of the decade.

The development of industry on the Continent and in the United States in the previous period had contributed to the great mid-Victorian boom. It created needs for capital equipment such as railway iron; it expanded the market for coal; with higher incomes Europeans could buy more consumer goods from Britain. A vast new outlet opened up for British capital and a wide range of specialized institutions and firms was established in London as a result. There was therefore a constant offset to any tendency for investment opportunities at home to dry up and an apparatus was built up which directed part of the income stream accruing to the wealthy into new investments abroad from which further income could be derived. In the cosmopolitan investing pattern which ensued newly industrializing, as well as primary producing, countries could turn to the London market for their requirements.

Some of the areas with which British trade and investment were carried on formed part of the formal or informal empire of the dominant economy. The colonies, especially India, were virtually captive markets and privileged fields for the investment of British capital. There were other parts of the world, too, especially in South America, which stood in a near perfect complementary relationship to the 'workshop of the world'.

The position held by British enterprise and capital in the primary producing regions of the world meant that they also profited from the spread of industry in Europe and North America. The industrializing countries had to increase their purchases of raw materials on the world market, that is to say from areas in which British capital was dominant. The financing and insuring of their shipments also almost invariably brought more business to the City of London which could offer unrivalled facilities of this kind.

As a result of her prior development of a thoroughly capitalist internal economy dependent upon an intricate network of credit, and then her leading role in world trade, Britain became the financial centre of the world, and the pound sterling the unit upon which the world monetary system turned. Through the extension of the gold standard, which was essentially a sterling standard, the world was endowed with a monetary system which permitted a remarkable degree of flexibility as well as stability. Currency stability and the free convertibility of monies was a heritage which lasted until 1914 as a result of the international position of Britain.

British prosperity and economic predominance were inseparably associated in the minds of the bourgeoisie with a quasi-automatic market system, individualist, competitive enterprise and a minimum of state interference, international free trade and the gold standard. In the main, despite some temporary demurring in some quarters, these attributes of capitalism in its heyday retained the allegiance of the bourgeoisie throughout the period which we now have to examine. There could have been no question of an alteration of the system which impinged upon these fundamentals.

Up to the 'seventies there is some strength in the assertion that decisions made in Britain, or by British subjects overseas, had more influence upon the shaping of the world economy than decisions made by foreigners had upon what happened in Britain. From then onwards, however, the reverse begins to be true. Long range changes in the world economy imposed a constant series of adjustments on those responsible for making decisions of economic significance in Britain. Their area of choice, as it were, tends to become constricted. The degree to which they understand what is going on and make the necessary changes conditions the extent of the adaptation which is made to forces which, for the British economy, are exogenous. Very little more precision than that can be given to a generalization of this sort for the moment.

The share of world trade and world industrial production assumed by Britain in the early 'seventies was of course abnormal. It was neither possible, nor perhaps desirable for her economic health, that such a proportion be maintained. On the one side, as other countries industrialized it was evident that Britain's share would inevitably decline; on the other, as this was a condition for further growth in the total volume of trade and industrial production, it was necessary if growth in Britain was to continue. Unless foreigners had more purchasing power the world demand for British goods could not go on increasing; in order to increase their pull on world demand they had to shift resources from agriculture to more productive outlets, that is, they had to industrialize. By its nature, industrialization tended to lead to the building up of industries in excess of the demands of the national economies into which the world was divided. For such industries to have a healthy base, therefore, they needed to be able to sell their commodities across national frontiers. To do this the firms involved had to manufacture more cheaply and sell harder than those already established, mainly British, industrial exporters. Hence, after 1870 or thereabouts, the spread of industrialization brought in its train intensified international competition in manufactured goods.

The spread of industrialization on a world scale thus created a new international environment for British enterprise, the features of which are naturally only clear in retrospect. Generally speaking, entrepreneurial and other decisions are taken on the basis of past experience and on the assumption that things will continue in the immediate future much as they had been in the immediate past. When this has been confirmed over a lengthy period well-established habits are formed which it is difficult to change even when, repeatedly, things do not turn out exactly as expected. Moreover, there may be other inbuilt inflexibilities which make adjustment to change difficult, or ways of maintaining income with the minimum of adjustment in the short run at the cost of an undiscernible long-term deterioration of the market position.

In the newer industrial countries entrepreneurs enjoyed the advantages of latecomers. As has been seen they were under pressure to keep down costs because they had to confront British competition if not at home (where protection was effective) certainly in the export market. They were able to begin with the most advanced equipment and had a wide choice in selecting the location of their plant and in laying it out. The chances were that they began without extablished industrial habits or inhibitions: for example, they accepted and may have sought bank participation and some form of government support. As newcomers they have small if any reserves upon which to fall back; the penalty for failure is bankruptcy. Competitive forces act rather sharply without the cushion of inherited wealth or an established market position. Again, in marketing the product the newcomer has to try harder; he begins with the standards set by the established firms and seeks to go one better. Hence the well-known cases of German firms studying particular markets very assiduously in order to suit more exactly than their established British rivals the needs of their foreign customers.

In Britain the pioneers now laboured under some disadvantages. Heavy investment had been made in the past not only in industrial equipment but also in infrastructure, such as railways and port facilities, which now represented a dead-weight of obsolescence.

It was obviously economically impracticable to begin again from scratch, tear down factories, relocate industries and scrap existing facilities. For one thing part of this investment had been fully amortized so that its use only entailed maintenance and replacement costs. Orthodox economic accounting therefore justified the continued use of wholly or partly obsolete equipment. The problem of 'moral depreciation' was bound to arise in an economy which had undergone rapid industrialization at an early stage of technological development. Continued technological advance, especially at a rapid rate, in competing national economies, made it still more acute if not necessarily more recognizable at the time. Thus, for two comparable industries, one in an earlier industrialized country and the other in a latecomer, the former would probably have a high proportion of old and obsolete equipment while the latter would be equipped and organized according to the requirements of the latest techniques. It does not follow that the latter would have a cost advantage because much of the old equipment had already paid for itself and the old industry might, therefore, very well be more profitable. If that were so its owners might not feel any particular spur to speed up their replacement of old equipment or to improve their organizations or methods. The more strongly entrenched their market position the more likely they would be to respond in a slow and lethargic way to the appearance of competition.

The familiar strictures on British entrepreneurship in this period must be seen in relation to this situation. The justification for a market economy lay historically in its ability to develop the productive forces more fully than any alternative system. The question which is really being raised as a result of the study of the behaviour of entrepreneurs in the older industrial countries is whether adherence to the profit principle in a market economy did not inevitably, at some point, tend to produce a slowing down of growth. This is bound to be the case unless it can be shown that businessmen could conceivably be, as it were, untrue to their object which, economically speaking, was the pursuit of profit.

But it has to be remembered that the entrepreneur was the product of complex environmental forces and could not be a purely economic man. Even if he were his decisions were geared mainly to short-run market situations and what he was perfectly justified in doing in the interests of his business on a limited time schedule might eventuate, if others in similar situations tended to do the same thing, in a long-run situation which represented a deterioration for all. For example, though it might be perfectly correct from an accounting point of view not to introduce certain technical improvements, in the longer run this might leave a whole national industry with an unmanageable proportion of old and obsolete machinery facing a well-equipped and technically progressive rival. Competitive forces might not be strong enough to prevent such a situation developing: the home market usually offered some shelter from outside competition because of transport costs, foreign markets might also be in some way sheltered or privileged and colonial markets even more so.

There are, then, the non-economic aspects to be taken into account. Under a system of private property economic decisions are influenced by the existence of accumulated wealth, by the desire to conserve or enjoy it as well as to add to it. In certain circumstances, and perhaps to a degree in all conditions, the businessman is a slave of accumulation. He must, to continue in business, make a profit and to make a profit he must invest part, or all, of the profit being made. The need for investment therefore imposes itself on him; only its extent, direction and character is a matter of choice. The selfmade man of the early Industrial Revolution was typically dedicated to accumulation: he ploughed back a high proportion of profits into the firm, taking out comparatively little for his own consumption. His sons and grandsons were not necessarily under such a pressing urge to accumulate. Inheriting the business as a going concern and a source of income they were already men of wealth and standing, susceptible to various social pressures which tended to separate their personal identity from that of the firm. Hence the tendency in the second and third generation for members of business families to diversify their interests and begin to behave like, or merge with, the existing leisured class of landowners. In a sense, too, the firm tends to be administered more like an estate and less exclusively as an instrument of profit-making and accumulation.

Where industries were dominated by a relatively small number of wealthy families there was no question of a shortage of capital for investment; it was more a case that income came in so steadily that it was treated as such. Discretion would dictate some diversification of holdings and a general tendency to live and to spend on a more lavish scale was practically irresistible. This could have meant a falling off in the quality of business leadership in the sense that it became less concerned with pushing forward to acquire a position than to maintain a position gained in the past. The industrial rich in general were more intent on enjoying their wealth, power and prestige than in pushing up the production indices. It is difficult to fault this behaviour as a response to actually prevailing conditions. In retrospect, and with hindsight, it can be shown that a multitude of responses of this kind, coupled with the technological falling behind already accounted for, had deleterious results for the rate of growth and competitive position of the established British industries and thus weakened the national economy as a whole.

Having said this, and the case can, of course, be made out in much more detail, it is difficult to see how, at the time, anything could have been done to alter or arrest the trend. There were, of course, contemporaries who discerned the weaknesses in British industry, warned about foreign competition or suggested remedies. About all that does is to provide some qualitative evidence for the view that there had been a change in the climate of business enterprise from the early days of the Industrial Revolution, that the pioneers had now become comfortable and conservative, jogging along in a routine way rather than searching restlessly for new sources of profit. Therefore, given the prevailing institutional structure, the predominance of the liberal ideology and the abhorrence for state intervention, the verdict must surely be that the relative industrial decline of Britain was an inevitable process. Numerous additional factors can be brought together for corroborative purposes.

What was remarkable, and has to be explained, was the lack of any pressure to change, or rather to change faster, because adaptation was going on all the time in a piecemeal fashion. Thus inside industry most of the habits acquired in the earlier stages of industrial technology were conserved. In the workshop the practical man was king. Training at all levels took place on the job. Industrial processes were learned and developed empirically; few of those concerned had any formal education in fundamental science and institutions for this purpose scarcely existed. Labour power was relatively abundant and adaptable, workers grew up accustomed to the needs of machine industry. At the time this was an evident advantage for employers. But wages were neither so high as to demand a continuous search for means to economize in the use of labour power nor so low as to encourage its wasteful use. The labour force was sufficiently skilled to be able to make use of general purpose machines and the traditional craft tools as well if not better than the workers of any other country. Mechanization was not stimulated by scarcity of skilled workers or by the existence of an unskilled labour force which could not have been employed except in factories equipped with automatic machinery. At the same time, in the urban areas, with which Britain was more highly endowed than any other country, there existed large reserves of labour for casual, heavy or low paid manual work from which employers derived an inestimable advantage.

In some fields, then, British industry lost its competitive advantages. There tended, too, to be less incentive to introduce new techniques and to develop new industries. A significant case in point was the iron and steel industry. The British industry had developed its position of world leadership in the period when wrought iron was the principal constructional material, and its structure, location and layout were determined by its rapid development in this period. With the development in turn of the Bessemer, the Siemens-Martin and the Gilchrist-Thomas processes—which made possible the utilization of the large deposits of phosphoric ores in western Europe and North America—the newer industrializing countries went rapidly ahead in creating a steel industry. The economic use of the new steel-making processes required large-scale, integrated plants strategically located in relation to ore and coal supplies and able to make use of the economies in fuel, heat, materials and waste gases which a series of minor technical improvements had made available. The British iron industry was composed of a relatively large number of competing firms with many scattered plants embodying big outlays and the older techniques. Coal was used rather wastefully and much production was geared to the specialized demand of users who wanted a high-quality product with known properties. In the changeover to steel the industry tended to conserve many of its existing characteristics and, particularly from the 'eighties, when foreign producers took up the Gilchrist-Thomas process, it lost ground rapidly relative to its competitors. Total U.S. production of pig iron and steel exceeded that of Britain by 1890; Germany overhauled Britain in pig iron in 1893 and in steel in 1905.

The diminishing British share in world output must be regarded to a considerable degree as inevitable. Other countries had an expanding home market as a result of their own rapid industrialization while the British market did not expand at the same rate. Not only were they able to supply all their own demand, without the need for British imports, but to enable their large new plants to operate profitably the steel-makers needed to break into the world market, which they did at Britain's expense. The main British weakness at this time was the failure to turn over to the large-scale production of cheap steels. To enable this to take place a bold programme of modernization in the steel industry would have been necessary. In the main the iron and steel makers sought to avoid this or were simply incapable of making a fresh start. The location and structure of the industry remained in 1914 surprisingly similar to what it had been in 1870. Known deposits of phosphoric ores were not exploited, the Thomas process being adopted only slowly. There was reluctance to scrap plant which was obsolete but not worn out and to invest in large-scale integrated plants. Less attention was paid to the application of metallurgical chemistry to large-scale production than in other countries. Combination and concentration went ahead more slowly and there was not the same intimate connection between the banks and the industry which had made possible the expansion of the Ruhr and Lorraine.

The steel industry is perhaps a classic case where the considerations already put forward seem to apply. It is possible to frame a convincing indictment of the business leaders in the industry for their lack of foresight, enterprise and energy. It is, however, to be pointed out that their decisions were limited by the institutionalized inertia of the plant layout and structure which they inherited; by the fact that they were not, like their foreign rivals, creating a new industry but trying to adapt an old one, encrusted with tradition and a momentum of its own, to quite new technological conditions. Like the owners of the older parts of British industry they were very much the products of their age and milieu—most of them could neither see nor admit the defects in the traditional policies to which they adhered. In any case, as already suggested, there was no sharp economic pressure or incentive to innovate or expand more rapidly on these secure and on the whole prosperous businesses. Caution was therefore the watchword. In the 'seventies and 'eighties this led to an underestimation of the competitive power of steel by the makers of wrought iron. In the nineties there was mistrust of Thomas steel and, all along, users tended to be conservative or to have justifiable technical reasons for distrusting products made by the new methods. In the years before about 1905 the state of the market again counselled caution about big new investments. It is not impossible, then, to find good reasons, if not excuses, for what seems like the technical lag of this particular industry. Even so, the steel makers surely displayed more than an excusable degree of complacency of the sort which had its origins in the period of Britain's undisputed industrial predominance. The old leadership was now passing away before the eyes of British entrepreneurs without them taking stock of the situation or being able to take effective action to prevent it. And as ground was lost it became more difficult to regain.

Such were the penalties of age, of 'maturity', in one key industry. The story was not very different in the others. As for the new industries the general picture is not so much that no advance was made but that the major developments in the practical applications of science and technology to industry in this period took place abroad. Of the reasons for this perhaps the only addition to the points already made which needs to be mentioned is the fact that Britain was already so well equipped with the old technologies that the scope for the application of new ones was more limited. For instance, the large investment in steam power plants and in gas lighting equipment and the availability of cheap coal reduced the incentive to develop electricity. The existence of a dense rail system lowered interest in the internal-combustion engine for road traction. The nature of the market and the distribution of incomes, which was still steeply unequal, meant that there was little incentive to develop the mass production of such an expensive consumer durable as the motor car. It was condemned to be primarily a rich man's toy. Of the other new industries those based upon the application of chemical science were probably the most important. In the field of synthetic dyestuffs and pharmaceutical products the Germans seized and held the lead, cornered and developed the major patents and secured a practically impregnable position in the world market. This success story was the result of a combination of superior scientific education, remarkable business acumen, available raw materials and a favourable legal climate (particularly the patent law). Whether by foresight or by luck capital and technique were directed into a field which was destined for growing importance. Neither the French nor the British industries were able to keep pace. As they fell behind it became more and more difficult to catch up.

It was not until the war, when British dependence not only on German chemicals but also on a range of other vital manufactured imports such as magnetos, hosiery latch needles and scientific and optical instruments became a strategic matter that anything was done about it. But was that surprising in the generally expansive and confident period which preceded the war? After all, if German producers had a comparative cost advantage, however acquired, in synthetic dyestuffs, did not this benefit consumers in Britain and conform to the principle of the international division of labour upon which the free trade policy was based? A British chemical industry could only be placed on a competitive footing, by a combination of tariff protection and government support. Neither of these were at all likely in the conditions which prevailed before the First World War. And it is difficult to prove, other than on strategic grounds, that it would have been desirable at the time to create a hot-house industry which market forces alone did not permit to emerge.

Certainly, before 1914 British capitalism was by no means in a desperate or parlous condition, however much historians have been tempted to find in this period the roots of the problems with which it is now afflicted. Capital was abundant and, trade cycle fluctuations apart, there was no lack of profitable outlets for it. The renewed world economic upsurge, after the halting advance of the 'Great Depression', enabled the great traditional industries to enjoy an unprecedented prosperity. More capital was attracted into these fields and the spur to diversify the industrial structure was correspondingly reduced. In retrospect this seems to have been a dangerous trend but at the time it was fully in accord with the normal response which profit-seeking investors and capitalists could be expected to make to market forces. In a situation of increasing world competition British businessmen were led into courses where the resistances were least. For example, they sought new customers for the products which they were accustomed to produce and sell to a greater extent than they found new products for their old customers. In its way this was a very rational response. In its effects it meant that the British export pattern continued to reflect dependence on the products of the older technology and was weighted towards the markets of the less developed areas of the world. This confirmed the tendency to direct capital into the old channels rather than to develop the newer technologies. It meant also that British exports contained a high proportion of the sort of goods which industrializing countries began at an early stage to manufacture for themselves.

The weaknesses which were involved in this continued dependence on the traditional export industries and the less developed countries appeared after the event, when the whole world economy had been disrupted by the effects of the First World War. The adjustments which were subsequently demanded were too large to be made all at once, with the result that the geographically concentrated traditional industries went into decline and were responsible for the distressed areas of the interwar period. However, had there not been a war the adjustments required would presumably have been spread over a longer period of time: other countries would not have industrialized so rapidly or in such isolation from the world market, the further emphasis on the old industries inherent in war demand would not have occurred, world investment and capital movements would have been different, and so on. After all, the First World War did mark an important hiatus in the world development of capitalism and imposed particularly acute strains on the industrial countries of Europe. The problems which subsequently arose were thus not exclusively British.

Returning to the character of the British economy in the 1870–1914 period, it is clearly one-sided to consider only its industrial aspect. British capitalism was deeply involved and completely integrated with the world market. Its prosperity depended upon the maintenance of a high volume of world trade and the continued existence of profitable investment opportunities on a world scale. Although the industrial base had to be maintained if the economy as a whole was to remain strong, a large and lucrative sector of British capitalism was concerned with the trade and finance of the world market. The institutions of the City of London were turned primarily towards the financing of world trade and raising capital for long-term overseas investment. It raised very little capital, relatively, for manufacturing industry where the strongholds were still occupied by the scions of old-established and wealthy families. The deeply rooted British interest in overseas capital investment meant that the total capital available for new investment tended to grow automatically. Taken on a national basis, therefore, new capital investment was provided from the proceeds of existing investment. There was, of course, a complex system of income flows whereby income was repatriated and directed to its recipients while savings—not necessarily of overseas origin—were mobilized and channelled into new flotations. Income from overseas investment was not necessarily available, when aggregates are considered, for ploughing into the domestic economy. There had in the first place to be reasonable profit expectations and the opportunity to invest. It can be assumed that, although the rate of return on overseas investment may not have been much higher than on home investment, additional increments of home investment would have resulted in a lowering of the rate of profit, which would have choked it off. This point might have been reached early unless or until the capital market adapted itself to handling a higher volume of home investment and new investment opportunities were opened up. But this is a might-have-been. As it was, overseas investment did play a functional role in the development of the national economy: it opened up supplies of raw materials and food stuffs and enabled them to be supplied at increasing quantities and at relatively low prices; it provided markets for the export trades for which home demand could not have substituted; it encouraged investment at home in food processing and handling, and in export manufacturing. These lines of involvement were so thoroughly part of the economy as it had developed throughout the nineteenth century that they could not be cut without catastrophe.

The balanced growth of the British economy depended on the mutilateral system of payments which tied it into the world economy and upon its ability to adjust to changes in world demand and payment flows. The keystone of this system was the existence of a large British capital stake in the world economy and the income flows which derived from it. Income from past investment and other invisible earnings enabled Britain to have payments deficits with the other advanced countries which represented, in fact, a market for their industrial products. Simultaneously, their surpluses with Britain enabled them to purchase industrial raw materials and foodstuffs from the primary producing areas which had been developed with British capital and with which Britain had a payments surplus. In this complex circuit of exchange, as Saul has shown, British investment income from India played a vital part. Free trade in Britain, meanwhile, gave other countries the opportunity of selling their surpluses in the British market in order to counterbalance their deficits in other parts of the world market. In this situation a certain international solidarity emerged, though it did not prevent, at the same time, vigorous competition for markets and investment fields and growing international tensions.

Although modifications in capital and income flows continually took place in the multilateral trading pattern it retained its principal outlines down to the First World War. It worked out very much to the advantage of British trade and finance as well as to the other advanced countries. However, its preservation depended, amongst other things, on continued long-term capital investment from Britain, the predominance of London as a financial centre, the maintenance of the gold standard and the free entry of commodities to the British market. Its preservation, until it was upset by war, was of mutual interest to the participants. For powerful vested interests in Britain it was a veritable condition for prosperity if not for survival. On the question of free trade, it was a matter which depended not only on the vested interest of all those sections of business which profited from a high volume of world trade but also on the support of the electorate, among a majority of which it enjoyed a quasi-religious status. To discuss the possibility of increasing home investment at the expense of foreign investment, encouraging home industry by tariffs, releasing financial policy from its orthodox attachment to the gold standard autonomism, or any change which damaged the interests of the City of London, would be to make a whole series of unreal assumptions. The British economy at this time formed a close-knit and coherent whole. One part could not have been changed without setting in motion a chain reaction, as a result of which nothing would have remained the same as at the start of the exercise. But where could such a change have come from? Only from an autonomous initiative on the part of private enterprise or of government, both of which were historically conditioned to a course of behaviour unlikely to change fundamentally except under extreme pressure—war, social crisis or economic breakdown.

There was, that is to say, once again, something inevitable about this pattern of development and about the subsequent course of the British economy. It was very much the prisoner of its history. But its history of economic leadership and continued maritime, financial and colonial power still contributed tangible economic benefits which, until we move on and consider the long-term results, have to be recognized. The period up to 1914 was for the bourgeoisie something of a golden age of prosperity and security when the society which it had built reached its apogee. This was in many ways true of Britain because, despite the evidence of the loss of industrial leadership, the worldwide interests in the sphere of trade, shipping, insurance and finance were still prospering.

The physiognomy of British capitalism on the eve of the world crisis which began in 1914 is that of an old, mature and rich economy, deeply involved in the world market, sedate and somewhat inflexible in the face of the new forces of change. It had been shaped in a peculiar economic mould constituted by a centuries-long process of the formation of capitalist relations and the pioneer character of her industrialization. Many of the advantages

of the early developer in the shape of accumulated wealth, a privileged position in world trade and finance, the possession of a large
colonial empire, were still retained. On the other hand, there was
carried over into the twentieth century a dead weight of institutions,
economic structures, technologies, habits of mind and behaviour
patterns which had crystallized out in the early period of industrial
advance and economic predominance. This was the case, for
example, in the field of business organization. Firms which had
once appeared to be large and progressive were now too small and
had become hidebound by routine. The old empirical methods
satisfactory in an earlier stage of technology when advance could
only be made by a kind of inspired tinkering and intuition were out-
dated in fields where there could be no efficient production without
continuous laboratory control.

On the Continent and in the United States this period saw the
rise of giant business units, trusts and cartels which made markets
increasingly imperfect. At the same time, the large volume of
capital needed to establish the giant plants in which the newer
techniques could be most economically employed brought closer
and more sustained association between manufacturing firms and
the banks. At least in the field of large-scale production the old
competitive capitalism was disappearing. The giant manufacturing
units supplied such a large proportion of the market, operating as
they did over a long range of increasing returns, that competition
was inherently unstable. To realize the maximum economies from
the more advanced techniques vertical concentration became a
pronounced tendency. Agreements to divide the market, to fix
prices or to merge completely replaced the old competitive tussle
between separate firms. Now, while all these tendencies did display
themselves in Britain they were much weaker than in the newer
industrial countries. The existing old established firms behaved in
an individualist and exclusive manner towards their British as well
as foreign rivals. There was, for example, a marked reluctance to
pool information or to discuss common technical problems. Where
employers came together it was more likely to be to present a
united front to the trade unions than to control the market. The
tendency for British industry to continue with the old techniques,
or to adapt only slowly to the new technologies, diminished the

effectiveness of one of the forces making for combination. In the strongholds of industry the family type firm still remained characteristic even where it was now concealed behind the façade offered by the Company Laws and made use of their facilities to achieve corporate identity and continuity. Since the capital market provided only a small proportion of industrial finance and the banks continued to maintain their traditional policy of non-involvement in long-term industrial investment or promotion, the financial pressures making for combination, which were important in other countries, were virtually absent.

If the momentum of the historically derived structures prolonged the life of individualist and competitive forces, public policies and opinion acted in the same way. The openness of the British market acted as a deterrent to the growth of monopoly. In fields exposed to foreign competition the scope for price maintenance was strictly limited. Raw materials came largely from foreign sources so that there was little basis for the rise of monopoly on the basis of control of physical resources. The coal industry, growing up in the early period of individualist capitalism, had always been highly fragmented and although there were some giant mining enterprises they could not pretend to control prices. The main price maintenance schemes and successful combinations before 1914 are to be found in industries able to be sure of the home market or having a product for which there were no close substitutes of domestic or foreign provenance. Thus, although there were clear signs of a decline of competitive forces in some fields the old individualist nature of British business remained basically unaltered. Public opinion, the courts, and the government were, moreover, suspicious of, and hostile towards, actions in restraint of trade. There was undiminished confidence in the virtues of competition.

If combination into giant integrated concerns and the growing interpenetration of industrial and banking capital were the hallmarks of the most advanced stage of capitalism, Britain could be said, in the years before 1914, to be definitely lagging behind. The country in which capitalism had its longest continuous history and whose society had been most profoundly transformed by the Industrial Revolution was not the one in which the inherent tendencies of industrial capitalism were worked out earliest to their

8

full conclusion. On the contrary, structures and habits derived from the earlier, pioneer stages were carried forward into an era where they appeared to be archaic vestiges. At the same time, their distant origin and involvement with the whole economic and social structure made them extremely deeply rooted and tenacious: they still conserved a good deal of vitality fifty years later.

Yet these archaic features, although they do include some remnants of a still earlier, precapitalist past – the monarchy, the hereditary nobility and the traditional pageantry and symbolism of 'Old England' – were essentially capitalist in their origin and nature. Moreover, Britain was the most thoroughly transformed of the industrial countries by the processes of industrialization and urbanization. The non-capitalist and preindustrial remnants were merely decorative. There had for a long time been no place for a peasant class or very much for independent small commodity producers in the artisan industries. The landed upper class, though it conserved some superficial 'feudal' traits, had long been integrated into a market economy. Its coalescence with the wealthy bourgeois families was now going on more rapidly than ever before. There were no special backward regions in which precapitalist relations retained their strength. The social structure was shaped in an urban mould to which the rural areas were increasingly obliged to conform. There was a much greater degree of homogeneity in consumer patterns than was to be found in other countries where geographical lines of development had been more uneven. Income distribution was still sharply unequal and at the bottom remained low. Wealth and income were the prime determinants of the placement of the individual and the family in the social pyramid; the older lines of status were nowhere so blurred outside the 'new' countries such as the United States. There was virtually no section of the population still clinging to self-sufficiency. To live, a money income was indispensable and if it did not come from property it had to come, as was the case with the great majority, from the sale of labour power in the market. A more complex and variegated occupational pattern on the basis of market relations probably existed at this time nowhere else in the world. This was the consummate expression of a free market economy still operating on mainly competitive lines and with the intervention of the state confined to fields such as education and factory legislation where the free operation of market forces had proved socially intolerable or unworkable.

To see the British economy in this period as only the seedbed for the problems which were to beset it in the twentieth century would thus be one-sided. As a result of its leadership in the creation of a modern capitalist economy, those who owned its industrial plants and business enterprises continued to enjoy definite advantages. Their accumulated wealth and the size of their income gave them a viability and room for manœuvre even in the face of setbacks and foreign competition which must seem enviable to their successors today. True, the apparent invulnerability of their position made them complacent to a degree, and slowed down the adoption of techniques, methods of organization and changes in policy which might have made the adaptation of British capitalism to the changes of the twentieth century less painful. To lay blame on the businessmen and the ruling class of the pre-1914 era for later misfortunes is easy for those who possess the advantage of hindsight. At the time they behaved as men of their stamp and class, in a particular historically determined position, could have been expected to do. It would have been remarkable, indeed, had they acted as a class, in response to market indicators and social pressures, in a fundamentally different way. What the history of the British economy in this period seems to show is that the classic forces of the market, the old-style capitalism, had become anachronistic. They could survive for so long in Britain only because of specially favourable conditions. Following the brusque snatching away of some of them by the war of 1914–18, a more or less thorough process of transformation had to begin, but it was far from completion when another war once again altered the whole world economy to Britain's disadvantage and removed some of the remaining assets from the past which had been cushioning the readjustment. To say that the roots of the problems of British capitalism lay in the period 1870–1914 contains an indubitable truth. In a way they have their origin still further back. But it would be unrealistic to separate them from the new climacteric in the economic history of world capitalism which followed the onset of war in 1914 and the general crisis in the system which it inaugurated.

Problems for discussion

1. How far can the weaknesses of the British economy in the period 1870–1914 be attributed to lack of entrepreneurial ability or zeal?

2. Examine the pattern of British foreign trade in the 1880s and trace the major changes which took place in it up to the First World War.

3. Why did Britain remain a free trade country in this period?

4. Was the amount of capital invested abroad by British citizens excessive?

5. Would it be true to say that in this period British industry was suffering from the disadvantages of having been first in the field?

6. What were the major sources of British prosperity in the pre-1914 period?

7. Account for the continued predominance of Britain in the field of international investment and finance.

8. How far can it be said that the problems of the British economy in the mid-twentieth century have their roots in the last quarter of the nineteenth century?

Appendix

This is expressly not a statistical or quantitative study but concentrates primarily on structures. The principal aggregates such as industrial and agricultural production, national income, foreign trade and length of railway line, as well as more sophisticated indices are to be found in the works cited in the bibliography. Many problems are involved in the measurement of economic growth in the nineteenth century and accurate intercountry comparisons are especially difficult to make. When an effort is made to translate a term which is essentially structural in origin into quantitative terms it becomes still more difficult. Is it possible to say when industrialization begins, to define it statistically in terms of a 'take-off'? Can the degree of industrialization be measured and different stages distinguished? On what basis is it possible to say that one country is more industrialized than another?

The approach by means of income per head and comparisons in terms of some international monetary unit to which the incomes of different countries may be reduced is perhaps now the most common. Combined with the breakdown of occupational distribution into primary (agriculture fisheries, etc), secondary (manufacturing and processing) and tertiary (services), it enables a general classification to be made. Once such distinctions are made countries may be placed in different stages of development according to their income levels. The works of Colin Clark, *The Conditions of Economic Progress* and W. G. Hoffman, *The Growth of Industrial Economies* show what can be done with modern statistical techniques.

Some other measures of the levels of economic development of the advanced countries have recently been offered by P. Bairoch in an article entitled 'Niveaux de développement économique de 1810 à 1910', *Annales: Économies, Sociétés, Civilisations*, 20e. année, no. 6, Nov–Déc., 1965. He has constructed some tables based on *per capita* consumption of the basic raw materials of nineteenth-century industrialism, the use of power, production of agriculture and utilization of railways. Such partial measures have the advantage of statistical material of a high degree of accuracy and inter-country comparability making it possible to establish an order of industrialization.

By way of example, then, here are Bairoch's tables for cotton, coal and pig iron in kilograms *per capita* for the countries dealt with in this book and reclassified.

Raw cotton, kg. per cap.

	1840	1860	1880	1900	1910
United Kingdom	7·3	15·1	17·3	18·7	19·8
Germany	0·9	1·4	2·9	5·8	6·8
France	1·5	2·7	2·6	4·5	6·0
Russia	0·3	0·5	1·0	1·6	3·0
Italy	0·1	0·2	1·1	4·0	5·4

(*Source:* Bairoch, Tableau, 3 modified)

Pig iron, kg. per cap.

	1810	1840	1860	1880	1900	1910	(steel) 1910
United Kingdom	20	54	130	220	220	210	150
Germany	2	5	14	53	130	200	220
France	4	12	25	46	65	100	100
Russia	–	3	5	5	25	31	38
Italy	–	1	2	1	1	8	28

(*Source:* Bairoch, Tableau 4)

Coal consumption kg. per cap.

	1810	1840	1860	1880	1900	1910
United Kingdom	600	1110	2450	3740	4070	4040
Germany	–	110	400	1170	2650	3190
France	40	130	390	740	1200	1450
Russia	–	–	–	70	190	300
Italy	–	–	–	100	150	270

(*Source:* Bairoch, Tableau 6)

The relative importance of the industrialization of the countries chosen for study can be seen clearly enough from these and the other tables Bairoch presents.

They can be complemented with a few figures of total output in 1913 in millions of tons:

	Coal	Pig iron	Steel	Population (mn)
United Kingdom	292	10·4	7·7	45 (1911)
Germany	190	16·7	17·5	64 (1910)
(1913 frontiers)				
France	40	5·2	4·6	39 (1910)
(1913 frontiers)				
Russia	35	4·6	4·0	175
Italy	0·7	0·4	0·9	36 (1914)

Proportions of the occupied population engaged in agriculture give a useful indication of the extent of industrialization. In the years immediately before 1914 the following approximate percentages may be offered.

France: 33%   Germany: 23·8%
Italy: 59·8%   Russia: 86%

On a world scale Bairoch suggests that the United States over-hauled Britain in level of industrial development by about 1900. Germany had overhauled France by 1880 and was catching up Britain, but in 1910 was still behind Belgium. Switzerland was ahead of France, and Italy and Russia, in that order, were behind Sweden and Spain. This placing does not take account of aggregate industrial power, which would require France to be moved ahead of Belgium and Switzerland. Italy and Russia were handicapped not only by the weight of agriculture in their economies but by the fact that it was only about one-fourth or one-third as productive as that in the U.S.A. in terms of labour expended. In other words economic development required a great increase in the productivity of agriculture as well as a reduction in its relative weight in the less developed countries.

Bibliographical Note

The economic history of the principal European countries is still not well covered in English. Despite the strongly established position of economic history in the British universities it tends in content to be focused exclusively upon Britain, to suffer from insularity or even parochialism. The volume of research or interesting writing on European economic development from this source is therefore disappointingly small. Many of the textbooks in use or recommended to students were written some time ago and, whatever their merits, they do not adequately reflect the latest trends in the subject.

There is now considerably more research on European economic history being done by Americans than by British academics and some of this is of a very high quality. However, this gives a probably exaggerated impression of the general level of interest in European economic history on the other side of the Atlantic. In fact economic history of any sort is much less strongly represented in American universities (with some notable exceptions) than is the case in this country. It is certainly not generally accepted as a necessary part of undergraduate studies in economics as is the case in most British universities.

Such need as does exist is therefore catered for by two or three general texts which, however good, tend not to reflect the present trends in the subject at all adequately. In the European countries themselves, especially in the West, there has been growing interest in economic history in recent years but even so the place of the discipline in undergraduate studies is still considerably inferior to that in Britain and this is reflected in the volume and quality of the literature which appears. Moreover, no doubt in large part because of the limited nature of the market in this country and in the United

States, very little of the new work in European languages has been translated into English.

The student of European Economic History, whether at the undergraduate or at a more advanced level, once he has acquainted himself with some general texts, unless he possesses one or more foreign languages, is confronted with a comparative paucity of monographic material. Some aspects of the subject are covered reasonably well, but there are big gaps, particularly, as might be expected, in the history of particular firms and industries or in regional studies. Of course, such studies are not always available in the language of the country concerned, let alone in English. In many ways, the student has therefore to make do with second best or reach what conclusions he can on the basis of fragmentary evidence. European economic history, especially comparative history, offers enormous scope for research and specialized study as well as for provisional synthesis of the scattered and partial conclusions which emerge from specialized work already done.

The aim of this bibliography is to offer a guide to the main works in English, especially those which have been found useful in writing the chapters which precede it. For useful surveys on orthodox lines there are two American texts in print, H. Heaton, *Economic History* (Harper & Row 1948) and S. B. Clough, and C. W. Cole, *An Economic History of Europe* (Harrap 1952). A more detailed account of the nineteenth century is to be found in W. Bowden, M. Karpovitch, and A. P. Usher, *An Economic History of Europe since 1750* (American Book Company 1937).

At a more advanced level there is the relevant section of the *Cambridge Economic History of Europe*, vol. VI, *The Industrial Revolutions and After* (ed. H. J. Habakkuk and M. Postan, Cambridge U.P. (1965), in two parts, of which the chapter by D. S. Landes, 'Technological Change and Development in Western Europe 1750–1914' is invaluable. A useful volume of documents edited by S. Pollard and C. Holmes entitled *The Process of Industrialization*, 1750–1870 (Arnold, 1968) appeared after the completion of this book. A second volume is in preparation.

At the point where economic history meets with the problems raised by economists concerned with growth and development there have been a number of interesting contributions. Selecting the most important by historians there is the influential work of W. W. Rostow, *The Stages of Economic Growth* (Cambridge University Press, 1960), whose ideas have, by implication been rejected, the essays by A. Gerschenkron collected in *Economic Backwardness in Historical Perspective* (Pall Mall Press 1966) which have influenced some sections of the present work and B. Supple's introduction to his collection of readings, *The Experience of Economic Growth* (Random House 1963). The Rostow thesis has been subjected to considerable criticism and some views on it will be found in the book edited by W. W. Rostow, *The Economics of Take-off into Sustained Growth* (Macmillan 1963).

Some suggestive works have been produced which integrate economic history with the broader forces of cultural and political development. Necessarily efforts of this sort are open to criticism: they have to take up firm positions on controversial questions and make judgments where the empirical evidence is often uncertain. However, by getting away from a narrow, over-specialized view of the field they serve a useful purpose, generate interest and reveal fruitful lines for future research. Of recent works in this category the following should be noted: E. J. Hobsbawm, *The Age of Revolution* (Weidenfeld & Nicolson 1962), which covers the period 1789 to 1848, C. Morazé, *The Triumph of the Middle Classes* (Weidenfeld & Nicolson 1966), which covers the whole of the nineteenth century and B. Moore, *The Social Origins of Dictatorship and Democracy* (A. Lane 1967), which draws upon a wide range of historical data in an effort to explain the political diversity of a number of countries including Japan, India and the U.S.A.

For students who want to begin with something more basic or require a handy resumé of essential factual material the works by A. Birnie, *An Economic History of Europe, 1760–1939* (8th edn, Methuen 1950) and W. O. Henderson, *The Industrial Revolution on the Continent* (F. Cass 1961), are useful but not inspiring. J. H. Clapham's classic, *The Economic Development of France and Germany 1815–1914* (4th edn., Cambridge U.P. 1936), remains an indispensable starting point for a study of these countries. Nevertheless, its very rigour can deter the student and it should be used in conjunction with the more adventurous treatments mentioned above.

As more general background reading for a course in European

economic history the following works should be mentioned: W. Sombart, *The Jews and Modern Capitalism* (n.e. Collier-Macmillan, 1963 with Introduction by B. Hoselitz), M. Weber, *General Economic History* (Collier-Macmillan 1961) and *The Protestant Ethic and the Spirit of Capitalism* (Allen & Unwin 1965). However wrong these books may be the theses which they stated have been a powerful stimulus to thought and to research. The Marxist view can be studied in *Capital* — substantial sections of volume I are concerned with economic history — and chapter 20 of volume III should also be studied. The only important general study by a presentday Marxist in this field is M. Dobb, *Studies in the Development of Capitalism* (Routledge 1946), which is, however, mainly confined to Britain though it does, in a limited way, draw upon the experience of other countries. Some parts of J. A. Schumpeter's *Capitalism, Socialism and Democracy* (Allen & Unwin 1965) are stimulating for the historian as are parts of K. Polanyi's *Origins of Our Time* (Gollancz 1945).

There are a number of works, in addition to those mentioned, which contain material relating to two or more countries. W. O. Henderson's *Britain and Industrial Europe 1750–1870* (2nd edn; Leicester University Press 1966) deals very competently with the influence of British technique, capital and entrepreneurship in European industrialization. H. Feis, *Europe the World's Banker* (New York, Kelley 1930), is a standard work on European capital exports. W. Ashworth, *A Short History of the International Economy since 1850* (2nd edn., Longmans 1962), is a useful textbook treatment. There is a statistical study of industrialization in W. G. Hoffmann, *Growth of Industrial Economies* (Manchester University Press 1958).

There is a vast literature on economic growth: for the student of economic history the following books are particularly useful in helping to provide a theoretical groundwork: W. A. Lewis, *The Theory of Economic Growth* (Allen & Unwin in 1955), A. J. Youngson, *Possibilities of Economic Progress* (Cambridge U.P. 1959), and N. S. Buchanan and H. S. Ellis, *Approaches to Economic Development* (New York, Twentieth Century Fund 1954).

On British industrialization there is now a constantly lengthening list of books and with the application of quantitative methods an entirely new approach has been developed. However, some of the older works continue to hold their own, especially P. Mantoux, *The Industrial Revolution in the Eighteenth Century* (1st edn. in French, Paris 1906; Methuen, University paperback), J. L. and B. Hammond, *The Rise of Modern Industry* (Methuen 1925; paperback edn. 1966), and T. S. Ashton, *The Industrial Revolution 1760–1830* (Oxford University Press 1948). The growth of economic history as a university discipline since the end of the Second World War has had as one of its main results a large number of books devoted to the period of the Industrial Revolution. However, there remains a strongly marked empirical strain in much of this work and a reluctance to draw general conclusions. The interpretation of the process continues to give rise to discussion and debate leaving the student with the impression that no firm conclusions have been, or perhaps can be, reached. Of recent works for the student the following may be mentioned: P. Deane and W. A. Cole, *British Economic Growth, 1688–1959* (Cambridge U.P. 1962), is a pioneer attempt to apply quantitative methods; P. Deane's own interpretation is contained in *The First Industrial Revolution* (Cambridge U.P. 1965), and M. W. Flinn makes a useful survey of the literature for the student in *The Origins of the Industrial Revolution* (Longmans 1966). All these works have their shortcomings and the criticism to which they have been subject show how far we still are from a consensus. For a more sceptical treatment in an introduction to a useful collection of essays, see R. M. Hartwell, *The Causes of the Industrial Revolution in England* (Methuen 1967). The same author has produced an outline for the general reader or beginner in the Historical Association pamphlet entitled *The Industrial Revolution in England* (rev. edn. 1966).

S. Pollard writes, authoritatively, amongst other things, on the sources of capital accumulation and the problems of recruiting a labour force for the early factories in *The Genesis of Modern Management* (E. Arnold 1965). L. S. Presnall's *Country Banking in the Industrial Revolution* (Oxford U.P. 1956) is the standard book in its field. On banking see also the chapter by Rondo Cameron in the book which he has edited entitled *Banking in the Early Stages of Industrialization* (Oxford U.P. 1967).

There are few general studies to accompany the chapter on the agrarian revolution, which used the term in the widest sense to embrace the transition from traditional to market-oriented agriculture. There are many detailed studies and a considerable field for differences of opinion about many aspects of agrarian change. For a good general history see B. H. Slicher van Barth, *The Agrarian History of Western Europe* (Edward Arnold 1963) and, for the nineteenth century, M. Tracey, *Agriculture in Western Europe* (New York, Praeger 1964). On France, M. Bloch's *French Rural History* (trans. J. Sondheimer, Routledge 1966) is a classic. The important studies of the French peasantry in the Revolutionary period by G. Lefevbre have not been translated in their entirety. Some relevant articles will be cited under France. The controversy over the English enclosures continues. The Hammonds' *The Village Labourer* (1911; n.e. Longmans 1966) is still essential reading. The modern school revisionist is well represented by J. D. Chambers and G. E. Mingay, *The Agricultural Revolution, 1750–1880* (Batsford 1966).

Apart from Clapham, *op. cit.*, only S. B. Clough's *France: a History of National Economics* (ne. New York, Octagon 1964) covers the economic history of France for the whole of the nineteenth century. The latter work remains useful but concentrates mainly on the policy of the state and the tariff and is now somewhat dated. A forthcoming work by the present author, *Economic Forces in French History*, attempts a more interpretative treatment with the help of recent research which has appeared both in French and in English.

A. L. Dunham's *The Industrial Revoltion in France 1815–1848* (New York, Exposition Press 1955) is a scholarly piece of research which tends to overwhelm the reader with its mass of factual material. The same author's earlier work, *The Anglo-French Treaty of Commerce of 1860 and the Progress of the Industrial Revolution in France* (Ann Arbor, Univ. of Michigan Press 1930) remains the standard work on the subject. Interest in French economic history has been maintained by a number of American scholars, notably Rondo Cameron and D. S. Landes. The former's work, *France and the Economic Development of Europe*, (2nd edn. Rand McNally 1967) contains a good deal of valuable information about the French economy but is principally a study of French investment and financial influence in other European countries. His chapter on French banking in the work previously cited is a useful and up-to-date summary. Further glimpses of the French financial scene can be found in D. S. Landes, *Bankers and Pashas in Egypt* (Heinemann 1958).

For attempts to explain the peculiarities of the French economy in the nineteenth century and its alleged retardation the student has to bear in mind the actual or implied comparison with the development of other countries. A stimulating starting point is provided by the brilliant article of F. Crouzet, 'England and France in the Eighteenth Century: A Comparative Analysis of Two Economic Growths' in R. M. Hartwell, *op. cit.* Different viewpoints on the following century are provided in S. B. Clough, 'Retardative factors in French economic growth', *Journal of Economic History*, Supplement, 1946. D. S. Landes, 'French entrepreneurship and industrial growth', *Journal of Economic History*, ix, May 1949. R. C. Cameron, 'Economic growth and stagnation in France', *Journal of Modern History*, xxx, no. 1, 1958, and T. Kemp, 'Structural factors in the retardation of French economic growth', *Kylos*, xv, 1962, fasc. 2.

An ambitious but not altogether successful attempt to tackle the problem on an explicitly comparative basis is provided by C. Kindleberger, *Economic Growth in France and Britain*, 1851–1950 (Harvard U.P. 1964). As a pioneer work of its type it deserves attention and it contains a detailed bibliography.

Apart from the article by Landes already cited, the French entrepreneur has been examined by him in 'French Business and the Businessman: a Social and Cultural Analysis', in E. M. Earle, *Modern France*, by J. E. Sawyer in 'The Entrepreneur and the Social Order: France and the United States' in W. Miller, ed. *Men in Business* (Harvard U.P. 1952; Harper Torchbooks) and by B. Hoselitz in 'Entrepreneurship and Capital Formation in France and Britain since 1700' in M. Abramovitz, ed. *Capital Formation and Economic Growth* (Princeton U.P. 1955). The French entrepreneur comes out of these comparisons rather badly and there is a danger of laying excessive blame upon him for the behaviour of the French economy and creating an unhelpful stereotype. P. Stearns shows in 'British industry through the eyes of French industrialists', *Journal of Modern History*, xxxvii, 1965, how afraid they were of British competition. All these studies give insufficient weight to the adjustment which French business made to its markets and competitive position and do not deal adequately with its successes.

Rostow's take-off thesis has been challenged very effectively by the leading authority on French historical statistics, J. Marczewski, in 'The take-off hypothesis and French experience' in Rostow, ed. *op. cit*. See also his article, 'Some aspects of the economic growth of France' in *Economic Development and Cultural Change*, xi, no. 3, 1961, for a statistical outline.

Of the other works in English which deal with particular aspects of French economic development the following may be mentioned. On agriculture: R. R. Palmer 'Lefebvre and the French peasants', *Journal of Modern History*, xxxi no. 4, 1959, F. L. Sargent, 'From feudalism to family farms in France, *Agricultural History*, xxv, no. 4, 1961, A. Davies, 'The origins of the French peasant revolution', *History*, xlix, no. 165, 1964, On the tariff, F. A. Haight, *A History of French Commercial Policies* (New York, Macmillan 1941) and E. O. Golob, *The Méline Tariff* (Columbia U.P. 1944). H. D. White's *The French International Accounts* (Harvard U.P. 1933) is useful but should be used with caution in view of R. C. Cameron's criticism in *France and the Economic Development of Europe 1800–1914* (Princeton U.P. 1961). K. A. Doukas, *French Railways and the State* (Columbia U.P. 1945) covers some aspects of an important subject. C. E. Freedeman's article, 'Joint stock business organisation in France, 1807–1867' in *Business History Review*, xxxix, no. 2, 1965, is useful.

Other background material may be found in articles in the book edited by E. M. Earle already cited, in S. R. Hoffmann, ed. *In Search of France* (Harvard U.P. 1963; published in U.K. as *France: Change and Tradition*, Gollancz 1963), in G. Chapman, *The Third Republic of France* (Macmillan 1962) and in the section on 'The French economy' in the E.C.E. *Economic Survey of Europe 1954.*

Apart from Clapham there is no general economic history of Germany in the nineteenth century, though some aspects are covered in W. O. Henderson, *The Industrial Revolution on the Continent*.

The early nineteenth century is dealt with best in T. S. Hamerow's *Restoration, Revolution, Reaction* (Princeton U.P.; O.U.P. 1966) but it is intended as an explanation of German political development not as an economic history. The later nineteenth and the twentieth century are dealt with more fully, but for the earlier period the student will have to depend to a large extent upon monographs. The main German works have not been translated, a fact which presumably reflects the low level of interest in German economic studies in the English-speaking countries.

On the period after 1870 see G. Stolper (and others in the new edition) *The German Economy 1870 to the Present Day* (Weidenfeld & Nicolson 1967), which, however, only deals in a rather summary fashion with the nineteenth century. The work by W. F. Bruck, *Social and Economic History of Germany from William II to Hitler* (Oxford UP. 1938) contains much useful material but it is presented as part of a philosophical approach which the reader may find heavy and indigestible.

Some stimulating points are made in comparing German economic development and structure with those of other countries in D. S. Landes's paper, 'The structure of enterprise in the nineteenth century' given to the Eleventh International History Congress, 1960, and included in its *Proceedings*. See also his chapter 'Japan and Europe: Contrasts in Industrialization' in W. W. Lockwood ed. *The State and Economic Enterprise in Japan* (Princeton U.P.; O.U.P. 1966).

W. O. Henderson attributes a more positive role to the Prussian bureaucracy than some of his critics in his works *The State and the Industrial Revolution in Russia* (Liverpool U.P. 1958) and *Studies in the Economic Policy of Frederick the Great* (F. Cass 1963). His study, *The Zollverein* (Cambridge U.P. 1939), is invaluable; see also A. H. Price, *The Evolution of the Zollverein* (Ann Arbor, Univ. of Michigan Press, 1949).

The special character of German banking is examined by R. Tilly in his chapter in Rondo Cameron ed., *Banking in the Early Stages of Industrialization*, and its origins are traced out more fully in his fine study, *Financial Institution and Industrialization in the Rhineland* (Wisconsin U.P. 1966). Clearly many more studies of this quality on German economic history are needed. Cameron's own book contains interesting sections devoted to German finance.

9

On the agrarian reforms see W. Conze, 'Agrarian reform in Central Europe' in G. S. Metraux and F. Crouzet, *The Nineteenth Century World* (Mentor, New American Library 1963), the summary in Tracey, *op. cit.* and F. Wunderlich, *Farm Labor in Germany 1810–1945* (Princeton U.P. 1961).

The impact of industrialization on the traditional German social structure provides the theme for a number of writers. T. Veblen deals with it in his characteristic and idiosyncratic way in *Imperial Germany and the Industrial Revolution* (Univ. of Michigan Press; Cresset 1966). For the student the book is likely to prove a disappointment since it does not deal, as the title might lead one to believe, with the actual process of industrialization. The writings of Gerschenkron already cited are important here. See the paper by R. A. Brady, 'The economic impact of Imperial Germany: industrial policy', *Journal of Economic History*, Supplement, *The Tasks of Economic History*, Dec., 1945. On similar themes see H. Rosenberg, 'Political and Social Consequences of the Great Depression of 1873–1896 in Central Europe' in *Economic History Review*, xii, 1943—this has been expanded into a book length study of the Bismarck era which has not appeared in English. Also, H. Lebovics, ' "Agrarians" versus "Industrializers": social conservative resistance to industrialism and capitalism in late nineteenth-century Germany', *International Review of Social History*, xi, no 1, 1967, which emphasizes the problems of adjustment.

The remaining monographic material is thin. J. J. Beer's thesis, *The Emergence of the German Dye Industry* (Illinois U.P. 1959) deals with and explains an important industrial success. W. Röpke's *German Commercial Policy* (Longmans 1934) is a useful summary from the point of view of economic liberalism. N. J. G. Pounds *The Ruhr: a study in historical and economic geography* (Faber 1952) is a valuable study by an economic geographer which contains some historical material on this key industrial area. There is also some historical material in the same author's collaborative study with W. N. Parker, *Coal and Steel in Western Europe* (Faber 1957). The impact of German competition in Britain is dealt with in R. J. S. Hoffman's *Great Britain and the German Trade Rivalry 1875–1914* (University of Philadelphia Press 1933; rep. New York, Russell 1964).

H. Kisch is studying the Rhineland textile industries in the earlier period, see 'Growth deterrents of a medieval heritage: the Aachen-area woollen trades before 1790', *Journal of Economic History*, Dec. 1964, xxiv.

The student of Russian economic history is fairly well served in English, on the whole more amply than in the case of Germany which has been scandalously neglected. Even in the Cambridge Economic History Russia is accorded two chapters, by Gershchenkron and Portal, while Germany is dealt with as part of Western Europe.

Thanks to the American Council of Learned Societies a substantial Soviet textbook has been translated, P. I. Lyashchenko's *History of the National Economy of Russia* (New York, Macmillan 1949). It is, or purports to be, a Marxist interpretation; made in the Stalin era, it thus tends to be rigid and doctrinaire but it is a very full, indeed invaluable, factual account. J. Mavor's book *An Economic History of Russia* (Dent 1914) was written before the Bolshevik Revolution made Russian economic history a field liable to passion and distortion. It provides a useful measuring rod for later work.

B. H. Sumner's *A Survey of Russian History* (2nd edn. Duckworth 1948; Methuen University paperbacks) deals with social and economic development. A number of chapters in C. E. Black, ed. *The Transformation of Russian Society since 1861* (Harvard U.P. 1960) are useful introductions to their field. M. H. Dobb, *Soviet Economic Development since 1917* (rev. edn. New York, International Publishers 1967) summarizes earlier development in Chapter Two. M. Miller's *The Economic Development of Russia, 1905–1914* (2nd edn., F. Cass 1967), is a useful guide to the period.

Most of these works include their own type of interpretation. The thesis put forward minimizing the role of serfdom in Russia's belated economic growth by A. Baykov, because it is unorthodox and thought-provoking, should certainly be read; it is in *Economic History Review*, 2nd series, vii, 1954–5, and is entitled 'The economic development of Russia'. See also the article by H. J. Ellison, 'Economic modernisation in Imperial Russia', which, however, is a mainly factual summary, in *Journal of Economic History*, xxv, Dec. 1965.

Statistics of Russian economic development are given by Gerschenkron *op. cit.*, but the field has been reworked more recently by R. W. Goldsmith in an article entitled 'The economic growth of Russia' in *Economic Development and Cultural Change*, ix, no. 3, 1961 (Johnson Reprint Corp., New York, 1966).

Agriculture has been necessarily accorded a good deal of attention because of the problem of serfdom. The situation before 1861 is dealt with on the grand scale by J. Blum, *Lord and Peasant in Russia* (New York, Atheneum 1964). Perhaps the best introduction to the later period remains G. T. Robinson, *Rural Russia under the Old Regime* (New York, Macmillan 1967). See also L. Owen *The Russian Peasant Movement* (New York, Russell 1963), D. W. Treadgold, *The Great Siberian Migration* (Princeton U.P. 1967) and G. L. Yamey, 'The concept of the Stolypin land reform', *The Slavic Review*, xxiii, no. 2, 1964. For Lenin's views see 'The agrarian question in Russia' in V. I. Lenin, *Collected Works*, vol. 15.

Olga Crisp's contribution to the collective volume on banking edited by Cameron is an excellent introduction to the field; see also her article 'Russian financial policy and the gold standard', *Economic History Review*, 2nd series, vi, no. 2, 1953–4.

The problems of labour recruitment have been dealt with by G. V. Rimlinger, 'Autocracy and the factory order in early Russian industrialization', *Journal of Economic History*, xx, Mar. 1960, and 'The expansion of the labour market in capitalist Russia, 1861–1917', *Journal of Economic History*, xxi, June 1961; and T. H. Von Laue's 'Russian peasants in the factory', *Journal of Economic History*, xxi, 1961.

The issues facing the autocracy at the turn of the nineteenth century are seen through the career of the outstanding statesman of the period in T. H. Von Laue's *Sergei Witte and the Industrialization of Russia* (Columbia U.P. 1963). The dilemmas of the Liberals are dealt with in G. Fischer's *Russian Liberalism* (Harvard U.P. 1958). V. I. Lenin's *The Development of Capitalism in Russia* (English translation *Collected Works*, vol. 3, Lawrence & Wishart, 1960) contains a mass of data besides a vigorous polemic against the Narodnik school. The literature of the other side is not so readily available but summaries are in the works already cited. There are numerous works on the nineteenth century revolutionary move-

ment, the intelligentsia and the pre-1917 labour movement which
shed some light on economic development. F. Venturi's *Roots of
Revolution* (London, Wiedenfeld and Nicholson; New York, Knopf
1960) is outstanding.

The list of works in English on Italian economic development is
the shortest of all. Until the appearance of S. B. Clough's *Economic
History of Modern Italy* (Columbia U.P. 1964) no general work
was available. Clough does not depart very far from an empirical
treatment but he has pointed the way. There is much economic
history in M. F. Neufeld, *Italy: School for Awakening Countries*
(New York School of Industrial and Labor Relations, Cornell
University 1965), though it draws heavily on well-known articles,
namely, A. Gerschenkron, 'Observations on the Rate of Economic
Growth in Italy', *Journal of Economic History*, xv, no. 9, 1955 (also
in *op. cit.*) and S. B. Clough and Levy, 'Economic growth in Italy',
Journal of Economic History, xvi, no. 3, 1956.

C. Seton-Watson, *Italy from Liberalism to Fascism* (Methuen
1967), which is an excellent general history, while modest about its
pretensions in the field of economic history, contains useful material.
See also D. Mack Smith, *Italy: a Modern History* ((University of
Michigan Press; Cresset 1959), R. Grew, 'How success spoiled
the Risorgimento', *Journal of Modern History*, xxxiv, 1962, and
J. M. Cammett, 'Two recent polemics on the character of the
Risorgimento', *Science and Society*, xxvii, no. 4, 1963.

There are some suggestive points in Gerschenkron, *op. cit.* On
the role of the banks see the recent article by J. S. Cohen, 'Financing
Industrialization in Italy, 1894–1914: the partial transformation of
a latecomer', *Journal of Economic History*, xxvii, 1967.

The literature on the Southern Question is not abundant in
English. See particularly, R. S. Eckaus, 'The north-south differential in Italian economic development', *Journal of Economic
History*, xxi, 1961, for a statistical analysis. Some of the basic
facts are in A. Molinari, 'Southern Italy' in *Banca Nazionale del
Lavoro, Quarterly Review*, viii, 1949, and F. Vochting – author
of a major work on the subject – 'Industrialization and pre-indus-
trialization in Southern Italy', *Banca Nazionale del Lavoro, Quarterly
Review*, xxi, 1952. For a general view of the problem in its social
setting and as part of a wider Mediterranean problem the student

will find G. Schachter, *The Italian South* (New York, Random House 1965), the most instructive introduction. V. Lutz is mainly concerned with contemporary problems (and favours emigration), see her *Italy, A Study in Economic Development* (Oxford U.P. 1962). For the leading Marxist contributor to the controversy see A. Gramsci, *The Modern Prince* (Lawrence & Wishart 1968), but important writing remain untranslated.

On other related topics the following are useful: R. Hostetter, *The Italian Socialist Movement (1860–1882)* (Van Nostrand 1958), and R. F. Foerster, *The Italian Emigration of Our Times* (Harvard University Press 1924), a sociological classic.

On the 1870–1814 period in British economic history there is an ever-growing number of specialist studies and a wide area of controversy. A selective list should therefore suit the student's need as most of the works cited include exhaustive bibliographies or references. J. H. Clapham's *An Economic History of Modern Britain*, vol. III (Cambridge U.P. 1938), is the indispensable standby and reference work but a good deal of important research has been done since it was published. W. Ashworth, *An Economic History of England from 1870–1939* (new edn. Methuen 1960), is a useful textbook but there is not much drama in the story and the views expressed are extremely moderate. R. S. Sayers, *A History of Economic Change in Britain, 1880–1939* (Oxford U.P. 1967), the most recent introductory text is also moderate.

A representative sample of new work is to be found in J. Saville, ed., 'Studies in the British Economy, 1870–1914', *Yorkshire Bulletin of Economic and Social Research*, xvii, 1965, and in D. H. Aldcroft, ed. *The Development of British Industry and Foreign Competition, 1875–1914* (Allen & Unwin 1968).

There is an abundant literature on 'the Great Depression'. The best starting point for the student is the article by A. E. Musson, 'The Great Depression in Britain, 1873–1896: A Reappraisal', *Journal of Economic History*, xix, 1959, which contains full bibliographical references up to that date. The pamphlet by S. B. Saul, *The Myth of the Great Depression 1873–1896* (Methuen 1969) appeared after the completion of this book. It argues strongly against the use of the term; difficult for the beginner, it contains a full bibliography. See also, D. Coppock, 'The climacteric of the a full bibliography. See also, D. Coppock, 'The climacteric of the 1890's: a critical note', *The Manchester School*, xxiv, no. 1, 1956, and 'The causes of the Great Depression, 1873–96' in *Manchester School*, xxix, no. 3, 1961. The interpretation by W. W. Rostow, now generally considered inadequate, is to be found in his *British Economy of the Nineteenth Century* (Oxford U.P. 1948). For an early critique see J. Saville, 'A Comment on Professor Rostow's British Economy of the 19th Century', in *Past and Present*, Nov. 1954.

For other views on Britain's problems in the period see Kindleberger, *op. cit.*, D. H. Aldcroft, 'The entrepreneur and the British economy, 1870–1914', *The Economic History Review*, 2nd series, xvii, no 1, 1964, J. Saville, 'Some retarding factors in the British economy before 1914', *Yorkshire Bulletin of Economic and Social Research*, May 1961 and F. J. R. Jervis, 'The handicap of Britain's early start', *The Manchester School*, xv, no. 1, 1947.

On the steel industry, D. L. Burn, *Economic History of Steelmaking, 1867–1939* (Cambridge U.P. 1940), is the classic study but see also T. H. Burnham and G. O. Hoskins, *Iron and Steel in Britain, 1870–1930* (Allen & Unwin 1943). S. B. Saul, *Studies in British Overseas Trade 1870–1914* (Liverpool U.P. 1960) is important. On agriculture see T. W. Fletcher, 'The Great Depression of English agriculture, 1873–1896', *Economic History Review*, 2nd series, xiii, no. 1, 1954, and C. S. Orwin and E. H. Whetham, *History of British Agriculture, 1846–1914* (Longmans, 1964).

For contemporary material see W. H. B. Court, ed., *British Economic History, 1870–1914: Documents and Commentary* (Cambridge U.P. 1965).

Foreign investment is covered in A. K. Cairncross, *Home and Foreign Investment, 1870–1913* (Cambridge U.P. 1953) – an indispensable book – and in C. K. Hobson, *The Expert of Capital* (New York, Barnes & Noble 1914), as well as in Feis, *op. cit.* For estimates of the volume of British investment overseas the computations of A. H. Imlah in *Economic Elements in the Pax Britannica* (Harvard U.P. 1958) should be consulted.

H. J. Habakkuk, *American and British Technology in the Nineteenth Century* (Cambridge U.P. 1962), will be found stimulating by the advanced student and is a first-rate example of comparative economic history. A comparison between Britain and Europe along the same lines would yield interesting results.

For up-to-date research the student should, of course, refer to *The Economic History Review*, *The Journal of Economic History*, *Past and Present* and the European journals such as *Annales*.

References and Quotations

p. 2. Rostow, W. W., *The Stages of Economic Growth* (Cambridge U.P. 1960).

p. 53. Crouzet, F., 'England and France in the Eighteenth Century: a Comparative Analysis of Two Economic Growths' in Hartwell, R. M. (ed.), *The Causes of the Industrial Revolution in England* (Methuen, London, 1967).

p. 65. Rostow, W. W., *op. cit.* and Rostow, W. W., *The Economics of Take-off into Sustained Growth* (Macmillan, London, 1963) especially ch. 7, Marczewski, J., 'The Take-off Hypothesis and French Experience'.

p. 125. Baykov, A., 'The Economic Development of Russia', *Economic History Review*, 2nd series, vii, 1954–5.

p. 125. Gerschenkron, A., 'Agrarian Policies and Industrialization: Russia 1861–1917, ch. viii of vol. vi of *The Cambridge Economic History of Europe* (Cambridge 1965).

p. 137. Gerschenkron, A., *ibid* and *Economic Backwardness in Historical Perspective* (Pall Mall Press, London 1966).

p. 146. Gerschenkron, A., *op. cit.*

p. 149. Rimlinger, G. V., 'Autocracy and the Factory Order in Early Russian Industrialization', *Journal of Economic History*, xx, i, 1960.

p. 149. Gerschenkron, A., *op. cit.*

p. 154. Miller, M., *The Economic Development of Russia, 1905–1914* (2nd ed., Cass, London 1967), p. 297.

p. 156. Goldsmith, R. W., 'Economic Growth of Russia' in *Economic Development and Cultural Change*, ix, no. 3 (Univ. of Chicago 1961; Johnson Reprint Corp. 1966).

p. 166. Clough, S. B., *Economic History of Modern Italy* (Columbia U.P. 1964), p. 67.

p. 167. Gerschenkron, A., *op. cit.*, ch. 4, p. 84.

p. 170. Clough, S. B., *op. cit.*, p. 129.

p. 176. Cohen, J. S., 'Financing Industrialization in Italy, 1894–1914', in *Journal of Economic History*, xxvii, no. 3, p. 382.

p. 194. Saul, S. B., *Studies in British Overseas Trade, 1870–1914* (Liverpool U.P. 1960), pp. 198–207.

Index

bureaucracy, in Russia *(cont.)*
  and Stolypin reforms, 143
  under Alexander II, 133, 135
  under Alexander III, 148, 151

capital, capital accumulation,
  need for, 186
  as a prerequisite for industrialization, 6, 7, 13, 179
  in Britain,
    and enclosures, 39
    and foreign investment, 19, 155
    and middle classes, 15, 57, 181
    family, 20, 57, 186
    industrial, 15, 20, 186
  in France,
    and bourgeoisie, 181
    and foreign investment, 72, 155
    industrial, 63
    used to finance government, 56, 57
  in Germany,
    and bourgeoisie, 99, 181
    and joint-stock companies, 100-101
    foreign investment in, 95, 98, 100, 155
    shortage of, 94-5, 98, 113
  in Italy, 151, 174, 181
  in Russia, 128, 139
    and bourgeoisie, 181
    foreign investment in, 72, 151, 155, 156
capital goods, 19, 25, 166
capital market, 66, 100-102, 138, 193, 197 *see* banks
capitalism,
  character of, 11-12, 16, 31
  family, 26, 63
  in agriculture, 40, 43-5, 48, 139, 146
  in Britain,
    and social structure, 198-9
    and world markets, 181, 195
    family, 26
    industrial, 2, 197-8
    pre-1914, 195, 197
  in Europe, 30, 31, 32
  in France,
    and the Revolution, 57, 78-9
    characteristics of, 72-3
    family, 63
    industrial, 26, 62, 63, 67-8
    structure of, 67, 68-70, 71
    weaknesses of, 72-3, 78
  in Germany,
    and nationalism, 116-7
    characteristics of, 81, 99
    industrial, 26, 62, 99, 113-4

  in Italy,
    character of, 31, 169, 170, 173
    industrial, 169-70, 174
    structure of, 168, 174
  in Russia,
    and autocracy, 135-6
    and ideologies, 134, 150
    industrial, 137, 138, 150, 151, 157
    structure of, 153, 157
    rate of development of, 40
capitalists, 8, 23, 156
Caprivi, G. L. 108
cartels, cartellization, 104, 114, 153, 196
Cavour, C. di, 162-3
chemical industry, 18, 50, 114, 191
Church, 43, 53, 121, 164, 166
City of London, 182, 193
Civil War, American *see* American Civil War
Clark, Colin, 201
Clough, S. B., on Italy, 166, 170
coal, coal industry,
  consumption of, 202, 203
  importance of, 11
  in Belgium, 10
  in Britain, 26, 188-9, 190, 197
  in France, 10, 62, 71, 72
  in Germany, 10, 92, 95, 102, 104
  in Russia, 125, 137, 150, 153
Cohen, J. S. on Italy, 176
Colbert, Colbertism, 54
colonies,
  Britain and, 29, 105, 182, 196
  competition for, 30, 52, 105
  France and, 52
  Germany and, 105, 116
  industrialization and expansion of, 3, 29, 116
  Italy and, 172 *see also* imperialism
commercial treaties, 69
company laws, 69, 197
Confederation of Germany, 1815, 96, 98-9
Continent *see* Europe
Continental System, 58
coqs du village, 140
corporative state, 176
Corso Forzoso, 164, 170
cotton, cotton industry, 18, 92, 137, 202
  see also textile industry
Crédit Lyonnais, 70
Crédit Mobilier, 66-7, 170
credit system *see* banks
Crimean War, 1854-6, 119, 123, 124
crisis,
  1857, 67